W9-BDB-689

Race
with
Destiny

The Year
That Changed
NASCAR Forever

David Poole

ALBION PRESS
Tampa, Florida

Library of Congress Cataloging-in-Publication Data

Poole, David, 1959–
   Race with destiny : the year NASCAR changed forever / by David Poole.
     p. cm.
   ISBN 0-9709170-3-1
    1. NASCAR racing—History. 2. Winston Cup—History. I. Title.

   GV1029.15 .P55 2001
796.72'0973—dc21

                   2001022940

Photographs on page 91 (bottom) and 94 (top) are courtesy of Tom Roberts. All other photographs are courtesy of *The Charlotte Observer.*

Interior design and typesetting by Sue Knopf, Graffolio

Published by Albion Press, Tampa, Florida.

Printed in Canada .

For Mama Sue,
who taught me that hard work
is the first step
in making dreams come true.

Contents

The Gathering

Alan Kulwicki had never let Tom Roberts down.

That thought reassured Roberts as he anxiously watched the elevator doors in the lobby of the Hilton in downtown Atlanta. It was just past 6 a.m. on Thursday, Nov. 12, 1992.

Just outside the front doors sat a white limousine. At 6:15, it was supposed to roll. But Roberts, who handled Kulwicki's media relations and sponsor commitments, wasn't entirely sure the NASCAR driver was even in Atlanta.

Roberts glanced at his watch, then stared back at the elevator.

Where was Kulwicki?

Davey Allison had been in and out of the Georgia capital earlier in the week, but that morning he was winding up a short vacation he hoped would clear his mind for the hectic weekend ahead. Allison was due back in Atlanta in time to sign autographs that night at a local Ford dealership.

Bill Elliott had slipped away too, flying to Bermuda with his fiancée, Cindy, for the first part of the week leading up to the Hooters 500, the 29th and final race of the season in Winston Cup, stock car racing's premier series.

Just 40 championship points separated Allison, Kulwicki and Elliott heading into the finale, creating the tightest championship battle in the circuit's history.

They formed an interesting trio of contenders.

Allison was a young, cocksure driver from one of NASCAR's most storied families. Kulwicki was a college-educated Wisconsin native who had let neither a lack of funds nor non-Southern roots limit his success. Elliott was a good old boy from the hills of north Georgia who had emerged in the mid-1980s as one of the sport's biggest stars.

While it had been a little chilly for Elliott in the islands, Atlanta's weather on that Thursday was simply awful.

The pouring rain was not good news for the people at Atlanta Motor Speedway, located 30 miles south of downtown Atlanta near the town of Hampton. Track officials already had enough to take care of that weekend.

A large white tent stood in the track's infield, adjacent to a media center that was becoming increasingly overcrowded each year as the sport's popularity grew. Stock-car racing had long enjoyed a devoted following in the South. Now, it was drawing attention from outside that traditional base. Live racing coverage had become a programming staple on cable television, especially ESPN, and the ratings were on their way up.

As the sport grew, so did the number of media outlets covering it. Reporters needed work space. The Atlanta press facilities had been more than adequate when no more than two dozen reporters covered the sport with any degree of regularity. Now, the media center was bursting.

Over the final two months of the season, the race for the 1992 championship had evolved into an epic battle. Allison, Kulwicki and Elliott had the best chances to win the championship and a $1 million top prize after the Hooters 500 that Sunday, but Harry Gant, Kyle Petty and Mark Martin all still had a mathematical shot too. Since the points system had first been used 1975, never before had more than three drivers come into the year's last race with a chance to be champion. This time, there were six.

All of that, however, was a glorified subplot for many because of the looming retirement of the man NASCAR fans know simply as "The King."

Atlanta Motor Speedway needed a tent for overflow media work space that weekend because Richard Petty, the Jack Nicklaus and the Babe Ruth of his sport, had announced 13 months earlier that 1992 would be his last year as a driver.

Petty's final season, his 35th on the circuit, was staged as a "Fan Appreciation Tour." The fans turned that around and made it a year-long celebration of a career that included 200 victories, nearly twice as many as anyone else in the sport, and a record seven championships.

Now, only one race remained.

The Hooters 500 had long been a sellout. Tickets for a new 12,000-seat grandstand added that year had been snapped up. When the track added nearly 18,000 seats in temporary bleachers in October, those tickets disappeared in a matter of days.

Nearly 800 media credential requests had poured in, some from outlets that for years barely had mentioned stock-car racing and had then buried it deep inside the sports section or at the end of the evening's highlights.

A giant going-away party for Petty was set for Saturday night, with more than 50,000 fans expected to gather to hear country music performers and to honor the one driver whose fame had transcended the sport's then-limited scope.

Before becoming an auxiliary media center for the weekend, the tent was set up to handle a Thursday afternoon news conference at which Petty would announce who would drive his car for the '93 season. Everybody who followed racing had known for weeks that it would be Rick Wilson, but the official announcement offered one more chance to hear Petty talk about his final ride and still figured to draw a crowd.

Two months earlier, it appeared there would be nothing to deflect the focus from Petty's farewell on the season's final weekend.

When Elliott finished second in the Peak Anti-Freeze 500 on Sept. 20 at Dover, Del., he built his lead in the championship standings to 154 points over Allison. Gant was third, 239 points back. A wrecked car left Kulwicki 278 points behind the leader and seemingly out of contention.

Had Elliott been so much as mediocre over the final six races, the mathematics of points racing would have given him a second career championship.

If he'd managed a string of top-10 finishes in the final weeks of the season, there would have been no points race drama on the final weekend. Four times in the five races leading up to the finale, however, Elliott's Ford had suffered unlikely yet crippling mechanical failures. The collapse was completed at Phoenix in the season's next-to-last race when Elliott suffered engine problems and finished 31st.

Allison came to Atlanta with 3,928 points through 28 races. If he won the Hooters 500 and led the most laps, he would earn the 185-point maximum available for any one race and finish with 4,113.

Kulwicki trailed Allison by 30 points, with Elliott 10 behind Kulwicki. If Kulwicki got 185 points in the final race, he would finish with 4,083. That meant Allison needed 155 points to clinch, giving him a magic number of fifth place, which is worth 155 points. Sixth place would do provided Allison led at least one lap, earning 150 points for the finish plus a five-point bonus for leading a lap.

Allison was trying to join Petty as the second son of a champion to win NASCAR's top prize. Allison's father, Bobby, won the 1983 title and had also finished second five other times.

Like any son following in his father's footsteps, Davey Allison faced the added burden of living up to expectations. But if the younger Allison felt that pressure, he wasn't showing it. He appeared calm, even detached from the approaching hoopla.

"The most important thing I learned from my father is not to get too wrapped up in it and put too much emphasis on it," Davey said that week. "If it's meant to happen it will, and if it's not, it won't.

"All we've got to control is the anticipation. If you just let it happen and try to do your best, and then you can do your best, then you've got to be happy with the outcome, no matter what it is."

Allison had been to the hospital as many times as he had been to victory lane that season. He had been in major crashes at Bristol and at Charlotte and in a particularly savage one at Pocono, the same track where four years earlier his father wrecked and ended his driving career —and very nearly his life.

After his Pocono crash, Davey was forced to give his car over to relief drivers after starting the next two races. Lingering effects from the wrecks had him driving in pain into the season's final days.

Kulwicki finished fourth at Phoenix and moved past Elliott into second in the standings, but he was still disappointed in the outcome of that race. Kulwicki knew that opportunities to win at this level were precious, and it annoyed him when he felt he had squandered one.

Now just 500 miles remained in a season that started nine months earlier with Allison winning the Daytona 500. If the front three contenders all faltered in the finale, Gant, Kyle Petty (Richard's son) or Martin could still steal away the title. But it would take an unlikely set of circumstances for one of them to pass all three of the Ford drivers out front.

There had been no race the weekend following Allison's win at Phoenix, giving the teams time to come to Atlanta for testing.

Elliott had the fastest test speed among the championship contenders, lapping the 1.522-mile track at an average speed of 178.475 mph. It was only slightly slower than the pole-winning speed from the race held earlier that year at the track.

Allison ran 176.123 mph and Kulwicki 175.615 mph. Though their speeds were slower there was little concern, since both had spent the day driving cars set up the way they would be for the 500-mile race, not for a one-lap qualifying run. The top lap speed under such conditions is not as important as the car's ability to run consistent speeds lap after lap, a more accurate measure of how the car might perform over a 500-mile race.

Elliott's speed was not the fastest overall in testing. Jeff Gordon, a 21-year-old driver preparing for his first career start, ran 181.130 mph as he tried to get a one-race jump on his rookie season in 1993. Gordon would race in a rainbow-colored No. 24 Chevrolet for a team being formed around him and crew chief Ray Evernham in one of NASCAR's top multi-car operations, Hendrick Motorsports.

History would ride with Allison on Sunday. Only once since 1975 had the leader going into the season's final race not won the title. Richard Petty had trailed Darrell Waltrip by two points entering the 1979 finale at Riverside, Calif., but Petty finished fifth that day to Waltrip's eighth. Petty's 11-point final edge had been the closest points margin in NASCAR history.

After the test on the previous Friday, Allison came back to Atlanta on Monday. He took his wife, Liz, and their two young children on a family outing to Callaway Gardens that day and arrived at his hotel late that afternoon.

Too late, in fact.

That night, Atlanta was christening its new indoor stadium, the Georgia Dome, with the hometown NFL Falcons facing the San Francisco 49ers. Tommy Allison, Davey's business partner and cousin, knew one of the San Francisco players from his college days and lined up tickets for the game.

With ABC's *Monday Night Football* in town, Winston Cup series sponsor R. J. Reynolds Tobacco Company worked corporate connections and arranged for Allison to appear in a halftime interview with former NFL star Frank Gifford. It was the kind of national exposure NASCAR craved as it worked to break out of its Southern roots and into the mainstream of American sports.

The interview was to be taped around 7 p.m., about two hours before the game's kickoff. But by 7 p.m., Allison had barely made it back to his hotel.

"By the time we left for the game, it was all we could do to get there before the kickoff," said Ty Norris, who worked for Sports Marketing Enterprises, the marketing arm of RJR. "We went straight to the booth, but they were into their pregame show by that point.

"So we missed out on a huge opportunity. We stiffed Frank Gifford."

Liz Allison, worn out from the day's activities, was ready to go back to the hotel shortly after halftime. But during the first quarter, the Allison cousins and Norris had used sideline passes and struck up conversations with some of the San Francisco players, who then invited the group to the locker room after the game.

Allison was excited about the chance to hang out with some of the NFL's most famous stars. Liz, however, was not. She was going back to the hotel with or without Davey, who spent the fourth quarter futilely trying to change his wife's mind.

While Tommy Allison and Norris went to meet Joe Montana and Jerry Rice, Davey and Liz Allison went back to their hotel.

Allison spent Tuesday dealing with the media responsibilities that come with being a contender for the Winston Cup title. He held a news conference at the Waverly Hotel and then participated in a teleconference with reporters from around the country. Norris also took him to various radio and television interviews in the Atlanta area, beginning at 7:30 a.m. and running into the early evening hours.

Allison, who had already begun growing a scruffy goatee he wore on hunting trips during his few weeks off each winter, then slipped back to Alabama for one last chance to catch his breath ahead of the biggest weekend of his career.

Tom Roberts had the same kind of day planned for Kulwicki on Thursday.

Roberts and Kulwicki had known each other for more than a decade, having met in 1980 when Roberts worked at Nashville Speedway and Kulwicki was racing in American Speed Association events. Twelve years later, Roberts had his own public relations company and Kulwicki was his client.

Roberts also was Kulwicki's friend, one who had been along for every step of a remarkable journey from obscurity to success the driver had orchestrated with intelligence and a dogged sense of determination.

The concept of spending a full day with the media in Atlanta on Thursday hadn't been a particularly hard sell to Kulwicki, even though it was something the driver had never done. Kulwicki was smart enough to know such a media blitz would bring great exposure for himself, his team and his sponsor, which was Hooters, an Atlanta-based chain of restaurants that also was the title sponsor for the season's last race.

Kulwicki also knew that dealing with the media on Thursday would allow him more time to focus on getting his car ready once he went to the track on Friday. Kulwicki needed that focus. Unlike almost all of the other drivers in NASCAR's top circuit, the 37-year-old native of Greenfield, Wis., made every important decision about his car.

Kulwicki was not only driver of the No. 7 Ford Thunderbirds, he also was team owner. He directed operations at Alan Kulwicki Racing and its 16 fiercely loyal full-time employees. Most major race teams had at least twice as many employees; some multi-car operations had three or four times that number.

Kulwicki drove his people hard, but never harder than he drove himself. Nobody who didn't buy heart and soul into working for the team stayed around long. For those who did, however, Kulwicki made sure they understood they were beating the odds and accomplishing remarkable things—fostering an intense bond that glued his team together.

Even though Kulwicki had agreed to the media day, Roberts knew he was pushing his luck with the ambitious schedule he had lined up.

Before sending the schedule to Kulwicki, Roberts called the team's shop just on the outskirts of Charlotte, N.C., and spoke to Cal Lawson, another of Kulwicki's tight inner circle and the race team's general manager.

"This is not going to be pretty, Cal," Roberts warned. "You've got to help me make this happen."

Predictably, when he saw what Roberts had planned, Kulwicki hit the roof.

Kulwicki called Roberts back, fuming. He had already agreed to give up part of Wednesday to participate in a teleconference. Now, Roberts was asking for too much more of his valuable time.

"What is this? Is this 6:15 a.m.?" Kulwicki asked.

"Yes," Roberts said.

"No!" Kulwicki said. "I can't do that!"

Kulwicki's voice rose an octave with every sentence.

"I'll have to come in on Wednesday night, Tom!" Kulwicki said. "I can't do that. My priority is this race car. We're talking about the last race!"

Roberts calmly explained again what he was trying to accomplish.

Kulwicki didn't care. All he knew was that leaving Charlotte on Wednesday would keep him from being at the shop until late that evening, tweaking the car's setup.

"I am not promising you anything," Kulwicki finally declared. "I may be there and I may not."

And then he hung up the phone.

Standing in the hotel lobby before sunrise on Thursday, Roberts hadn't spoken with Kulwicki since that abrupt end to their phone call.

Late Wednesday, Roberts had called the shop and found out Kulwicki had left that afternoon. There was a room in Kulwicki's name at the Hilton for Wednesday night, so at least the reservation hadn't been canceled.

All Roberts could do now was wait.

R. J. Reynolds had offered to provide Kulwicki a limousine for the day, but Hooters provided its own for the driver representing a chain that advertised itself as "delightfully tacky" and used attractive young women in revealing attire—tight T-shirts and bright orange "hot pants" —as waitresses. It was an image the decidedly untacky Kulwicki learned to live with after the company's sponsorship had come along in desperate hours early in the 1991 season.

Waiting on Kulwicki that morning with Roberts were Wayne Estes, a public relations agent for Ford who had helped Roberts set up the day's schedule, and Mark Brooks, the earnest 25-year-old son of Hooters chief executive officer Bob Brooks. The elder Brooks had assigned Mark to oversee the company's motorsports involvement, and Mark's eager beaver attitude had rubbed many of the team's members the wrong way.

The limo Hooters sent that morning was plain white, unadorned by the company logo that features an owl with eyes behind the two O's in the name to make them suggest the parts of the female anatomy for which "hooters" is common slang. The limo was accompanied, however, by two "Hooters girls" wearing the trademark waitress's uniform to serve as "hostesses" for the day.

Just before 6:15 a.m., the last member of the traveling party finally made his appearance.

A wave of relief came over Roberts as the lobby elevator doors opened and Kulwicki stepped out. He said nothing to Roberts about being upset over having to come to town the night before. Kulwicki was there now; it was time to go to work.

To someone with no interest in racing, Kulwicki could have easily been mistaken for a typical businessman heading off to a meeting in one of downtown Atlanta's corporate offices. Kulwicki always dressed neatly, even when he went into the sometimes-grimy garages at race tracks.

Kulwicki stood 5-foot-9 and weighed 160 pounds, fairly typical for professional race car drivers, who don't have to be tall like a basketball star or bulked up like a pro football player. Kulwicki always paid close attention to his black hair, keeping it carefully groomed.

The only thing that might have made him stand out in the Atlanta hotel lobby was his accent—more precisely his lack of one. Kulwicki was from Wisconsin, so he didn't have a Southern accent like so many of his fellow NASCAR competitors.

Roberts got the driver a cup of coffee and they were out the door, starting the day with a series of radio interviews in the morning drive-time hours.

In between stops, Kulwicki called from the car to the shop, checking with Lawson and Paul Andrews, his crew chief, on final preparations on the car the team would race on Sunday.

Early that morning, Roberts remembered to ask his driver a question about preparations for the annual Winston Cup awards banquet in New York that would follow the season.

A production company that worked with ESPN on its motorsports coverage was preparing videotape montages of the highlights for the championship contenders. The champion's highlights would be set to music and used as part of the awards presentation in New York.

Roberts asked Kulwicki what song he'd like to have used if he won the title.

Kulwicki said nothing.

"If you were around Alan a lot, sometimes you would say stuff and wonder if it was registering or not," Roberts said. "If he had something else on his mind, it might go in one ear and out the other. Sometimes he did hear you and was just thinking."

Roberts decided it was a question he could come back to later.

After the radio interviews, the limousine headed toward a Hooters restaurant in Jonesboro, Ga., a suburb on the highway leading toward the track. Newspaper reporters were gathered there for their turn at the most unlikely of the championship contenders.

As they walked from the parking lot to the restaurant, Kulwicki turned toward Roberts.

"'My Way,'" Kulwicki said.

"What?" Roberts asked.

It had been hours since Roberts had posed the musical question he wasn't even sure Kulwicki had heard. He certainly wasn't expecting an answer at that moment.

"'My Way,'" Kulwicki said. "The song. You asked me what music I would want them to play on a video. 'My Way.'"

Roberts said okay, knowing it was a good choice. Virtually every aspect of Kulwicki's life, and certainly everything in his racing career, had been done on Kulwicki's own terms.

About the same time, Elliott arrived at the Holiday Inn Crowne Plaza on Ashford-Dunwoody Road for a news conference for the state's anti-drunk driving program. Elliott, a native of Dawsonville, Ga., was the program's spokesperson.

Richard and Kyle Petty were heading for the track for the 1 p.m. news conference in the infield tent. Richard Sowers, the speedway's public relations manager, tried to talk Richard Petty into putting a scare into reporters who'd been writing for weeks that Wilson would be named as Petty's replacement. He wanted Richard to have Kyle step up as the next driver when the big moment came, just to see what the reaction would be. The Pettys declined to play along.

After his lunch and interview session at Hooters, Kulwicki began his afternoon with trips to area television stations.

Roberts knew that by mid-afternoon the questions at every stop would have long since become redundant, so he inserted a surprise into the itinerary. Kulwicki's schedule, the one that had prompted Wednesday's rancorous phone conversation, showed a 2:30 p.m. meeting that had been identified only as "Hooters Meeting."

The limousine arrived at a hotel and Roberts led Kulwicki toward a meeting room. The doors opened and the group inside burst into applause, standing to welcome their visitor. At the front of the room stood Bob Brooks, the Hooters CEO. The crowd cheering Kulwicki consisted mostly of Hooters franchisees, some of whom had at first been only lukewarm to Brooks' idea of sponsoring a race team.

Many NASCAR drivers would have killed their public relations man for pulling such a surprise. The very idea of standing up before a crowd and speaking extemporaneously would petrify those who need a prepared list of "talking points" to say a 30-second hello at a reception.

Kulwicki, however, was different. He had a gift for such occasions. Despite his reservations about the Hooters image, he also had a genuine appreciation for the opportunity Brooks' company had given him to pursue his dreams, and welcomed the opportunity to express his gratitude.

No driver-owner had won the Winston Cup championship since 1979, when Richard Petty rallied in the final race to edge Waltrip. Comparing Kulwicki's team to Petty's was in no way a fair analogy. Petty Enterprises was a cornerstone operation in the sport's history. Kulwicki's team was a devoted band of underdogs, battling Elliott's team, owned by NASCAR legend Junior Johnson, and Allison's team, owned by master engine builder Robert Yates, toe-to-toe for a title.

Brooks thanked Kulwicki for coming to the meeting and for his kind words.

"Is there anything that we can do to help you this weekend?" Brooks asked.

Kulwicki pondered the request for a moment.

"Is there any way possible you could arrange to have a masseuse meet me at the hotel tonight after we finish?" Kulwicki asked.

Brooks chuckled. A professional masseuse was certainly not among the favors the stereotypical NASCAR driver might ask for.

"I'm sure that can be arranged," Brooks said.

The day was far from done. After more television interviews in the afternoon, Kulwicki joined a number of drivers at a large autograph session and charity auction early in the evening at the site of Georgia's state farmers' market. From there, about the same time that Allison went to his appearance at the Ford dealership, Kulwicki returned to the Jonesboro Hooters to sign more autographs for fans from 8 to 10 p.m.

After nearly 16 hours of interviews, autographs and photos, Kulwicki climbed back in the limo and headed back for the hotel where the day had begun.

The Hooters girls had been dismissed. The limo driver, Kulwicki and Roberts rode along in darkness.

Roberts felt good about the productive day, especially the meeting with the Hooters folks that Kulwicki had seemed to particularly enjoy. There was little conversation, but Roberts knew his driver well enough to know Kulwicki had seen the value of the exercise.

Kulwicki stared out the dark tinted windows as the limo headed toward the bright lights and tall buildings of downtown Atlanta.

He was tired, but he knew that every interview, every autograph and every handshake during his long day was part of what it took to be a top Winston Cup driver. If he was going to continue to be his own car owner, to have things done the way he wanted them to be done, he knew he would have to work at those things even harder as the sport, and his fame, continued to grow.

Earlier that afternoon, Kulwicki's race car had been loaded into the large truck—a "transporter" in NASCAR jargon—for the nearly 4-hour ride toward Atlanta. Even though Kulwicki had not been there, he knew that every part had been checked and rechecked. He also knew that he would check them again personally the next morning.

Back at the Hilton, Kulwicki said good night to Roberts and slid out the door. He started inside to see if Bob Brooks had made good on his promise to have a masseuse come by.

Just before the driver closed the door, Kulwicki turned and leaned back into the limousine.

"'My Way,'" Kulwicki told Roberts. "That's the song. 'My Way.' And it has to be the Frank Sinatra version."

His Racing Highness

While Alan Kulwicki, Davey Allison and Bill Elliott were in Atlanta to race for a championship, Richard Petty was still the star of the weekend's show.

It has been said that the world's first automobile race was most likely held on the day after the world's second automobile was made. Richard Petty's history in American motorsports doesn't go back quite that far. It only seems that way.

As much as the corporate image-makers who guide stock-car racing today don't like to talk about it, NASCAR's lineage traces directly to bootlegging, one of the Southeast's leading industries in the 1930s and 1940s.

Untaxed whiskey, called "moonshine" because it was made in illegal stills under the cover of darkness, was delivered by men driving cars souped up so they could quickly complete long delivery routes and outrun the sheriff or revenue agents trying to stop them.

It is impossible to know for sure when the first group of moonshine runners decided to see whose car was the fastest, with a few bets on the line to make things interesting. But almost as soon as those contests began, crowds began coming to watch. Before long it occurred to someone to start organizing these competitions at rings built for horse racing at the county fairgrounds and charging admission.

Some of these early promoters would offer a prize of, say, $500 to win— then pay perhaps a tenth of that after saying that not enough tickets sold to pay the promised amount. Sometimes nobody got paid at all —by the time the race ended and the arguments about who had won were over, the promoter had absconded with the receipts.

On Dec. 12, 1947, a man whose filling station on Main Street in Daytona Beach, Fla., had become a hangout for local racers convened a meeting of men who wanted to bring some honesty to the sport. Given the bootlegger heritage of the sport they were trying to regulate, it was perhaps fitting they met in a bar atop Daytona's Streamline Hotel.

William Henry Getty France wanted to clean up stock-car racing and bring it to the masses. To do that, he felt that the word "stock" was an important part of the equation for success, and his reasoning was simple genius. By requiring that cars raced under his group's sanction be new models of standard street cars, France forged an enduring connection between the sport and its fans.

The National Association for Stock Car Automobile Racing was incorporated on Feb. 21, 1948. NASCAR sanctioned races featuring modified cars that year, but on June 19, 1949, France's organization held its first race in what it called the "strictly stock" division in Charlotte.

The series now known as Winston Cup was born that day on a three-quarter mile patch of red Carolina clay near where Charlotte's airport now sits.

And Richard Petty was there. Two weeks shy of his 12th birthday, the boy who would one day end the greatest career in stock-car racing history in the 1992 Hooters 500 at Atlanta bummed a ride home from that first race.

Richard's father, Lee, borrowed a new Buick and drove it from his home in Level Cross, N.C., to race that day. Other members of the Petty clan followed along in the family car.

During the race, Lee Petty caught a rut in the track's dirt surface and crashed, destroying the borrowed Buick. The women went back home in the family car, leaving Richard to hitchhike. Lee stayed back to arrange to have the wrecked car towed to Level Cross.

On Oct. 2 of that year, Lee got the first of his 54 career NASCAR victories at Heidelburg Speedway near Pittsburgh. Racing soon became the family business for Lee, his wife, Elizabeth, and their two sons, Richard and Maurice.

Richard was 17 when his father won his first NASCAR championship in 1954. Lee won the championship again in 1958, the year that Richard began his career as a driver, racing for the first time in July at Canadian National Exposition Speedway in Toronto and finishing 17th.

Richard, at 6-foot-3, was taller and more angular than his father was. While Lee was by no means portly, he did look much sturdier than his son, whose long arms and legs make him seem downright spindly. Before Richard started wearing custom-made cowboy hats virtually every time he stepped out in public, those who saw him looked at a head full of black hair curled in a seemingly random pattern.

Lee won the 1959 championship, too, and had his best season. In 42 races he won 11 times, finished second five times and was in the top 10 a total of 35 times.

Two of Lee's 1959 victories were particularly noteworthy. He won the first Daytona 500 in a photo finish over Johnny Beauchamp at Bill France's monstrous new 2.5-mile superspeedway that still reigns as the most famous stock-car track in the world.

Then on June 14 at Lakewood Speedway in Atlanta, it appeared that Richard had won for the first time in his career. After his son took the checkered flag, however, Lee sped around the track one more time and then pulled into victory lane to protest, claiming Richard had been given credit for one lap too many.

After checking scoring records, race officials ruled in the elder Petty's favor.

"I didn't really question it since it was family," Richard would say years later. "I guess I'd still be there arguing about it if it was someone else."

Richard Petty won his first NASCAR race at 22 in 1960, at the Southern States Fairgrounds track in Charlotte. The setting for his first victory was fitting since Lee had won the inaugural NASCAR event on the half-mile dirt track in 1954. But 1960 would be the fairgrounds track's last year of hosting NASCAR races because earlier that year the 1.5-mile paved Charlotte Motor Speedway had opened.

Richard won three races and finished second behind Rex White in the 1960 championship race. Lee won five times that year and finished sixth, his worst finish in 12 seasons of racing.

Lee won again at Jacksonville, Fla., in November of that year in a race counted as the second event of NASCAR's 1961 season. But three months later at Daytona, while running in a qualifying race for the 1961

Daytona 500, Lee's No. 42 hit Beauchamp's car as they tried to avoid another driver's spin. Lee's car flew over a guardrail and landed more than 100 feet away in the parking lot.

Among other injuries he had a punctured lung and a broken leg, and he spent four months in the hospital recovering. He would make six more starts before finally retiring in 1964, but the Petty family's mantle had passed from father to son.

Richard wore it well. He won seven titles from 1964 to 1979. He won the Daytona 500 in '64, '66, '71, '73, '74, '79 and '81. No other driver has ever won NASCAR's biggest race more than four times.

Petty won an unbelievable 27 times in 48 races in 1967, winning 10 straight from Aug. 12 to Oct. 1 in an era when two or three NASCAR races were sometimes held in the same week. In the subsequent seasons he won 16, 10 and 18 times.

It was during this remarkable period of dominance that sportswriters covering the sport began using the nicknames that would stick with him throughout his career—"King Richard" and, simply, "The King."

NASCAR's modern era dawned with the 1972 season, one year after R. J. Reynolds Tobacco stepped in to sponsor the points fund. All races shorter than 250 miles were dropped. The final race on dirt had been held at Raleigh, N.C., in September of 1970—and Richard Petty won that.

There had been 46 races in 1971. In 1972 there would be just 31. It didn't matter. Petty won 21 races in '71 and eight the following season, winning the championship both times. He also won the last title using the old points system in '74 and the first using the new system the following year.

Over the course of his career, Petty survived horrible crashes that left his body broken. He endured manufacturers' boycotts that at times left him without a car to drive, like one in 1965 that caused Petty to miss 33 races after NASCAR banned Chrysler's "hemi" engine. He raced generations of champions and was the primary rival of such great drivers as Bobby Allison, Cale Yarborough, Fred Lorenzen, Ned Jarrett, Buddy Baker and Bobby Isaac.

Petty's most formidable foe was David Pearson, a South Carolinian whose prematurely gray hair and cunning skills behind the wheel earned him the nickname "Silver Fox."

Petty and Pearson waged some of the most legendary battles in racing's history. From 1973 to 1977 alone, Petty and Pearson finished first and second in 63 races, with Pearson winning 33 of those.

One of their most famous 1-2 finishes came in the 1976 Daytona 500. On the final lap Pearson, who would win 105 times in his career to rank second only to Petty on the all-time list, drove his Mercury past Petty's Dodge off the second turn. Petty fought back and, coming off Turn 4 dove inside and pulled up alongside Pearson.

As they sped toward the finish line, their cars made contact. Pearson's car nosed into the wall, bounced off and clipped Petty's. Both cars skittered into the infield grass. The rivals' cars had been the only ones on the lead lap, but neither had crossed the line to win the race.

Petty's car stopped perhaps 100 yards short of victory and he couldn't get the engine going. Pearson, telling his team over his radio, "The bitch hit me!" bumped his car along a few feet at a time by pressing the starter repeatedly to get the checkered flag and the victory.

Three years later, Petty's Daytona luck evened out. On the final lap of the 1979 Daytona 500, Yarborough and Donnie Allison crashed on the backstretch on the final lap as they raced for the apparent victory. Petty, who had been running third, swept by to take the lead.

Moments after Petty crossed the finish line, Yarborough and Allison began a fistfight on the backstretch. Bobby Allison, Donnie's brother, stopped to join the fracas. A national television audience watching the first live flag-to-flag broadcast of the race on CBS that day ate it up. NASCAR's future as a hot television commodity was born and Petty got his sixth Daytona 500 victory.

His seventh Daytona 500 win in 1981 was the 193rd win of his career. Victories at North Wilkesboro, N.C. and Brooklyn, Mich., later that year made it 195. After going winless in 1982, he won three times in 1983 —at Rockingham, N.C., Talladega, Ala., and Charlotte—to reach 198.

At the end of that season, Richard left Petty Enterprises to drive for the first time in his career for another car owner—Mike Curb—and carried the No. 43 he made famous to victory at Dover in May of 1984 for his 199th win.

The milestone 200th win would be a story almost too good to be true. On July 4, 1984, Petty beat Yarborough back to the yellow flag by a matter of inches and won a Firecracker 400 that ended under that caution. President Ronald Reagan, who had given the command to fire the engines at the start of the race from on board Air Force One on his way to Daytona, watched the improbable finish from a seat in the track's control tower.

With Petty driving for Curb, the family-run Petty Enterprises team had shut down in 1985. But Richard revived it the following year and marked his 1,000th career start at Michigan in 1986. He finished second at Atlanta later that year and was second at Bristol, Tenn., the following season.

But as his 50th birthday passed that July, days when his car ran competitively began to grow scarce. His qualifying performance waned, too, and NASCAR instituted a rule by which a former Winston Cup champion could gain a provisional starting spot in a race for which he had been unable to qualify. Critics quickly nicknamed it the "Richard Petty Rule."

Petty's skills on the race track clearly diminished over those final seasons, but the trait that truly set The King apart, the grace with which he dealt with the demands of fame, endured. It has been said that nobody in sports history has been interviewed more times than Richard Petty, and that no athlete has signed more autographs. Petty's autograph was no easy task, either, since he signs his name in an elaborate, looping style that takes far longer than the straight-line scribble many athletes deliver.

Because Petty is so tall, his trademark cowboy hat can still frequently seen bobbing from inside the middle of a tightly bunched group moving through a garage area as The King signs his name a few dozen more times.

So while it came with no shock, there was a sense of sadness on Oct. 1, 1991, when Petty announced the 1992 season would be his last as a driver. The news conference was held at the Petty Enterprises shop in Level Cross, next door to the house were Lee Petty lived. The A-frame from the reaper shed where the family had first started working on cars remains part of the roofline of the headquarters.

"It's not a farewell tour because I'm not going anywhere," said Petty, who would stay on as the car owner. It was billed, instead, as a "Fan Appreciation Tour."

That name was more than a mere marketing slogan. Petty's connection with the fans was important to him, and on the final weekend of his career *The Atlanta Journal and Constitution* gave him a chance to write a farewell to those fans in a special race day section.

"I wish I could have done more the last few years and given the fans more to cheer about," Petty wrote. "We've tried hard, but racing's changed over what it used to be and it takes a whole heck of a lot to not only get on top, but to stay there.

"It's really the fans, though, that have meant the most to me. . . . When you stop and think about it, fans have really been responsible for what racing is today. They're the ones who pay our salaries. When they buy tickets to the races or go out and buy the products that our sponsors make, it's their way of showing their loyalty.

"They should be standing up on podiums and taking bows and being recognized. Not Richard Petty. I'm not the kind of cat who likes to stand up and take bows."

The fans, however, would insist. If Petty was "The King" of stock-car racing, his final season turned into a royal jubilee.

Every week, especially during the second half of the season as he raced at tracks for the final time, Petty and his wife, Lynda, were showered with honors and gifts and with cheers from fans who simply didn't want to let them go.

It began at Daytona, with Petty starting 32nd and finishing 16th in the 500. As would be the practice at all 29 races that season, Petty's car was allowed to run in front of the entire field on the first parade lap before the start of the race.

It became quickly apparent that the Fan Appreciation Tour would become a business bonanza. Twelve major sponsors paid $225,000 apiece to pay for the advertising and arrangements of the tour and special appearances that ran Petty ragged all season. A similar number of companies paid smaller fees as associate sponsors. In return, most of the companies ran special promotions or sold commemorative items that the racing public gobbled up.

There were, for example, 43,000 miniature replica race cars produced for each of the 29 races on the schedule. Each batch of the No. 43 Pontiacs had stickers identifying the race for which they were produced. Priced at $12, plans were to sell them only at the tracks on the weekend of each event. At Daytona in February, people bought them by the carton and resold them for three times the original price. Crewmen for other teams lined up at tracks during the early portion of the season to purchase the cars for themselves or to resell at a premium.

By midseason the market had cooled. At 43,000 cars per race, a 29-race schedule produced a total inventory of 1,247,000 miniature cars —hardly the kind of scarcity that creates large increases in value. Some of the inventory for each race was made available by mail order and sales picked back up.

In the end, the overall success of the merchandising of Petty's final season formed a framework for the NASCAR collectible industry. Dale Earnhardt and his marketing advisors would, over the remainder of the 1990s, perfect the idea of running a different paint scheme for certain races, allowing the production of a new line of die-cast cars to sell to fans who already had models of the car in its primary colors. That idea wasn't all that far removed from Petty's final season in 1992.

There had almost been one last competitive highlight for Petty during the final season. At Daytona in July, the site of the 200th victory and so many other great moments in his career, Petty ran 188.961 mph on his qualifying lap.

The longer that stood as the fastest speed, the more excited the crowd became. Then Sterling Marlin, driving a Ford owned by Junior Johnson, ran 189.366 mph and bumped Petty off the pole. Petty hadn't started first in a race since winning his 127th career pole—another of his records —at Bristol in 1979.

"I may need a bulletproof vest," Marlin joked. Darrell Waltrip said that in this case Marlin was "like the guy who shot Santa Claus."

Petty did start on the outside of the front row that day in a race that then–President George Bush witnessed, and led early in the race before fading into the pack.

Finally, after nine months of adulation and adoration, it was time for the Tour to end. There would be the one last race on a November Sunday at Atlanta, a track where Petty had won six times, and it would be done after 1,185 career starts.

Before that final curtain call, however, Petty had to confirm the selection of Rick Wilson to take over as driver of his car at the Thursday afternoon news conference.

Wilson was 39 and had raced in 174 Winston Cup races without a win, although he'd fallen just a few feet short of beating out Bill Elliott at Daytona in July 1988. The Stavola Brothers team had fired Wilson after the Daytona 500 earlier that year. Ted Musgrave, Hut Stricklin and road racing champion Tom Kendall had also been interviewed for the job as Petty's replacement.

As the rain pounded down outside the large tent in the Atlanta track's infield, Petty ceremonially handed a steering wheel to Wilson.

"The tent had a canvas floor on it," Sowers said. "But the floor had sunk down into the mud and we were standing in water up to the tops of our shoes. I was afraid that when 'The King' touched the microphone he was going to get electrocuted."

Petty fielded a few questions about Wilson, who had a one-year contract. "I'll never be able to fill his shoes," Wilson said of Petty, "but I'm grateful to be able to fill his seat."

Petty spent the rest of the afternoon answering questions he'd answered a dozen times before that year. Because the last weekend had finally arrived, however, reporters hung on Petty's words.

"I started off hoping at the beginning of the year that it would be a really long year," Petty said. "I hoped it would take a long time to get it over with. But toward the end of the year the quicker I'm trying to get it over with.

"This last year has developed into something a lot bigger than I anticipated. It involved a lot more people completely away from racing and situations I never dreamed about. . . . We've been getting busier and busier and doing more and more things and gotten further and further away from the race car. . . . I'm looking forward to surviving between now and when the race is over."

Petty said there was no sadness creeping in as the final race approached.

"All the people I've met and the all the things I've done through the years we'll roll up into a big ball so I can look at the whole picture," he said. "There haven't been any sad times and I'm not looking for any."

When Petty announced that Wilson would drive his car in 1993, he also announced that Wilson would not use the No. 43. Wilson's cars would carry the No. 44, continuing the progression that began when Richard took his number following his father, who drove the No. 42.

That progression never would have started if Richard had gotten his way.

When preparing for his first race back in 1958 the No. 43 was not Richard's first choice. His father was No. 42, and Richard wanted to take those digits and reverse them. But another driver already was using the No. 24.

The number was available, however, in late 1992 as Jeff Gordon prepared to make his first Winston Cup start. The irony that Gordon got the number Richard Petty first wanted would become more evident as Gordon's career progressed.

Petty's final season was reaching the climax fans had been anticipating for more than a year. That, combined with the unprecedented battle for the championship with its three compelling lead characters, left little room for much else to draw attention as the '92 season drew to a close.

Davey, Awesome Bill and Kool

I n some ways the three primary challengers for the 1992 championship could not have been more different. Yet they also all shared some uncanny similarities.

Davey Allison and Alan Kulwicki, for example, were both devout Catholics in a sport that begins most of its events with very public—and very Protestant—prayers.

Allison grew up in Hueytown, Ala., and Elliott in Dawsonville, Ga. Both towns are in the heart of the region where NASCAR rooted before spreading like the fast-growing kudzu vine indigenous to the South. But in many ways Elliott was as much an outsider as Kulwicki, the Wisconsin native.

Allison grew up in the sport. He spent his childhood at tracks where his father, Bobby, and his uncle Donnie were racing. He spent hours playing with sons of other drivers—among them Ned Jarrett's son Dale, whose racing fate would one day become forever entwined with the legacy of his boyhood pal.

Elliott's father was a major force in driving his sons toward a career in the sport. Kulwicki's father was a race engine builder, but did as much as he could to divert his son's interest in the sport.

Allison was by far the most outgoing of the trio. Elliott disliked the attention that came with his success in racing. Kulwicki enjoyed being recognized for his accomplishments, but found it difficult to balance the demands that recognition placed on his time and energy with his desire to keep making his car race better.

All three were talented drivers, but for Allison and Elliott their abilities seemed more intrinsic, more natural. Kulwicki had a natural feel, too, but perhaps because he had more formal education than virtually any successful driver in NASCAR history, his contemporaries believed Kulwicki's talent was more deeply rooted in strategy and in his knowledge of the machine he was driving.

"Davey had big balls and a tremendous heart," said Michael Kranefuss, who directed Ford's NASCAR racing operations. "He was a fighter and had a lot of natural ability. With Alan you never knew if he was a natural driver because of the way he designed the race in the car. He could carry a car that was wounded. But I would be hard pressed to say he was as much a natural racer as Davey. They got the same results in a different way."

The points leader coming into the Hooters 500 was the oldest of Bobby and Judy Allison's four children. Davey Allison was born Feb. 25, 1961, in Hollywood, Fla., one day before that year's Daytona 500.

Bobby Allison began driving full-time in 1966, and even when Davey wasn't with his father at the track, his mind was. Young Davey's grade school records included notes from teachers who complained that the boy spent too much time daydreaming about race cars and too little time concentrating on his school work.

At age 12, Davey went to work in his father's race shop, earning 50 cents an hour for sweeping floors and sorting nuts and bolts. He wanted to go racing but his parents demanded he get a high school diploma before getting behind the wheel.

On track to graduate in 1979, Davey borrowed a 1972 Nova from uncle Donnie and raced for the first time on April 22 at Birmingham International Raceway, finishing fifth in a race in the limited sportsman division.

On May 5, in his sixth career start, Davey got his first victory at Birmingham. The next day at Talladega, Ala., Bobby won the Winston 500.

Right after graduation, Davey went to work full-time in his father's shop. He started building a car of his own, a '67 Chevy Nova, under

Bobby's strict orders that he could work on it only after 5 p.m.—once he was off the clock for dad's team.

That was no problem for Davey, for whom work was as natural as breathing. While playing football, basketball and baseball in high school, Davey also got a part-time job bagging groceries. He often worked at the store until 9 p.m., then went to his father's shop for several hours before going home for a quick nap and the trip to school to start another day.

The boundless capacity for work, combined with a keen desire to follow his father into Winston Cup, was a perfect formula for success. Five victories in his first season of limited sportsman racing were only the first signs of his potential.

Like pencil marks on the doorway charting the growth of a child, Talladega Superspeedway, the 2.66-mile track where fans had a passion for home-state drivers—the "Alabama Gang"—came to mark the progression of Davey's career.

He got his first superspeedway pole and victory in an Automobile Racing Club of America race there in 1983. He made his first Winston Cup start there in 1985 and filled in for an injured Neil Bonnett in July of 1986, starting and finishing seventh and leading at two different points in the race.

Allison's popularity quickly spread far beyond his home state track and its loyal fans. While he had his father's intense determination, Davey also had a natural friendliness that was contagious. His rarely contained boyish grin and his dancing eyes instantly revealed a playful nature. Virtually every one of his frequent attempts to grow facial hair resulted only in making him look even younger.

His father's competitive fire had often boiled over in anger and bitterness—more than once in his career, Bobby's temper contributed to him losing rides in cars that he had taken to victory lane. But Davey seemed to channel his drive into his time behind the wheel.

In 1987, Davey was ready for a full-time shot in the big leagues in Fords owned by Ranier-Lundy Racing. He won the pole for the season's second race at Rockingham, the first of his rookie-record five poles that year.

On May 3, once again at Talladega, Davey won for the first time in just his 14th Winston Cup race. Two races later, at Dover, Del., he won again. No Winston Cup driver had ever won twice in his rookie season.

The next year, Bobby won the Daytona 500 and Davey finished second. It was one of the most memorable outcomes in NASCAR history, but it would be the last time father and son would race each other so closely for a Winston Cup win.

On June 19, 1989, Bobby Allison's driving career came to an abrupt end.

On the first lap of a 500-mile race at Pocono, his car blew a tire going into the track's treacherous second turn. He hit the wall and turned sideways in front of traffic, with Jocko Maggiacomo's car slamming into the driver's side.

It took 20 minutes for Allison to be extricated, with Davey stopping to check on his father several times as the race continued under yellow.

Bobby had a broken left leg, but the most serious problem was a head injury. He was unconscious when he was taken from the car and airlifted to a hospital in Allentown, Pa. Allison stayed there until Aug. 1, when he was flown to a rehabilitation center in Birmingham and began to learn to walk all over again.

Allison finally went home to Hueytown in early October, but his days as a racer were over after 84 career wins in more than 700 races. The head injury had resulted in memory loss that left Bobby's mind still clouded at times during his son's run for the 1992 title.

Davey, after receiving assurances that his father was still alive and that doctors said he had a chance to recover, finished fifth at Pocono on the day of Bobby's crash. He won at Michigan and at Richmond later that year, and then won two more races in 1989 after Robert Yates bought out Harry Ranier and took charge of the race team.

After a winless 1990, Allison won five times in 1991—including the Coca-Cola 600 at Charlotte in May the weekend after winning The Winston, the sport's annual all-star race also held at the Charlotte track.

Allison finished third behind Earnhardt and Ricky Rudd in the '91 points race and came into '92 with every intention of joining Elliott in becoming the only Ford drivers to win the championship since David Pearson's back-to-back titles in 1968 and 1969.

Chrysler became the sport's dominant manufacturer in the early 1970s and Ford began using its Mercury nameplate in NASCAR. From the time the "modern-era" schedule began in 1972, it was more than three years before a Ford went to a Winston Cup victory lane—Buddy Baker won at Talladega in May of 1975.

Baker won twice more at Talladega and once each at Atlanta and Riverside, Calif., in the space of a calendar year, but after May 1976 the next Ford win came at Atlanta in March 1978 with Bobby Allison driving. Allison carried the Ford banner until 1981, when the manufacturer began working its way back into the NASCAR mainstream.

Dale Earnhardt, the 1980 champion in Chevrolets who would come to be that company's signature star later that decade, ran Fords owned by Bud Moore for two seasons—'82 and '83. But the man who would become the manufacturer's next headliner was a red-haired Georgian who began his career with a race team he, his brothers and their father poured their time, their talents and their resources into.

Bill Elliott, born Oct. 8, 1955, was one of George Elliott's three sons. Among the businesses George owned over the years was a junkyard, where Bill and his brothers Dan and Ernie would each pick out an old heap and work on it to get it running. They then raced each other around a makeshift track set down among the junkers, with Bill usually finishing first.

George Elliott later owned a Ford dealership in Dahlonega and put his sons to work there. Dan ran the parts department while Ernie, who had earned an engineering degree, worked on the cars in the shop along with Bill.

George also owned race cars that ran on short tracks around Georgia and Tennessee, and by the time Bill was 16 he was driving them. Ernie built the engines and Dan prepared the cars out of a shop in what had been an elementary school in Dahlonega.

When the NASCAR circuit came to Atlanta, the Elliotts would go and dream big dreams. They took a car to Charlotte in 1974, but Bill failed to qualify for a race in the Sportsman series, which became the Grand National series after the top circuit dropped that name in favor of Winston Cup. He failed similarly in 1975.

Early the next year, the Elliotts took a well-worn Ford Torino they bought from Bobby Allison and went to North Carolina Speedway in Rockingham to try to make the show. On Feb. 29, 1976, Bill made his first start and finished 33rd, earning $640.

The Elliotts raced as often as they could afford to over the next few years, impressing many in the sport with their dedication and work ethic. But while George's business ventures helped him make a good living, at least by the standards of the north Georgia hills, his pockets weren't deep enough to finance a full-blown, full-time racing effort for his three boys.

Harry Melling's pockets were. The Michigan businessman sponsored Elliott's car for one race in 1981, then bought the team at the end of that season. Melling largely limited his role in the team to providing the resources—such as a primary sponsorship from Coors beer—to allow Bill, Ernie and Dan to display talents that had been hidden by their meager means.

Bill ran 21 races in 1982, finishing second three times, and the full schedule for the first time the following year, with four more second-place finishes. It was apparent he was on the verge of breaking through, and on Nov. 20 in the final race of that '83 season at Riverside, Calif., he got his first career win in his 117th race.

Ford began to notice the Elliotts, too, and gradually increased its support for what began as a ragtag team of relatives and volunteers. In 1984, the support began to pay off. Elliott won at Michigan, at Charlotte and at Rockingham, finished second four times and wound up third in points behind Terry Labonte and Harry Gant.

In 1985, there was only one word to describe the Elliott team's performance.

Awesome.

The media couldn't resist the rhyming nickname and "Awesome Bill from Dawsonville" kept giving them reasons to use it. He won the Daytona 500. He won at Atlanta and then Darlington. And when he won the Winston 500 at Talladega, the plainspoken Georgian found himself smack in the middle of a media circus.

Time and inflation have diminished the impact of the $1 million bonus R. J. Reynolds first offered in 1985 for winning three of the sport's big four races —the Daytona 500, the most important race; the Winston 500 at Talladega, the fastest race; the Coca-Cola 600 at Charlotte, the longest race, and the Southern 500 at Darlington, the most historic race.

Until that point, the most any NASCAR champion had won in a single season was $873,118 by Waltrip in 1982. After his win at Talladega, Elliott was eligible to win a $1 million bonus just for winning the Coca-Cola 600 at Charlotte three weeks later.

There was no reason to believe he wouldn't, either. Elliott won the weekend after Talladega, at Dover, and headed for Charlotte with momentum on his side. Working against him, however, was the media deluge that awaited him.

Before the first win at Riverside in 1983, Elliott had developed a fan following. Drawn perhaps to the wide-eyed innocence he and his brothers brought with them to the track in those early days, fans took to Bill's round face and the shocks of reddish-orange hair that ringed it. Fans love an underdog, and NASCAR fans especially love one who sounds like a lot of them. When a Southern race fan says Elliott's first name, it has at least two syllables—Beee-ull.

As popular as he was, however, Elliott in 1985 was still far from being polished in his dealings with writers and broadcasters. He certainly wasn't ready for 600 week at Charlotte—perhaps nobody could have been.

Elliott's run for the $1 million bonus was on tap for Sunday, one day after the first running of The Winston, an all-star race among drivers who'd won races the previous year that paid a $200,000 first-place prize of its own.

All of that swelled the number of reporters covering the Charlotte race weekend, perhaps for the first time approaching the media swarm that would become normal at the sport's biggest races a decade later. And every one of those reporters was there to do a major story on Bill Elliott.

The small group who regularly covered Winston Cup was accustomed to a level of unlimited access to drivers that can barely be imagined in today's world of professional sports. Often, reporters and drivers would spend their days away from the track hunting or fishing together and parts of their weekends at the track sitting around hotel dining rooms or bars swapping stories.

Perhaps that all began to change in May of 1985 at Charlotte. The crush on Elliott and his team was simply too great for the usual situation to work. Pylons were erected and guards were posted around the garage stall where the Elliotts worked on the No. 9 Ford. The team's siege mentality became part of the story.

"I was pretty resentful of the media," Elliott recalled. "A lot of the people didn't write exactly what I said and I blamed it a lot on the media. I couldn't communicate well. I didn't know how. It became a situation I let get to me."

The Elliott story fizzled in the Coca-Cola 600. He had a tire go down and a lug nut came loose inside the wheel, ripping a hole in a brake line. He finished 18th, 21 laps behind the winner, Waltrip, who had also won the inaugural running of The Winston.

With the Charlotte fiasco behind him, Elliott won twice at Pocono and twice at Michigan before going to Darlington for the Southern 500 and his final shot at the $1 million bonus. Once again all eyes focused on Elliott, but the lessons the team and NASCAR had learned in May helped everyone handle the attention more effectively.

Elliott dodged disaster all day in the Southern 500 and edged Cale Yarborough by less than a tenth of a second for a dramatic victory. Fireworks, balloons and confetti—the latter in the form of fake $1 million bills bearing Elliott's photo—exploded in victory lane.

Elliott left Darlington with a $1 million check and a 206-point lead over Waltrip in the points race before the pattern that would haunt him again in 1992 began to take shape.

Waltrip won at Richmond and Elliott ran 12th, losing 53 points off his lead. The next weekend at Dover, Elliott lost 69 laps while his crew replaced the rear-end housing after he broke an axle and hub. Elliott's lead was down to 86. Elliott wrecked at Martinsville, too, and Waltrip climbed to within 23 points. North Wilkesboro was next, and things only got worse. Just 118 laps into the race, Elliott was done—his car had a broken flywheel. Waltrip finished 14th but took the points lead.

Elliott hung in over the next three races, actually winning again at Atlanta to go into the final race of the season just 20 points behind Waltrip. But in the finale at Riverside, Calif., an $8 part in his transmission broke and Elliott finished 31st again. Waltrip ran seventh and won the title by 101 points—a 307-point pickup over the final eight races.

For years afterward, critics would point to Elliott's loss in the '85 championship race as evidence of the flawed nature of NASCAR's points system. Elliott won 11 times while Waltrip won just three races. But Elliott finished in the top five in just five of the 17 races he did not win. Waltrip had six runner-up finishes and six third-place runs and his consistency won out.

The winner of a Winston Cup race gets 175 points. Second place is worth 170, third worth 165, fourth 160, fifth 155 and sixth 150. Seventh place pays 146 points and a four-point difference per position goes down to 11th, which is worth 130. From that point, the difference is three points per position, with 41st being worth 40 points.

Qualifying pays no points. Winning a race pays no additional points, either, except for a bonus of five points for leading at least one lap. Since every race winner has to lead at least one lap—the final one— first place in a Winston Cup race is worth at least 180 points—175 for first plus the five points for leading. There's also a five-point bonus for the driver leading the most laps, so the maximum available in any one race is 185 points.

If a runner-up leads the most laps he earns 180 points—170 for second, five for leading a lap and five for leading the most laps. In that case, the winner and the second-place driver get the same number of points. There should be no way, the system's critics contend, for a runner-up to get the same number of points as a winner.

Elliott's 1985 collapse kept Ford from ending a string of 10 straight championships by General Motors-built cars—six of them, including the one in '85, with teams owned by Junior Johnson—but his season still was a publicity bonanza for the company. Not every Winston Cup race had live television coverage that year, and in many of the important ones that did, Elliott won. He'd won $2,433,187, an almost unthinkable total to long-time followers of the sport.

Regardless of the points arithmetic, Elliott was the dominant name in motorsports in 1985 and every one knew that "Awesome Bill," or "Million Dollar Bill" as he was called after the Southern 500 victory, drove a Ford Thunderbird.

While there's little statistical evidence to support a direct correlation between racing and retail—the adage of "win on Sunday, sell on Monday"—Elliott's season did at least give Ford fans and company officials something to smile about.

Elliott won only twice in 1986, but won six more races in 1987 and finished second to Earnhardt in points.

Finally, in 1988, he got the championship that had eluded his grasp. He took the lead with a second-place finish at Bristol, then won at Darlington and Dover to build a 127-point edge over Dale Earnhardt and a 139-point over Rusty Wallace. The win at Dover was Elliott's sixth of the season, and although he didn't win again he did protect his lead to finish 24 points up on Wallace, ending the season out with a conservative but intelligent 11th-place finish at Atlanta to close the door.

Winston Cup's annual awards banquet is held each year at the

Waldorf-Astoria Hotel in the heart of midtown Manhattan, a few blocks from Times Square.

That's about as far away from the moonshining hills of the Appalachians as you can get, which is why the banquet is held in New York. The sport craves acceptance into the mainstream and seeks to gain it by going "uptown" for its annual celebration. Still, it's always something odd to see the Richard Pettys and Junior Johnsons of the world decked out in black-tie formal wear.

With Elliott as champion, the 1988 banquet had the feel of a "Ma and Pa Kettle" movie. Elliott went along with the image, saying his biggest worry about the 75 or so people he'd brought with him was that they might go home with sunburns on the roof of their mouths from holding them open as they walked around.

By the end of the 1991 season, however, things were not the same in Dawsonville, where the folks sound an old fire-engine siren at the local pool hall to celebrate every Elliott victory.

Bill and his first wife, Martha, had divorced. The pressures of keeping up with the sport's financial and technological growth began to wear on the Elliotts. Bill won three races in '89 but just one in 1990 and again in 1991. So when Geoffrey Bodine left Johnson's team to drive for Bud Moore after the 1991 season, Elliott left his Dawsonville roots behind and moved into Johnson's No. 11 Fords.

One year before Elliott's arrival, Johnson had decided to go back to a two-car team. His search for a second driver had centered on a strong-willed racer from Wisconsin whose determination and work ethic had made him widely respected in the garage, despite the fact few people really seemed to know him well at all.

Alan Kulwicki liked it that way. Born Dec. 14, 1954, in Greenfield, Wis., he had an upbringing in racing even if it did not come from a traditional Southern background. His father, Gerald, built engines that won six U.S. Auto Club stock-car championships, so like Allison and Elliott, the younger Kulwicki's exposure to motorsports began early.

Alan's exposure to tragedy started early, too. When he was in the second grade his mother died. Gerald moved Alan and his brother, Kenny, in with their grandmother, who died five years later. A year after that Kenny, who suffered from hemophilia, also died.

Alan ran in his first stock-car race at age 19 at a track in Hales Corners, Wis. Later that year, at Leo's Speedway in Oshkosh, he won for the first time. But Gerald Kulwicki knew how hard it could be to make a living in the business, so he did little to encourage his son's desire to race.

"At times I resented the fact that he didn't want me to race and did little to help my career," Alan recalled later. "I always felt he could have pulled some strings, but he never did. He never invested his own money in my cars, but I could always go and ask him questions. He just had a different perspective. He knew how difficult it was to be successful and he didn't want me to get hurt. I was all he had left."

Gerald wanted his surviving son to be exposed to opportunities beyond racing and encouraged him to get an education. Kulwicki went to the University of Wisconsin at Milwaukee, earning a bachelor of science degree in mechanical engineering in 1977. He kept right on racing, however, winning championships at Slinger Speedway and Wisconsin International Raceway while studying and then working as an engineer for two years after graduation.

Kulwicki turned to racing full-time in 1979, eventually moving into the American Speed Association, a breeding ground for future NASCAR stars like Wallace and Mark Martin.

It was at an ASA race at Winchester, Ind., in 1980 that Tom Roberts first noticed Kulwicki. On a trip to gather information for an upcoming race at Nashville Speedway, where Roberts worked in public relations, he struck up a conversation with Becky Robbins, wife of ASA patriarch Rex Robbins, at a Holiday Inn in Muncie, Ind.

"Becky started telling me about Alan Kulwicki," Roberts said. "Her direct comment was, 'Tom, I always told him he was too smart to be a race car driver.' I decided I needed to find out a little bit more about this guy. I noticed him at the race track, and I found out about his background and more or less just eyed him from a distance that weekend."

Roberts wrote a press release entitled "Kulwicki—Soon to be a Household Name." Racing trade publications picked it up and printed stories based on what Roberts wrote. Kulwicki read one, found out who had been behind getting him noticed and called Roberts to express his gratitude.

The two agreed to have dinner together when Kulwicki came to Nashville for the race. At a cookout for the drivers, crews and local media, Roberts sat down with Kulwicki for the first time.

"Why did you do that?" Kulwicki asked Roberts, wanting to know why Roberts had picked him to do the story on.

"I don't know," Roberts said. "It just seemed like you were in control of everything around you at the track. And you seemed to work so hard on your race car."

Kulwicki liked the answer. He liked people who noticed how dedicated he was.

People who would meet him later in his career would often feel that Kulwicki decided within the first few minutes after meeting a person if he liked them or not, then spend months testing the accuracy of that first impression.

Kulwicki raced five full seasons in the ASA, winning 12 poles and five races. NASCAR, however, was his ultimate goal. In 1983 Jim Braun, who owned Kulwicki's ASA team, rented a Winston Cup car for Kulwicki to drive in a race at Charlotte Motor Speedway.

Kulwicki knew every bolt on the cars he drove in the ASA series, but the Cup car wasn't his and it took him a while to figure it out. In early practice sessions, the car was nine seconds off the pace. As Kulwicki kept working on it, adjusting the shocks and springs and making other changes, that gap narrowed quickly. But before he got the chance to qualify, insurance issues arose and the team withdrew.

"That hurt my confidence," Kulwicki said. "I suspected it was the car but never knew for sure. There have been a lot of excellent drivers who have had a terrible time trying to adapt to Winston Cup cars."

Kulwicki came back in 1984 to run in Grand National races at Charlotte, Atlanta, Bristol and Milwaukee. He finished in the top five in three of them and in the top 10 in all four, restoring his faith in his abilities.

In 1985, Kulwicki lined up a five-race Winston Cup deal in cars owned by Bill Terry and sponsored by Hardee's, a chain of fast-food restaurants that also sponsored Kulwicki in the ASA.

His first Winston Cup start came Sept. 8 at Richmond International Raceway. On his first-round qualifying lap, Kulwicki drove too far into the third turn before letting off the accelerator and smacked the wall with the rear of his car.

"Let's just load it up and go home," said Terry, who didn't have a backup car for Kulwicki to run in.

"We can fix it," Kulwicki said.

Friends helped Kulwicki beat the dents out of the sheet metal and repair the damage to the suspension and the rear end. Kulwicki earned the 25th starting spot in second-day qualifying and finished 19th in the race. He raced at Dover, Charlotte, Rockingham and Atlanta later that year, with a 13th at Charlotte his best result.

But that was enough for Kulwicki to dive into NASCAR full-bore. He returned to Wisconsin and sold his short-track equipment. He loaded up an old Ford truck to head south, but days before his planned departure a fire burned out the truck's electrical system. Kulwicki rewired it and then set off for his new life, saying later that if anybody had been trying to give him a warning, he was determined not to heed it.

In addition to the tools and furniture on his truck and the money from the sale of his short-track cars, all Kulwicki had was a one-race deal for the Daytona 500, the first race of the 1986 season in the car owned by Terry. When he got to Florida in February, Kulwicki's name was misspelled over the window of the car.

In practice at Daytona, Kulwicki was running behind Bobby Hillin's car when it blew an engine. Kulwicki spun in the oil and hit the wall.

Volunteers from other race teams helped repair the car in time for his 125-mile qualifying race, in which Kulwicki needed to finish 15th or better to earn a spot in the 500. Coming off the final turn on the final lap, Lake Speed and Dick Trickle drafted their way past Kulwicki and knocked him out of the top 15 and out of a starting spot for the 500.

Kulwicki went to the next race at Richmond, the site of his first start the previous year, to try again. His qualifying speed was seventh fastest before rain came with three cars left to qualify. Under NASCAR rules, the qualifying times were washed out and the starting field was set based on the previous year's points and on postmarks on the team's entry forms for those that didn't get in on points. Terry had been late mailing in the team's entry, so Kulwicki didn't make the race.

Kulwicki was furious that a postmark had cost him the chance to race. He knew the only way he could control something like that, the only way he could be in charge of his racing destiny, was to be responsible for such details himself. He bought the car from Terry and took his career into his own hands. If he failed, he would have only himself to blame.

He would do things his way.

At Rockingham on March 2, 1986, Kulwicki made his first race as a driver-owner. He started 27th and finished 15th. Stuart deGeus, the marketing director for Quincy's, the chain of steakhouses that had signed the one-race sponsorship before Daytona, was there that day to hold the signboard marking the spot for Kulwicki to stop on pit road. He enjoyed it so much the one-race deal got extended to 15 races. Eventually, the deal covered all 23 races in which Kulwicki competed that year.

The entire deal was worth about $200,000. Kulwicki had one car, the one he'd bought from Terry, and two engines leased from Prototype Engineering near Chicago. Those engines were shuttled back and forth by air freight each week, with Kulwicki racing one and then sending it to be refurbished while racing the other the next week.

He rented shop space in Kannapolis, N.C. He found an apartment —Kulwicki had been living in motels near Terry's home base of Greenville, S.C., since the move from Wisconsin—and hired his first two full-time employees. He changed his car number from 32 to 35.

He named his car "Sirloin." The Quincy's folks were less than thrilled to learn the car had earned that nickname because it was so tough— "tough" wasn't exactly a word it wanted associated with its primary product. But Kulwicki made it work.

At Talladega in May, Kulwicki topped the 200 mph mark in qualifying but still wasn't fast enough to make the field for the Winston 500.

Quincy's had bought 150 tickets to the race and invited franchise-holders and top customers to attend. It could have been a disaster for the sponsor, but Kulwicki turned it around. On the morning of the race, Kulwicki had his car moved from the garage to an area behind the grandstands near where the Quincy's clients were to be seated that day. Instead of hiding from them after failing to make the race, Kulwicki met his sponsor's guests warmly, shaking hands and signing autographs.

"I want to thank you for your support," Kulwicki said. "We didn't go fast enough to make the race this weekend, but this race team has been running better and better each week and you folks have helped make that possible for us."

Kulwicki was at his best in such moments, thanks in no small part to the college education his father had encouraged him to get. Kulwicki had an intuitive feel for the business side of racing. He also was telling the truth. A week earlier, Kulwicki had finished fourth at Martinsville, Va.

By season's end, he had finished 18th or better 18 times and completed 94.7 percent of the possible laps in his 23 starts. Kulwicki was named rookie of the year, beating out Michael Waltrip for the honor despite the fact that Michael's brother, Darrell, as the defending series champion, was on the panel that chose the rookie award winner.

Wallace, his old rival and friend from the ASA days, helped steer sponsorship from Zerex anti-freeze toward Kulwicki's team for 1987. Kulwicki's car number changed to 7—because the number was shaped like the first letter of the new sponsor's name—and in that season's third race at Richmond he earned his first career pole. He finished the year with three poles and ran second to Dale Earnhardt at Pocono, Pa., in July, losing the lead on the final lap.

The next year at the banquet in New York, Wallace suggested Paul Andrews when Kulwicki said he was looking for a good crew chief. Andrews got the job and Kulwicki won four more poles in 1988 and finished second at Darlington in March and at Martinsville in September.

Finally, on Nov. 6 at Phoenix, in his 85th career Winston Cup race, Kulwicki got his first career win. After taking the checkered flag and coming back around the track on a cool-down lap, Kulwicki turned his car around on the frontstretch to make another victory lap, this time going clockwise in the opposite direction from which the race had been run.

When he got to victory lane, Ford's Preston Miller asked him if that was a "Polish victory lap."

Kulwicki repeated the remark in his postrace interview and the name stuck. Fans loved it, but NASCAR officials were not amused. Worried that people scurrying around the track at the end of the race might not expect a car coming from the wrong direction, Kulwicki was advised not to repeat the celebration. Kulwicki said he wouldn't, at least not until he won his first championship.

He won six poles and ran second twice in 1989 finishing 14th in points for the second straight season and going over the $1 million mark in career earnings. But he didn't win again until October of 1990 at Rockingham. By that time, changes in the company's corporate structure had led Zerex to decide not to continue its sponsorship for 1991.

Kulwicki began looking for a new sponsor. He had assembled an intensely loyal team around him, people who had bonded in an "us-against-the-world" spirit that Kulwicki cleverly cultivated. He talked to anyone who would listen about how good he thought his team could be with the proper backing. He liked being in charge.

"When I first came here, I just wanted to drive for somebody else," Kulwicki said. "I did it that way out of necessity. By the time I got other offers, I had so much invested in this team, I didn't want to give up on it."

With Johnson looking to add a second team for 1991, however, Ford officials saw the opportunity to pair Kulwicki with Junior Johnson.

Ford liked having Kulwicki in its camp and felt it could capitalize on his blue-collar image more as he became more successful. If Kulwicki could win races on a shoestring budget the way he had, the Ford racing brass was licking its chops in anticipation of what the driver could do with a major sponsor's resources and Johnson's legendary guidance.

Johnson had never won a championship in his driving career, mainly because he paid more attention to chasing victories than points. But he'd made up for it by winning six titles as a car owner, three straight with Cale Yarborough driving from 1976 to 1978 and three with Darrell Waltrip in 1981, 1982 and 1985.

Robert Glenn Johnson Jr. was born in Wilkes County, N.C., in June 1931. Farming and moonshine whiskey were the family's businesses. Junior remembers having to climb over stacked cases of illegal whiskey to get to his bed. Federal revenue agents would occasionally raid the house and destroy the inventory—once busting up a record of more than 7,000 cases in a single stop.

He'd started running moonshine at age 14 and had already begun his NASCAR career when, in 1956, he was arrested along with his dad for manufacturing liquor. His father got three years in prison and Junior got two years. Junior wound up serving a little more than 11 months of his sentence at a prison in Ohio before being paroled.

Junior was arrested along with his brothers and his mother in 1958, but this time Junior won acquittal using his NASCAR driving schedule as his alibi—how could he have been running moonshine and racing at the same time?

Johnson won his 50th career race on Oct. 3, 1965, at North Wilkesboro, the track where he'd first raced as a 17-year-old plowboy in 1949. He made eight more starts in 1966, again with the final one coming at North Wilkesboro, then retired as a driver and began his career as a car owner.

From 1967 to 1992, Junior Johnson-owned cars won 137 races and six championships. Some of the greatest drivers in the sport's history—LeeRoy Yarbrough, Bobby Allison, Cale Yarborough, Darrell Waltrip, Neil Bonnett, Geoffrey Bodine, Terry Labonte and Elliott among them—found success in his cars.

Along the way, Johnson became the definition of the clichéd legend in his own time. In 1964, an article by Thomas Wolfe in *Esquire* magazine dubbed him "the last American hero" and led to a 1973 movie starring Jeff Bridges as "Junior Jackson."

As Kulwicki searched for a new sponsor in late 1990, Ford officials pressed him to take Johnson's ride. Friends told him he would be crazy to turn the offer aside. Still, Kulwicki held off. He was waiting to hear the final answer from his potential sponsor, General Foods, which was looking to use its Maxwell House coffee brand to back a team.

Finally, Johnson needed an answer. He had Sterling Marlin, son of former racer Clifford "Coo Coo" Marlin, as Plan B in case he couldn't convince Kulwicki to come on board.

It all came down to a day in early September of 1990.

Kulwicki was in the office of his shop in Charlotte with one of Ford's top racing officials sitting with him, phone in hand. On the other end of the line was another Ford official, with Johnson in his office near North Wilkesboro, N.C.

"Tell that boy he needs to come drive for me," Johnson said to the Ford operative in his office.

The message was duly relayed.

"I really think I'm going to get this sponsor, and if I do I still want to keep this team going," Kulwicki said.

That message was relayed, too.

"You tell him that if he's waiting on Maxwell House, he's wasting his time," Johnson said to the Ford man in his office. "I've already got them signed."

Kulwicki first felt disbelief, then betrayal. The answer was no. He would never drive for Junior Johnson, not after this.

Ford officials pleaded with him to reconsider. Michael Kranefuss, the head of Ford's racing program, would later say Kulwicki was "a complete idiot" for turning Johnson down. Wayne Estes, the Ford public relations man who had come to be one of Kulwicki's good friends, drove from his home near Atlanta to the next race at Richmond just so he could stop by in Charlotte to ask Kulwicki if he was sure he was making the right decision.

Kulwicki was positive.

So at the start of the 1991 season, Marlin was in the Maxwell House car owned by Johnson. Kulwicki, meanwhile, had no sponsor and no real prospects on his horizon. He told people working for his team they were free to pursue whatever opportunities came along since the future of Alan Kulwicki Racing was so uncertain. It was a testament to the loyalty Kulwicki had fostered that hardly anybody went anywhere.

American soldiers were at war in the Persian Gulf that February and R. J. Reynolds arranged to have five cars in the Daytona 500 carry colors of each of the nation's military branches. Kulwicki carried the U.S. Army's colors and finished eighth.

At Richmond and Rockingham, his white car carried only the AK logo of Alan Kulwicki Racing on its hood where a primary sponsor's logos would go. He finished fifth at Richmond and 17th at Rockingham, then went to Atlanta hoping for a miracle.

He got one.

Kulwicki won the pole for the March 17 race. Hooters, meanwhile, had decided to give NASCAR a try in the race in its home city of Atlanta, sponsoring a car driven by Mark Stahl. When Stahl didn't make the race, the company signed a one-race deal with Kulwicki and had its logos moved from Stahl's car to Kulwicki's.

Kulwicki finished eighth. Hooters signed on for two more races. Kulwicki qualified sixth at Darlington and fifth at Bristol, and although he didn't finish well in either race the Hooters deal was extended for the remainder of the season.

Kulwicki continued to qualify brilliantly—he won four poles and started in the top 10 in all but four of that season's races. On Aug. 24 he won at Bristol. Three weeks later, Hooters and Kulwicki announced a three-year sponsorship deal that gave his team a level of security it never had before.

When Kulwicki was pulling the Grand National car to Charlotte to make his first run in that series, a trucker on a citizen's band radio called to ask what driver the car belonged to. A crew member answered with Kulwicki's name.

"Alan who?" the trucker said.

"Never mind," said the crewman, "the driver is Special K."

When that story got around back in ASA territory, public address announcers picked up on it and the name stuck.

Michael Waltrip called Kulwicki the "Polish Prince" during their run for rookie of the year in 1986. Jake Elder, a veteran crew chief nick-named "Suitcase Jake" himself because of his propensity for changing jobs, called Kulwicki "Slider" because the driver was able to "slide in" fast laps in qualifying and win poles.

Many of those closest to Kulwicki came up with yet another nick-name during the years Zerex was sponsoring his car. Because the prod-uct was designed to keep his engine cool, because Kulwicki's driving style was cool and calculating, and because it was the first syllable of his last name, they just called him "Kool."

Kulwicki also had his own personal mascot. From the very early days of his career, he started wearing a patch of the cartoon character Mighty Mouse on his uniforms and having them painted on his cars.

It fit the "little guy against the world" image that he felt most com-fortable with.

"I fight the bad cats," Kulwicki said.

Before he came to Atlanta to try to conquer the racing world on the final week of the '92 season, Kulwicki asked Estes to ask if he could take the first two letters off the car's model name on the nose of his No. 7 Thunderbird. Nobody at Ford had any problem with that.

So on Friday morning, when his team unloaded the car from its trans-porter, there was Mighty Mouse on the nose of Kulwicki's car in place of the letters "TH."

In the Hooters 500, the underdog second-place driver in the Winston Cup standings would be driving a Ford "UNDERBIRD."

28 Down, One to Go

Each NASCAR weekend begins with a motorized ballet.

In a typical week, trucks carrying the cars drive in late Thursday from the teams' shops, many of which are based within a 50-mile radius of downtown Charlotte. They gather at truck stops or park in campgrounds near the tracks to spend the night.

Before sunrise Friday, they line up in the order they will be parked in the garage area, which is set up as a meritocracy. The reigning champion's transporter comes first, followed by teams in the order of the points standings going into the previous race.

On Nov. 13, 1992, Dale Earnhardt's transporter was first in line at Atlanta Motor Speedway. The Atlanta lineup order was set Sunday morning at Phoenix, before that day's race changed the standings, so Bill Elliott's truck came next with Davey Allison's, then Alan Kulwicki's and the others behind them.

Each team's transporter carries two race-ready cars. First is the "primary" car, the one it plans to use that week. The second is a backup that will be brought out only if the primary car is damaged too badly in a practice or qualifying incident.

Teams are not allowed to change to the backup car on a whim; NASCAR must agree that the primary is too badly damaged to be repaired for the race and the team must pay a second entry fee of $2,000 for the backup car.

Work areas in the garage are also assigned to each team based on the points standings, keeping most cars relatively close to their transporters through the weekend.

On a typical weekend the teams practice from mid-morning until early afternoon Friday, working to get their cars ready for qualifying later in the day.

Winston Cup racing changed its rules and went to a single round of qualifying in 2001. In 1992, the top 20 positions were filled in first-round qualifying on Friday. Saturdays began with an early-morning practice session followed by second-round qualifying, where the remaining spots were filled on the starting grid.

Drivers who had failed to make Friday's top 20 could stand on their first-round speeds or requalify in hopes of going faster. Teams confident their speed would be good enough to make the race often stood on first-round laps to begin changing their cars to get them ready for the race.

Most teams have special engines, built to deliver more horsepower without enduring the punishment of a long race, and employ dozens of other adjustments for qualifying that won't work in the race. Going fast enough in the first round to be assured of making the race allowed the teams to begin changing their setups on Friday afternoon to use Saturday's practice sessions to work on their race packages.

In 1992, many tracks allowed an additional midday practice session after second-round qualifying and before the "support race"—most often a Busch Grand National event, which runs about half of its schedule in conjunction with Winston Cup dates. A final one-hour Cup practice, commonly called "happy hour," followed that race.

Sunday is, of course, race day.

The garage area opens five to six hours before the green flag, and crew members who are responsible for mechanical duties on their race teams are lined up when the gates open. Most teams have additional crewmen who come in only for Sunday to be part of the over-the-wall crew on pit stops.

Every team runs through a detailed checklist, making sure none of the car's parts has been damaged in some unseen way in practice.

Many times a driver and his crew chief will talk after the final practice Saturday and decide that major changes need to be made before race time. In other cases a drastic change in weather might require a new approach to race day, since engines, tires and other vital factors in how a car behaves on the track might be vastly different in warm, sunny weather than in cool, cloudy conditions.

Two hours before the race, drivers and crew chiefs attend a mandatory meeting with NASCAR officials, where reminders about pit road speed limits and other rules are covered. Any driver who fails to attend this meeting must start the race at the back of the field. The driver's meeting is followed by a chapel service. About 30 minutes before the race, the drivers assemble to be introduced one-by-one to the crowd. Again, any driver failing to appear at introductions is banished to rear of the starting field.

After introductions, many drivers sneak off to the bathroom. Once the race starts, there's no time for that kind of pit stop until the checkered flag falls. There's no need, either. It's warm inside the cars and with the fire suits the drivers wear, perspiration and concentration take care of that issue.

As the crowd listens to a prerace prayer and the national anthem, the drivers are already inside their cars hooking up to two-way radios and cooling systems that pump fresh air into their fire-retardant suits and thickly padded helmets.

Each driver's seat is built to fit snugly. A safety harness with belts twice as wide as belts used in a typical passenger car is locked down and pulled tight, securing the driver in place to prevent him from banging around inside the car in case of a wreck.

At the command of "Gentlemen start your engines!" from a politician, sponsor representative or some other VIP each driver flips switches or mashes a button—there are no keys to these cars—and a motor capable of creating more than 700 horsepower rumbles to life.

During the parade laps the pace car in front of the field runs at the speed that will be used for that day's pit-road limit. The cars running behind it at the same speed check their tachometers to see how many rpm their engine is turning at that speed. Since the race cars have no speedometers, this is how the drivers judge their speed as they come in for a stop. Pit road speed limits vary from 35 mph at tracks with short, tight pit roads to 55 at tracks with longer, wider and straighter pit lanes.

Inside the engine, hundreds of moving parts work under the highest possible stress. The failure of even one part can instantly end a team's day. Chassis setups are so finely tuned that one turn of bolts used to shift weight toward one side or the other can make a car handle in a completely different way. One pound of air pressure in one of the tires can be enough to make a car just good enough to pick up several positions, or even earn a victory.

In 1992, the teams had already done all of that 28 times before coming to Atlanta for the race that would determine that year's champion.

Allison fulfilled a childhood dreams to start the year in February, winning the Daytona 500 four years after finishing second in the race to his father. He did it in a backup Ford after crashing during a practice session four days before the race.

In the 500, he avoided a big crash that took out Elliott, Richard Petty, Earnhardt and several others on Lap 92. Allison led the final 98 green-flag laps and began his early season hold on the points lead.

Elliott had won one of the two 125-mile qualifying races on the Thursday before the Daytona 500. After his wreck in the main event, he and new car owner Junior Johnson became the season's first big story by winning the next four races.

Elliott dominated at Rockingham, lapping all but two cars, but Allison was second. Elliott won at Richmond, banging bumpers with Kulwicki over the final 10 laps and beating him to the checkered flag by less than 2 feet.

Pit strategy or luck, depending on how you looked at it, paid off at Atlanta. Superior gas mileage had allowed Elliott to go farther without making a late-race pit stop, and when a time caution came out he pitted under the yellow. Elliott wound up nearly a full lap ahead of his challengers and won by more than 22 seconds.

At Darlington, Elliott concentrated on minimizing tire wear and took the lead for good when Harry Gant had to make a late stop for new tires.

Allison finished fourth at Atlanta and Darlington and still led by 48 points, but on April 1 his grandfather Edmund Jacob Allison died of cancer at the age of 87. Until the illness kept him away for the past year, "Pop" Allison had been a constant presence at the track, pulling for his grandson or watching Alabama driver Hut Stricklin pilot the car of the team that Bobby Allison owned.

Davey Allison and Stricklin, ironically, qualified to start side-by-side on Row 3 for the Food City 500 that weekend at Bristol. But Allison was penalized a lap for pitting outside his stall on Lap 270, then 12 laps later crashed and suffered painful rib injuries. Sterling Marlin, who had dropped out early, took over as a relief driver and brought the No. 28 car home in 28th.

Kulwicki won at Bristol, his second straight win at the half-mile short track, giving him four career victories. Elliott spun out just past halfway and managed a 20th-place finish, but Marlin's relief helped Allison hang on to the points lead by 29. Kulwicki was up to fifth, 99 points behind.

The day after Bristol, Dave Marcis and Dick Trickle took one of the most important trips in NASCAR history, traveling to Indianapolis to test Dodge cars being used in the International Race of Champions all-star series at Indianapolis Motor Speedway.

Ostensibly a trial-run for a possible IROC race to be held at America's most famous race track as part of Indianapolis 500 pole qualifying day, the presence of full-fendered cars at the Brickyard, where open-wheel racers had competed since 1911, created a stir. Clearly something much bigger was in the works.

Rumors about stock cars at Indy swirled the next weekend at North Wilkesboro, where Allison showed his grit in a memorable performance.

Jimmy Hensley qualified the car on Friday and ran most of the practice in it on Saturday. He was also there for the race on Sunday, standing by to get into the seat if Allison needed relief because of his sore ribs.

Hensley stood by all afternoon.

"Jimmy was standing in the pits, in uniform, helmet in hand, for 400 laps," said Larry McReynolds, Allison's crew chief. "I knew there was no way Jimmy was going to get in that race car.

"Davey stayed in it, never complained and won the dad-gum race. After the race, the pain on his face was unbelievable. He sat down beside that car with a towel around his neck for most of victory lane, doing interviews and posing for pictures. But he did the job he needed to do for 400 laps."

Later that afternoon, after Allison's car passed inspection, McReynolds walked to the parking area with his wife, Linda, to find their car and head home.

"I wish you would look over there," McReynolds said to Linda, shaking his head.

Allison was sitting on a suitcase in the bed of his pickup truck on pit road, surrounded by about 300 race fans. Bad ribs and all, Allison stayed until every last one of those fans had an autograph.

Allison's ribs were better two weeks later when the circuit ran at Martinsville, Va., but he crashed again late when overheated brakes caused a tire to blow, sending him into the outside wall in Turn 2. Mark Martin won that race and Allison barely held his points lead over Gant, who finished fifth to move within 16 points.

At Talladega, Allison got back on track by winning the Winston 500 to earn two shots at the Winston Million, something nobody had won since Elliott in '85. Allison beat Elliott by two car-lengths at Talladega to give Ford a sweep of the season's first nine races. Counting the final four races of '91, Ford had won 13 straight.

Next up was Charlotte Motor Speedway's two-week celebration of speed. May of 1992 was particularly festive at Charlotte, because the 1.5-mile oval was debuting brand new lights for the May 16 running of The Winston all-star race. The track had spent $1.7 million on an ingenious system that used large mirrors to reflect light onto the track while minimizing glare for the drivers, and promoted its first race under those lights with the slogan "One Hot Night."

The Winston is a special, non-points event with a field limited to those drivers who have won races or who qualify with finishes in a preliminary event on race night for those who otherwise are ineligible. Its format is designed to mimic the style of Saturday night dirt-track racing, so racing under the lights was a natural development for the event.

Allison had won The Winston in 1991 and qualified fastest for it in '92. He won the first 30-lap segment, after which the field was inverted. Kyle Petty won the second 30-lap segment, allowing him to start first in the final 10-lap segment where $200,000 awaited the winner.

Petty built a lead over the first few laps of the final segment, but Darrell Waltrip's spin brought out a yellow and bunched the field for a restart.

Dale Earnhardt grabbed the lead at the green flag and held it until the final turn of the final lap, where Petty and Earnhardt made contact and Earnhardt's Chevrolet spun, taking him out of contention.

Allison, who had been running third, made up ground quickly as Petty and Earnhardt dueled and Petty let off the accelerator to avoid

Earnhardt's spin. Coming off the final turn and heading for the finish line, Allison had momentum and wheeled his Thunderbird to the inside as Petty tried to block him.

A crowd of more than 130,000 cheered wildly as Allison crossed the line less than half of a car-length ahead.

Within a moment, the cheers turned into an eerie hush.

As the top two cars crossed the finish line, they bumped. Allison lost control of his Ford and slid through the trioval, then slammed the wall, driver's side first.

As rescue vehicles began rolling toward Allison's crumpled Ford, McReynolds took off in the same direction. Allison had been knocked unconscious briefly during the crash, but was coming around when McReynolds got there.

"I can still see him slumped over in the car," McReynolds says. "I knew he wasn't hurt hurt, I knew he was knocked kind of coo-coo."

McReynolds was worried about his driver, but he was also worried about something else, too. As the rescue workers cut Allison out of the car, McReynolds kept checking the scoreboard to see what number was going to be posted at the top.

"It seemed like it took about two hours, and it was probably two minutes," McReynolds said. "Finally, they flipped that No. 28 up top. It was like, 'Yes!'"

Allison had a concussion and several other injuries. Instead of going to victory lane, he got a ride in an ambulance to the infield care center and then to the hospital, where he would spend the night.

"What happened?" Allison asked McReynolds on the ride to the infield care center.

"You won the race, Davey," McReynolds said.

"You're shittin' me," Allison said.

"No, Davey, you won the race," McReynolds repeated.

"You're not shittin' me?" Allison asked again.

"Davey, I wouldn't shit you about something like that," McReynolds said. "You won the race."

The victory was worth $300,000—$50,000 for the pole, $50,000 for winning the first segment and $200,000 for the final segment—but the price was very high. Allison, still not 100 percent after the rib injury at Bristol, was banged up badly again and the car he had destroyed in the wreck was his team's best.

The car, nicknamed "007" because it was the seventh chassis built by the Robert Yates team, had raced five times at Charlotte and won four times with one second-place finish. And Charlotte wasn't the only place where the car was strong.

"When we took it to a race track, we'd roll in the gate the competitors would ask, 'What car have you got?'" McReynolds said. "We'd say, '007.' They'd say, 'Oh, God.' We won so many races with that car."

The team had thought about saving "007" for the Coca-Cola 600 and the shot at $1 million, but elected to use its best car in The Winston with hopes of using it again the following weekend in the 600.

"Our attitude, and I think it was the reason we got along so good, was that our next race was The Winston and we were going to take our best piece to The Winston, no question," McReynolds said. "So we took it, sat on the pole and won the race. But we paid a big price winning it. It put Davey in the hospital and tore '007' all to pieces."

Later that night, with Allison at the hospital, McReynolds was back at the team's transporter when Tim Brewer, Elliott's crew chief, walked up.

"Brewer, we're in trouble," McReynolds said. "We're out of race cars."

Allison's team had one new car sitting at the shop, a car it would now have to use for the 600 the following weekend. It had a speedway car—the kind used at Daytona and Talladega—and a road-course car ready for an up-coming race at Sears Point. And that was all.

"That ain't no problem," Brewer said to McReynolds. "I've got a car up there that we haven't run this year. Why don't you come get it?"

Brewer, whose team was racing Allison for the championship, was offering the competition the use of one of his team's cars as a backup in case the new car McReynolds had waiting in the shop got wrecked before "007" could be fixed or a replacement could be finished.

The new car pressed into service for Allison in the 600 was No. 10 in the Yates inventory. While Allison tried to mend from the injuries he'd suffered in The Winston, fellow Alabama driver Neil Bonnett, now a television analyst after retiring as a full-time driver after the 1989 season, drove the practice sessions as the team tweaked it for qualifying.

Allison was ready to go in time to qualify and practiced for the rest of the week. Car No. 10 wasn't as good as "007," however, at least not with a hurting Allison driving it, and the first shot at the Winston Million slipped by as Allison finished fourth in the 600.

Earnhardt, the two-time defending points champion, won the 600 and broke Ford's winning streak by edging Ernie Irvan, also in a Chevrolet, by three car-lengths. Petty was third. Kulwicki finished seventh and Elliott was 14th. While Allison hadn't won $1 million, he had padded his points lead to 111 over Elliott.

At Dover the following Friday, teams had terrible difficulty getting their cars to work well on the tires that had been supplied for that weekend's race. Kulwicki, who'd made it through his rookie season with just a one-car inventory, wrecked two cars in practice and had to have a third car trucked north in time to make the field for the Budweiser 500.

Gant won the race by stretching his final fuel load for 98 laps. He actually ran out of gas on the backstretch on the final lap and coasted across the finish after cutting off his engine. Allison was penalized for exceeding the pit-road speed limit on his final stop, but finished 11th and held the points lead as Gant moved past Elliott into second.

Irvan won at Sears Point, where Allison damaged his car in a spin and crash on Lap 10 and wound up finishing 28th to see his points lead shrink to 28 over Earnhardt, who had moved into second.

The big news that day, however, was not the race in northern California. Back in Florida, William H. G. France died at the age of 82 after a prolonged illness. "Big Bill" France had in 1972 turned over the job of running NASCAR to his sons, Bill Jr. and Jim, but there had never been any question that ultimate power in the sport remained where it always had been, in the hands of the man who had started it all.

Kulwicki won the season's first trip to Pocono, rallying past Elliott and Martin late in the race. Elliott finished third and Allison was fifth. Allison, driving for the first time in a new car that the team built as a clone of "007," dominated at Michigan and tied Elliott for the season's lead with four wins. Kulwicki ran third and Elliott 10th, and Allison led by 67 points as the circuit took a weekend off at midseason.

The day after the Michigan race, Allison, Elliott, Earnhardt, Irvan, Martin, Petty, Ricky Rudd, Rusty Wallace and Darrell Waltrip went to Indianapolis Motor Speedway to participate in what officially was called a Goodyear tire test.

Nobody bought that explanation. If there were no plans to race stock cars at the Brickyard, why did Goodyear need to test tires? Since the

April IROC test there had been great speculation that Winston Cup racing would soon come to Indy. The June test made it clear that it was no longer a question of if, but when.

"The test at Indianapolis was a pretty neat deal," Elliott remembers. "It had so much history in the other type of cars, I really didn't know what to expect. It had so much history behind it, so being among the first guys to go up there and run on it was pretty special."

Thousands turned out to watch the stock cars on the track. The drivers signed hundreds of autographs and were positively giddy about being at Indy. Kyle Petty took his video camera and pointed it out the window at the cars in front of him as they went around the track the first few times. Although speedway officials asked the drivers not to do any racing, Earnhardt, Petty and Rudd couldn't resist and ran inches apart down the track's famous front straightaway.

It would not be until August of 1994 that NASCAR's top circuit finally raced in the inaugural Brickyard 400, but the seed was planted. Racing at Indy was one more sign, and a very important one, that the circuit the late "Big Bill" France had founded had arrived as a mainstay on the American sports scene.

After Richard Petty's near miss of the pole for the July 4 race at Daytona, Irvan dominated, leading 118 of 160 laps on a day where temperatures reached into the mid-90s. Petty succumbed to the heat and needed a relief driver on his way to a 36th-place finish. Elliott was fifth and Allison was 10th, with Elliott moving to within 46 points of Allison's lead. Kulwicki finished 30th but stayed third in points.

The week before the next race at Pocono, it was almost as though Allison's body had a premonition of peril it was about to face. He spent Wednesday and Thursday nights in a hospital in Charlotte, having checked himself in after suffering severe headaches, nausea and high fever for several days. Allison was worried he was having some kind of delayed reaction from the crash in The Winston.

"You aren't supposed to wake up from a wreck like that," Allison said after traveling to Pocono on Friday morning, only to have that day's time trials rained out. "It was big time bad. But the doctor did a scan and X-rays . . . and they showed I was completely healed from the crash. Those injuries had nothing to do with this."

Allison joked that the diagnosis turned out to be SSV—some sort of virus.

In that Sunday's race, Allison started back in the field after having his qualifying lap disallowed by NASCAR because the front air-dam on his Ford was too close to the ground.

It looked like it wouldn't matter. Allison came quickly through the field and had the lead when, on a pit stop under yellow just past the halfway point in the race, an air gun broke delaying the tire changers. Allison was mired in traffic when the race restarted and frustrated because he knew his car was fast enough to lead.

He had led 115 laps and was on his way back to the top spot on Lap 150 when, entering the same Turn 2 where his father had crashed so savagely four years earlier, Allison dove inside as he chased the leaders—Kulwicki, Rudd and Kyle Petty. Waltrip followed Allison into the hole and his car hit the left rear of Allison's Ford.

Allison's car turned sideways and went into the grass, flipped backward and began a violent barrel roll as parts spewed into the air. One piece of the flying debris ended up embedded in the bodywork of a safety truck parked near where the car finally came to rest on its top after rolling 11 times and bouncing off an inside guardrail.

McReynolds got on the radio.

"Davey, are you okay?" he asked.

There was no response.

McReynolds then heard the team's spotter over the radio.

"It's Davey," the spotter said, "and it's bad."

McReynolds looked at car owner Robert Yates, who was listening to other drivers describe the scene to their crews as they drove by.

One said the only thing the rescue crews needed was a body bag. "Davey has to be killed," the driver said. "He can't survive this deal."

Gary Nelson, a veteran crew chief who had gone to work that year as a NASCAR official, was near where the accident took place and among the first to get to the car once it came to rest. Allison had dirt and other debris in his eyes from the crash and followed Nelson's voice as he struggled to get free of the wreckage.

McReynolds hurried to the track's infield care center and saw Allison being unloaded from the ambulance.

As bad as the driver looked, McReynolds was relieved. Allison was alive, but had bruised his right eye socket and had broken his right collarbone, his right arm and wrist. The right arm flew outside the car after the roof had been peeled away in the crash and apparently was crushed against the guardrail as Allison's wild ride neared its end. For future races, Allison's team installed a net inside the car under the roof to keep appendages inside in case the roof ever got peeled away again.

Brian VanDercook, the team's public relations agent, talked his way inside the infield care center and used his radio to tell Yates, McReynolds and the rest of the team that their driver was alive, awake and talking to doctors.

Given what Allison had been through, that was indeed good news.

Waltrip came in for gas on the yellow after the crash and stayed out when the rest of the leaders came in later. He led the rest of the way for his 82nd career win.

Allison was credited with a 33rd-place finish. Elliott was 13th and took the points lead for the first time, nine up on Allison, who had been taken to the same Allentown hospital where his father had spent weeks recovering from his 1988 crash. Kulwicki finished third and was now just 47 points back.

McReynolds and the crew went to the hospital to see their driver.

In the hallway, Davey's mother, Judy, came out to meet them.

"Guys," Judy Allison said, "I want to tell you that he doesn't look like himself. He's swollen pretty badly."

VanDercook had already seen the driver.

"The only part of him that was recognizable was his nose," he said. "That, and his voice. If he hadn't said, 'Hi, Brian,' with that voice, I would not have recognized the man. It was amazing."

McReynolds steeled himself but still was surprised when he walked in and could barely recognize the young man with whom he spent many hours every day.

"Bless his heart," McReynolds recalls. "His little ol' ears looked like they were all the way on the back side of his head."

Any of McReynolds' doubts about the identity of the specimen there on the bed with all manner tubes and monitors hooked to him were erased when Allison spoke.

"I am going to get that son of a bitch," Allison said through clenched teeth. "I am going to get him." Allison was talking about Waltrip. Instead of worrying about the pain from his injuries, he was already thinking about exacting revenge on the man he believed had caused the wreck.

McReynolds asked Allison what the driver wanted the team to do about getting ready for the next weekend's race at Talladega. He was asking Allison who the driver wanted the team to line up to take over the car until Allison was able to return.

"What do you mean what do you need to do?" Allison said, rising up on the bed against the equipment holding him down. "Get your asses on that airplane, go back home and get my car ready. I will be there on Friday, and we will qualify that thing."

McReynolds left; partly believing Allison would never be able to get in the car the next weekend and partly knowing the Allison determination would somehow prevail.

Allison was in the hospital until Friday morning, but was discharged in time to fly to the airport located just behind the Talladega Superspeedway backstretch.

Bobby Hillin Jr. had been recruited to drive the car in Friday's practice and qualifying, but the plan was still for Allison to start the race on Sunday. Under NASCAR's rules, the points earned by a car's finish in a race go to the driver who's in the car at the time of the green flag. A driver contending for a championship could practically be in a body cast, but if he could manage to get in the driver's seat and get the car around the track for one lap, he would be the driver of record.

The team wanted Allison to try to make it until the first yellow flag so it wouldn't lose a lap stopping under green, which would have been particularly costly at the 2.66-mile Talladega track. NASCAR wanted Allison to get out of the car immediately after the green flag. Based on Allison's battered condition, it was difficult to argue with that position. Allison was actually spending his nights in a Birmingham hospital, then coming to the track during the day and summoning the courage to appear to be all right.

"He knew the politics of the garage area," VanDercook said. "He had seen and learned from his father's mistakes and his successes, as well as some of his own. He knew what concerns NASCAR would have. He knew what their responsibilities were, but he also knew he was in Alabama. He knew that was a plus for him."

Still, Allison came to the track on Saturday wearing dark sunglasses. When he took them off, he looked like a character from a horror movie, his eyes still almost completely red from the after-effects of the Pocono wreck.

Outward appearance aside, Allison figured to have difficulty driving many laps at all. His right hand was in a cast from the broken wrist, leaving him with little grip strength.

"We had to put Velcro on the palm of his the racing glove pulled over his cast and on the shifter," McReynolds said. "The only way he could shift was to have his hand Velcroed to the shifter."

Allison practiced the car capably on Saturday, mollifying NASCAR's concerns slightly. Officials still wanted the driver change made promptly, however, and McReynolds knew that if the race began with a long stretch of green-flag laps the pressure would intensify.

"There wasn't a cloud in the sky that day," McReynolds recalls. "But on Lap 11 one of those 30-second July rain showers came and a caution came out. The rain didn't last a minute, but it was enough for them to throw a yellow and we got Davey out of the car and Bobby in it."

Hillin, at the back of the pack on the restart because of the length of time it took to make the driver switch, hooked up in the draft with Irvan and began making up ground in chunks. Hillin wound up with a remarkable third-place finish. Irvan won, his third victory in six races, with Marlin second. Elliott finished fifth but fell one point behind Allison.

After an open weekend Kyle Petty won the rain-delayed, rain-shortened race at the Watkins Glen road course in New York, with Dorsey Schroeder, a driver with a road-course racing background, providing Allison's relief. The rain cut short Schroeder's bid to make up ground and he managed only a 20th-place finish, and Elliott took a 17-point lead by finishing 14th. Kulwicki stayed in the hunt with a seventh-place finish.

The return trip to Michigan in mid-August offered a great opportunity for Allison, since he had been so dominant there in June and since his injuries were beginning to heal. Jim Sauter was on standby as a relief driver for the Champion 400, but Allison planned to drive the entire race for the first time since Pocono.

Davey and his wife, Liz, flew from Alabama to Michigan early Thursday afternoon in the plane Allison owned. McReynolds and Yates were booked on a commercial flight from Charlotte to Detroit later that day.

"I left the shop to go home to clean up," McReynolds said. "I got home and my wife, Linda, said I needed to call the secretary back at the shop."

The news was awful. Clifford Allison, Davey's brother and the younger of Bobby and Judy's two sons, had been killed in a crash during a Grand National practice session at the Michigan track.

When McReynolds and Yates arrived in Michigan, they began searching for their driver. They found him that evening at a friend's house.

"Why don't we find somebody to practice and qualify the car?" McReynolds suggested. The crew chief could only imagine how hard it would be for Allison to drive off into the same turn where his brother had been killed not 24 hours earlier.

Allison paused, then looked at his car owner and his crew chief. The determination was beginning to show once again.

"Let me tell you guys something," he said in measured tones. "My brother got killed and I loved him, but I came up here to do a job. And I am going to do that job. We are going to win this race on Sunday, then I will go back home on Monday and bury my brother."

On Friday, Davey qualified third fastest in his Ford. He finished fifth on Sunday in a race Gant won with another bit of fuel conservation strategy. And on Monday, Davey Allison went to his brother's funeral.

Waltrip won at Bristol for the 12th time in his career in the next race, the first race held on the track's new concrete surface. It was a big week for Waltrip; the victory came just days after the birth of his daughter Sarah. It was big week for Elliott, too. He finished sixth while Allison wrecked once again and finished 30th. Elliott's lead grew from 37 to 109 points with Kulwicki, who finished fifth at Bristol, 133 back.

As it had every year since 1950, Labor Day weekend meant the Southern 500 at Darlington, stock car racing's version of Boston's Fenway Park. Steeped in history, the egg-shaped oval is considered one of the best tests of a driver's skill and nerve. The 1992 Southern 500 also had Allison's bid to win the Winston Million bonus adding spice to the traditional festivities.

When Elliott had won the $1 million in 1985, the number on the roof of his car had been accidentally affixed upside down. McReynolds had the No. 28 affixed to Allison's Ford that same way this time, trying to think of everything possible to help his driver collect the bonus.

Allison's car was clearly strong enough to win, too, but as the 400-mile mark approached in the 500-mile race, it was running low on fuel.

In July in Alabama, a thunderstorm had saved McReynolds when he wanted to get Hillin in the car and Allison out. In September in

South Carolina, however, the threat of rain left the crew chief facing a difficult call.

McReynolds motioned one of the team members over to him and hollered toward him over the din.

"Go check the radar," he ordered.

The team member ran off toward the NASCAR truck, which had a weather radar monitor. A few more laps, and a few more gulps of fuel, passed before his return.

"It looks good," the team member said.

There was a giant blob of green surrounding the dot on the screen representing Darlington. The runner McReynolds had dispatched hadn't looked at weather radar very often. He didn't know that green represented rain. After all, green meant "go" on the race track.

Instead of taking any risk of Allison running out of gas, the bad information about the weather clinched McReynolds' decision to bring Allison on in for his pit stop.

Waltrip stayed on the track, hoping his fuel would last until the rain arrived. Only a few laps after Allison had pitted, 405 miles into the race, Waltrip got his wish. The rain came and the race was stopped. Although the rain abated relatively quickly, NASCAR officials decided the track couldn't be dried in time for the race to be completed before dark. Waltrip was declared the winner.

Not only did Allison fail to get the victory, the timing of the rain and his pit stop dropped him to fifth. Elliott finished third and gained 10 points to extend his lead to 119. Kulwicki was eighth and fell another 28 behind the leader. The challengers lost more ground the next week at Richmond, where Rusty Wallace won, as Elliott finished 14th, Kulwicki 15th and Allison 19th despite spinning his car out twice.

If July's wreck at Pocono had been Allison's turning point in the season, Dover in September would be the one for Elliott and Kulwicki.

The June race at the one-mile track, where he wrecked two cars in practice, had been a nightmare for Kulwicki. The fall race turned out even worse. He crashed his primary car in practice again, then won the pole in his backup Ford. But in the race he was involved in a wreck with Chad Little and finished 34th.

By day's end, he was 278 points out of the lead and almost ready to declare himself out of the championship contest.

"It was almost as if everybody in the back of their minds knew the run for the championship was over," Tom Roberts recalls. "But Alan just wouldn't say it."

After his wreck, Kulwicki rode to the infield care center in a safety vehicle, where he was quickly checked and declared okay. He then walked to the team's transporter.

"Alan walked in and all of the guys on the team were standing there," Roberts says. "One of the guys walked up to him and sort of hugged him, saying it would be okay as long as Alan was all right and we would be able to continue racing."

Elliott was having a much better day at Dover. His Ford was strong and he was in the lead when he came for his final pit stop with about 35 laps left in the 500-lap race. As Elliott's car came down pit road, there was debate about whether to change all four tires, just two tires, or to take fuel only without changing any tires.

A car runs faster on four new tires because they offer better traction, and better traction almost always translates into better speed. It takes about 15 seconds, however, to change four tires. A two-tire change can be done in 10 seconds or less, so if a team thinks its car will run well enough on two new tires it may elect to make the shorter stop to gain positions on the track.

In late-race situations like the one at Dover, a third option comes into play. Elliott didn't need to have his fuel tank filled; he needed only enough fuel to make the final few laps. Without changing any tires, he could have gotten enough fuel in four or five seconds and then returned to the track with the lead.

Johnson made the call. "Four tires," he said, ending the discussion.

Elliott disagreed, but sitting in the car he had no choice but to wait until his car came down off the jack and he could go back out to race.

Ricky Rudd assumed the lead and came in on Lap 481 for his final stop, taking only gas. He came back on the track and was still six seconds ahead of Elliott, but on the fresh tires Elliott gobbled away at the difference. At the checkered flag, he wound up about 50 feet short of catching Rudd.

In the big picture, Elliott's second-place finish was as good as a win. He left Dover 154 points ahead of Allison, who finished fourth. Johnson had been thinking of the points race when he made the four-tire call, saying he didn't want to risk having Elliott run over a piece of debris that could cut a hot, worn tire and cost the team no worse than a second-place finish.

Elliott, nonetheless, was upset. He pulled his car to a stop at the gas tanks, where the top-five finishers are required to stop after the race. Crew chief Tim Brewer walked over to the car and leaned in to talk to the driver. Their exchange was clearly heated, but in the postrace din nobody could hear what they were saying.

Reporters covering the race knew Elliott would be in no mood to talk, but they needed comments about the four-tire decision for their stories. Estes could feel them looking at him. It was his job to collect postrace quotes from Ford drivers and then hand them out to reporters. He dutifully went to Elliott's transporter.

Elliott was sitting on the steps leading from the working area of the truck to a driver's lounge that's located just behind the truck's cab. He was angrily biting into a sandwich when Estes walked up.

"Don't you say a word to me," Elliott said.

Rain backed the next two races up to Mondays, and Geoffrey Bodine won both. He led the final 43 laps to win at Martinsville and then led 312 of 400 laps the following weekend at North Wilkesboro in a race run without a single caution flag.

Elliott's fortunes were as bad as the Sunday weather on those two weekends. He blew an engine after just 159 laps at Martinsville and finished 30th in a 31-car field. Kulwicki finished fifth and Allison was 14th and both made up considerable ground. At North Wilkesboro, the lack of cautions prevented Elliott's team from adjusting an ill-handling car and he finished 26th, eight laps down. Allison finished 11th and Kulwicki 12th. Elliott's lead drooped to 67 over Allison and 144 on Kulwicki.

Mark Martin won the following week in Charlotte. Elliott was running sixth with 39 laps to go when a part in the suspension system broke and his car hit the wall in Turn 4. Elliott spent 18 laps on pit road having it repaired and then ran 16 more laps before giving up on the day. He finished 30th while Kulwicki finished second and Allison ran 19th. Kyle Petty finished third and moved back into the picture along with Martin and Gant.

Elliott's lead was 39 over Allison and 47 over Kulwicki. Martin was fourth, just 91 points behind Elliott and three ahead of Gant. Petty was

106 out of the lead and pulled in closer the next week with a dominating win at Rockingham, leading 484 of the 492 laps, for his 11th top-10 finish in 12 races. Elliott stopped the bleeding with a fourth-place finish, however, and upped his lead back to 70 over Allison, 85 over Kulwicki and 94 over Petty.

While everyone had noticed Elliott's struggles, it was also true that Allison's team had missed several chances to regain control of the points race. The No. 28 car hadn't finished in the top 10 in any of the races where Elliott had trouble, and the driver and crew chief were getting frustrated.

McReynolds rode home from North Wilkesboro in a van with Yates.

"Man, we need to do something," McReynolds said. Mike Laughlin, one of the sport's top chassis builders, had been urging McReynolds to try a new kind of car he had developed, a "low-snout chassis."

"What do you think about me calling Mike to see if he can convert one of our cars over?" McReynolds asked Yates. "We could run it at Phoenix. We'll go test it somewhere first and see if we can get ourselves out of the hole we're in."

Yates was willing to try anything, and Allison was game, too. McReynolds picked car No. 10, the one Allison had raced in the 600 in Charlotte after destroying "007" in The Winston, and sent it to Laughlin's shop.

McReynolds took the converted car and one Allison had raced at North Wilkesboro to Richmond for a three-day test. Halfway through the first day, Allison was sold.

"You might as well put the old car in the truck," he said to McReynolds. "That's my race car right there." He pointed to the converted No. 10.

"Okay, Davey," McReynolds said. "But let's be sure."

Allison's mind didn't change over the remaining days of test. The low-snout car was his primary car for Phoenix.

The confidence the team had in that decision waned during practice on Saturday at Phoenix. Allison was not happy and the team changed virtually everything on the car looking for a better combination. With five minutes left in the final practice, McReynolds finally tried a heavier spring on the right-rear suspension.

"That's what I have been looking for," Allison said.

He was right. Allison took the lead on Lap 283 of a 312-lap race when Martin came in for his final pit stop. Two laps later, a yellow flag came out allowing Allison to pit under caution and trapping Martin back in traffic. Allison went on to get his fifth victory of the season and the 18th of his career.

Elliott, meanwhile, had another horrible day. A cylinder head cracked on his Ford's engine and the car began to overheat badly. He limped home in 31st place and, for the first time since Watkins Glen, lost the points lead to Allison. He dropped to third, 40 behind the leader and 10 behind Kulwicki, who moved up to second in the points by finishing fourth.

Kulwicki, however, was not at all happy with his seeming good fortune. He was fuming that a problem on his last pit stop cost him a chance to win. He and Andrews yelled at each other over the radio as the laps wound down, with Andrews ultimately telling Kulwicki the team was doing the best it could. The tension was palpable.

After the checkered flag Kulwicki went back to the transporter lounge to take off his uniform. Angrily, he pulled off his gloves and fired them toward the closet where his gear would be stowed for the trip home.

Roberts knew this mood. "I knew the best thing to do was to stay out of the way and let him blow off the steam," Roberts said.

Mark Brooks didn't have that much history with Kulwicki. Mark had been appointed by his father to handle the marketing side of the Hooters team's sponsorship. The crew, almost all of whom had poured sweat and blood into the team's success, had worked up a healthy resentment for young Mark and his knack for working his way into the frame anytime a photo was taken or a television camera showed Kulwicki and the car.

Brooks walked into the transporter as Kulwicki was stewing. He offered a few words of encouragement that Kulwicki was in no mood to hear.

"Get out of here!" Kulwicki said, glaring at Brooks. "I don't want to talk now and you are not making things any better."

Brooks tucked his tail and left, speechlessly.

Roberts later found him sitting in a corner of the track's media center, head bowed and almost in tears.

"He has no right to talk to me like that!" Brooks said.

"I know," Roberts said. "Alan doesn't mean it when he's like that. He just felt like we should have won the race."

"I don't care!" Brooks said. "He still has no right to talk to me like that. We sponsor that car!"

"I know," Roberts said. "I know. But trust me. Everything is going to be fine."

The Stars Align

The atmosphere was electric as teams gathered Friday morning at Atlanta Motor Speedway. The season-long fight for the championship had come down to the last 500-mile race, and every detail took on enormous significance.

Confidence surged through Davey Allison's team after the win at Phoenix, but Larry McReynolds worried the confidence might be getting out of hand.

Allison wanted to drive the same car he'd won with at Phoenix, the No. 10 chassis that had been converted into a low-snout. McReynolds was wary of the choice. Low-snout cars are designed for races on short tracks, not 1.5-mile tracks like Atlanta.

Allison was insistent during the test on the open weekend before the finale. "That's my car right there," Allison said.

"Davey, that's a low-snout," McReynolds said.

"I don't care," Allison said. "That's my car."

Looking back, McReynolds second-guesses himself.

"I just don't think we tested smart," he says. "We didn't make any long runs and our confidence was so high in that car because it had won Phoenix and it took us out of the hole we'd been in all summer."

So, when the team arrived in the Atlanta track's garage on Friday morning, No. 10 was unloaded as Allison's primary car.

Alan Kulwicki's team took out its "Underbird," which was also a Mike Laughlin-built chassis. The team had raced it in 27 previous events since February 1989, most recently at Charlotte in October when Kulwicki had won the pole and finished second in the race.

Elliott's team was trying to unload its Ford, too, but there was a problem. The team couldn't get the transporter's rear hydraulic gate to lower. The cars are stowed in a compartment at the top of the transporter, then pushed back onto a gate that lowers to ground level, where the car is then pushed off. A switch malfunctioned and the team had to take off the hoses supplying fluid to the hydraulic system to make repairs before the car could be unloaded.

In light of the mechanical problems it had faced over the final two months of the season, this was not the way the team wanted to start the climactic weekend.

Much of the media hadn't arrived at the track when Elliott's team was working to solve that problem. Reporters were instead attending an 8:30 a.m. news conference at the Atlanta Airport Hilton where Maxwell House was announcing its sponsorship of a Winston Cup team that would debut at Daytona in 1993. Bobby Labonte, Terry's younger brother, who had won the 1991 Busch series championship and finished second in that division in '92, was introduced as the driver for the team owned by Bill Davis.

Davis had planned for Jeff Gordon to drive his cars in Winston Cup. But as Davis and Labonte met the press that morning, Gordon was at the track getting ready to climb into a Chevrolet owned by Rick Hendrick for his first Cup qualifying run.

Like Kulwicki, Jeff Gordon's racing roots were nontraditional for NASCAR. He was born in Vallejo, Calif., on Aug. 4, 1971. His parents divorced when he was just three months old. Several months later his mother, Carol, met John Bickford, who built race cars and worked in the auto parts business. John and Carol went to Vallejo Speedway on their first date and took along Jeff, who'd just turned 1, and his older sister, Kim.

John and Carol were married and the family moved to a neighborhood where many of the kids were racing BMX bicycles. Jeff got a bike when he was 4, but Carol Bickford had seen too many kids get hurt and told Jeff he couldn't race. Bickford saw his wife's point and bought Jeff a quarter-midget racer. It took the better part of a year for John and Jeff to convince Carol that the little race car would be safer than racing a bicycle.

Gordon's first laps inside his quarter-midget car came on a track his stepfather cut into weeds that had grown up around a fairground in Vallejo. Night after night, Jeff drove the car around and around the little path. He started entering races and winning them. By age 8, he was the national quarter-midget champion. He won the title again at age 10.

Gordon soon outgrew quarter-midgets and was ready to graduate into sprint cars. In the sprint-car crazy Midwest, specifically the area around Indianapolis, 14 was the minimum age for racing. So Bickford moved the family to Pittsboro, Ind.

By the time Gordon took high-school driver's education, he had won more than 100 races in cars built by legendary Indianapolis chassis builder Bob East. In his high school classes Gordon sometimes sat next to people wearing Jeff Gordon T-shirts purchased at one of the Indiana tracks where he raced.

Gordon won the U.S. Auto Club's midget series title in 1990 and the Silver Crown championship the next year. He also began to attract attention outside of the Indianapolis area by racing in a series of races aired nationally on ESPN.

Two decades earlier, Gordon's career would have almost certainly progressed through the USAC sprint-car ranks toward a career of driving open-wheel "champ" cars on the Indy-racing circuit. But by the beginning of the 1990s, the cost of racing in the Indianapolis 500 and its sister events was rising and political infighting in the ranks of open-wheel racing's sanctioning bodies was beginning to fester. Opportunities for young American drivers were drying up.

Gordon's career path changed after he came to North Carolina to participate in a stock-car driving school run by Buck Baker at North Carolina Speedway in Rockingham. It was an epiphany. Gordon had found his calling.

He came to Charlotte in the fall of 1990 to test a Busch car. By the start of the 1991 Busch Grand National season he was driving the Davis-owned cars and winning rookie of the year with 10 top-10 finishes in 30 starts. He won one pole, but didn't win a race.

On a Saturday at Atlanta in March of 1992, Rick Hendrick was walking toward Turn 1 on his way to a luxury box when he noticed a car in the Grand National race smoking its rear tires on every lap as it went through the turn. Hendrick expected the car to wreck any moment, but it didn't.

Gordon was driving it, and on that afternoon he got the first of his three Grand National wins that season. Hendrick was impressed and began looking into the possibility of adding the young driver to his Chevrolet team.

Hendrick had fielded three Winston Cup teams from 1987 to 1990, but had cut back to two, with Ricky Rudd and Ken Schrader driving, when Darrell Waltrip left to start his own team in 1991. If Gordon were available, Hendrick thought he might be the guy with whom to make it a trio once more.

Hendrick wasn't alone in recognizing Gordon's talents. Davis knew if he was to keep Gordon, he would also have to fend off overtures from Ford team owners Junior Johnson and Jack Roush. Davis went to work trying to line up a sponsorship deal that would keep Gordon with his team.

In May, Davis and Gordon traveled to Minneapolis for a meeting at the headquarters of Target, the national chain of department stores. From Davis' perspective, things went quite well. The people from Target seemed receptive to the idea of sponsoring a NASCAR team, but since it would be a new venture for them there were still questions to be answered before the deal got a green light.

In the elevator on the way down from the meeting at Target's head-quarters, Gordon leaned over to Davis. "There's something I need to tell you," Gordon said.

In the lobby, as other members of the party chatted excitedly about the meeting, Gordon and Davis found a quiet corner. That was when Davis first learned that Gordon would begin his Winston Cup career at Hendrick Motorsports.

Gordon says he didn't feel Davis was close to a deal that would allow them to go Cup racing in 1993. Hendrick, meanwhile, had made him a solid offer that would allow him to make the move to the sport's highest level. Gordon took it.

Ford officials knew that Gordon had been weighing options all spring, but still were surprised when the news started seeping out. They howled in protest, saying Gordon's contract gave Ford right of first refusal for his services. Gordon said there was no such stipulation. Ford threatened to take legal action but never did.

Gordon finished the Busch season for Davis, winning a series record 11 poles and adding victories in May and October at Charlotte—and first saw his future wife, Brooke, in victory lane. Brooke Sealy was "Miss Winston," one of several models hired by R.J. Reynolds to pose and smile with drivers for promotional photos reminiscent of the days when a race winner got a victory lane kiss from a "beauty queen" clothed in a bikini or hot pants and hip boots.

Gordon finished fourth behind Joe Nemechek, Bobby Labonte and Todd Bodine in the '92 Busch standings. Then Gordon came back to Atlanta in November and, for the first time, climbed into the rainbow-colored No. 24 that would eventually carry him to stardom beyond the imagination of anyone who would see him race that weekend.

"I know it's hard for a young guy to come in and jump into the ranks of the talent that's in Winston Cup racing," Hendrick said of Gordon that weekend. "I think Jeff will lead races. I think he will get to the front . . . and I'm really confident that if he can get up front, I think you'll see some spurts of greatness.

"Of all the young guys I've seen and the talent I've seen come along, he has impressed me more than anybody. I'm really excited about him long-term. I don't think we need to gauge him by what he does this weekend or next year. It's going to take a little bit longer than that."

Gordon's first qualifying lap at Atlanta was nothing spectacular. After testing at better than 181 mph a week earlier, some considered him a threat for the pole in his first race. But Gordon went out seventh in the qualifying order and ran just 176.521 mph, which at day's end was only the 31st best time.

Gordon's lap was better than Richard Petty's was. The King, who went out 27th, ran just 175.318 mph in his Pontiac, putting him 36th on the first-day chart.

"I messed up," Petty said. "I missed the groove in Turn 1 and I couldn't get back in the gas until I got on the backstretch. The car is way better than that. . . . At least this part of the weekend is over with."

Allison went out first among the title contenders and ran 178.400 mph, putting him 17th on the starting grid. He remained confident in his choice of the converted short-track car for the weekend.

"That's all we could do today," he said. "We'll race good from wherever we start because this car feels good."

Kulwicki went out 35th in the qualifying session and ran 178.743 mph, putting him 14th on the starting grid. Kulwicki wasn't thrilled with his speed, saying he had run faster laps five times in practice earlier in the day, but had to live with it.

Clinching a $40,000 prize for being the season's top pole-winner made the lap go down a bit easier. He won the award, sponsored by Budweiser and worth $30,000 to Kulwicki and $10,000 to the team, by winning six poles that year. Sterling Marlin had won five. Had Marlin won his sixth pole at Atlanta Marlin would have won the postseason award because he would have won the tiebreaker—Marlin had been second fastest twice during the season to none for Kulwicki.

"Well it's about time I won that thing!" Kulwicki said. "I've won about 24 poles since I started this and I've always been a contender for this award, always been up there—but not quite. It feels good to finally win it."

Elliott's was the 50th car to qualify and he ran a lap at 178.977 mph that was good enough for the 11th starting spot, the inside position on Row 6 in the two-abreast starts used in NASCAR. Marlin, his teammate, would be on the outside of that row on Sunday.

"That's about what I've been running all day," Elliott said. "It has been right around that no matter what we did. We tried new tires, used tires, old tires."

Mark Martin, 113 points behind Elliott going into Sunday, ran 179.622 mph in his Ford to earn a spot on the second row outside of Earnhardt. Kyle Petty was 20th fastest at 177.735 mph and got the last spot, while Harry Gant's lap at 176.657 mph left him 29th fastest.

The front-row positions went to an unlikely pair.

The second-fastest qualifier was Brett Bodine, the middle of the three racing Bodine brothers, at 179.900 mph in a Ford owned by drag racer Kenny Bernstein. His older brother, Geoffrey, was eighth fastest in the Bud Moore-owned Ford. Younger brother Todd had not yet made it to NASCAR's top division.

The pole-winner was Rick Mast, a 35-year-old driver who traded a cow to get his first race car back near his tiny hometown of Rockbridge Baths, Va.

Mast, driving car No. 1, an Oldsmobile owned by Richard Jackson, ran 180.183 mph to break the track record and earn his first career pole in his 92nd start. It was also the final race that Mast would be driving an Olds—General Motors was pulling that brand out of the sport in 1993 and Mast's team had decided to switch to Fords.

"I got through turns 1 and 2 perfect," Mast said after his lap. "I said to myself, 'Man, if you get around the other end that well, you might have a shot at this thing.' But the car got loose and I had to back off a little bit. I thought, 'Oh, man, you blew it.'"

Mast's comment was a good example of the language racers speak, one that can sound like Sanskrit to those who've never heard the terminology.

Drivers, for the most part, talk in terms of lap times and not speed. It took Mast 30.409 seconds to complete his pole-winning lap around the 1.522-mile track. In referring to the lap, Mast would call his lap "a forty-one." That's referring to the portion of the lap time to the right of the decimal—41 hundredths, rounded off from .409, would be a forty-one.

During the race, crew chiefs or some other crew member call out lap times to their drivers virtually every time by. That's especially critical for a driver who's leading and needs to run consistent laps to keep from wearing out his tires or losing ground to a driver behind him who is driving smoother, more consistent laps.

Mast spoke of turns 1 and 2 at Atlanta, then said he wanted to get through the "other end" just as well. At most oval tracks, drivers consider the first two turns as basically one section of the track, then the other two turns as another section. There are tracks where individual turns demand special attention and one track, Pocono, has three distinctly different turns and three straightaways of varying lengths.

When Mast said his car got "loose," he meant the back end of the car showed a tendency to lose grip as the car turned. Greatly exaggerated, the feeling would be like the one a driver on the street might get if the car hits an icy patch—the tires are not gripping the surface of the road and therefore the car is on the verge of being out of control.

A driver who speaks of "chasing the car up the race track" is fighting a loose condition, because he has to correct the steering several times as he goes through a turn. If a car is too loose, the driver must "back off," lift off the accelerator, until he gains control. If he keeps the accelerator to the floor, he's most likely headed for the wall.

The opposite condition is called "tight." Again greatly exaggerated, this is the feeling one might get trying to steer a car with a failed power steering system. A tight race car doesn't want to turn when it goes into a corner; the driver has to muscle it around. Again, if a car won't turn the driver has to slow down to make it through the turn.

The challenge, therefore, is to balance a car's myriad chassis and handling characteristics so it will run smoothly through the turns. When everything is perfect, or at least close to it, the driver can make the car go right where he wants it to go on the track.

At least for a while, that is.

Sometimes a driver's car will work great on new tires, then will fall off dramatically as the tires become worn. Other times, a car will be significantly slower until the new tires have a few laps on them, then will run better once the pressure of the air inside the tires builds up as the tire warms up from wear.

A driver who is particularly adept at conserving his tires might run lap times a few tenths of a second slower than others on new tires, then pick up ground on competitors late in long runs. That's because his lap times are staying about the same while the ones going faster on new tires slow down more as their tires wear, or "go away."

Mast, a colorful, likeable fellow with a quick wit and a sharp mind, knew that being the pole-winner for Richard Petty's last race would be, if nothing else, a nice footnote to his driving career.

"Nobody can imagine what it means to Rick Mast to be sitting on the pole at Richard Petty's last race," Mast said. "It's just a dream come true. Most of the drivers here were little kids listening to the races and Richard Petty winning. He was always my hero."

Mast also clearly understood his place in the garage area's pecking order.

"Let me put this in perspective for you," he said. "Here I come in off the track and I see everyone holding up one finger and cheering. I don't know if they're cheering because I have the fastest time or because the car didn't wreck off Turn 4. I come in the garage area and get out of the car and everybody tells me I have the fastest time.

"I get out and see this horde of reporters coming at me. I think, 'Okay, I'm going to talk now.' They come right by me like that and I turn around and there they are at Richard Petty's car. That told me exactly where I stand in the scheme of things."

The idea that Mast could defy monstrous odds and stay up front on Sunday never got serious consideration. By the time reporters had their stories filed for Saturday's editions he was already an afterthought.

Only one more day remained before a race that was already assured of being one of the most memorable in NASCAR history, regardless of how things turned out.

Elliott put the capper on the day.

"Kulwicki runs good here," he said. "Davey runs good here. It's just about going to take misfortune of some kind to make the difference. If anybody has any misfortune at all, they'll just eliminate themselves. It's just that simple. We all want it, but that's not going to make any difference.

"You look at 100 different things and you'll find places where you could pick up 20, 35, 50 points. The rest of these guys could have done the same thing with their seasons. As many cars as there are in this deal, it's …"

Elliott then flipped an imaginary coin in the air.

His next words hung in the autumn air like smoke from all the fires in the campgrounds surrounding the track.

"It could come down to the last lap."

"Green Flag!
Green Flag!"

Aweek before he came to Atlanta for the Hooters 500, a fan mailed Alan Kulwicki a card. "Live, love and do your best," it read. "To God, leave the rest."

Kulwicki loved that kind of stuff.

In 1990, when asked about his reputation for being a perfectionist, he had said that he had come to realize that nothing could be perfect.

"I've got a saying worked out for that," he said. "The pursuit of perfection is a frustrating waste of time. No one is perfect. The pursuit of excellence is commendable and worthwhile. Therefore, strive for excellence and not perfection."

Kulwicki had a million of them.

"The dictionary is the only place where you'll find success appearing before work," he sometimes said.

Kulwicki held himself to exacting standards, and expected those around them to meet them, as well. Cal Lawson, his close friend and the manager of his team, knew this about Kulwicki, but still was surprised to find out just how deep that trait went.

Lawson and Kulwicki had been out together in Charlotte one night and Kulwicki had met a young woman. Kulwicki talked with her privately for a while, and when they parted at evening's end Kulwicki had a new phone number to add to his already impressive collection.

Lawson was driving home when he saw Kulwicki fiddling with his wallet and taking out a neatly folded piece of paper.

"What's that?" Lawson asked.

"Nothing," Kulwicki said. "Just a list."

"A list of what?" Lawson said.

"Just a list," Kulwicki said.

Lawson pressed his friend, who finally admitted that it was a list of traits he considered attractive in a woman—a checklist of sorts.

"He had all kinds of stuff on that list, like the length of her fingernails and whether she wore bows in her hair," Lawson said. "Alan didn't like women who wore bows in their hair. He thought that was too Southern."

Kulwicki chose carefully when allowing himself to get close to anyone, perhaps because the deaths of his mother, his grandmother and his brother had taught him at a young age how painful it could be to lose someone you loved.

When he hired a new person for the team, Kulwicki spent the first few weeks taking stock. If the new person didn't fit in—didn't pass Kulwicki's test—the new person didn't stay around. Those who did make the grade, though, could not have hoped for a more loyal backer.

"Alan was a very tough individual, tough to work for and tough to be around," Lawson said. "He was demanding. But I was a Marine. Nobody likes to be treated poorly by a superior, and Alan tended to do that. . . . You don't know how many times I would want to wring his neck. But he had a way with me. He wouldn't really apologize, but he'd say, 'Hey, let's go get a bite to eat.'

"Everything he did and everything he said, there was a thought process behind it. He didn't say it just to be saying it or do it just to be doing it. There was a reason behind it. Alan literally worked 24 hours a day, seven days a week, 365 days a year, whether he was in the shop or out going to dinner. He was working all of the time."

One person who hadn't stayed long at Alan Kulwicki Racing was Ray Evernham, the crew chief who now was leading Jeff Gordon's move into Winston Cup.

Evernham came to work for Kulwicki's team shortly after the end of the 1990 season. He went to Daytona with the team for the first race of 1991, but left the team before that race. Evernham and Kulwicki were too much alike to share the same shop—both knew exactly what he wanted to do to a car and neither had honed his skills at compromise. While their talents would eventually take them both to the top of their profession, they never could have got there together.

Of all of Kulwicki's sayings, perhaps his favorite was one he had borrowed from Vince Lombardi, the legendary coach of the NFL's Green Bay Packers in Kulwicki's home state of Wisconsin.

"Obstacles," Lombardi had said, "are what you see when you take your eyes off the goal."

To some, it had seemed that Kulwicki had taken his eyes off the goal of winning the '92 championship after falling 278 points behind. Kulwicki said he never gave up, but was trying to be honest about the situation.

"For two-thirds of the season I thought we would be a legitimate contender," he said. "There was only one time—right after the Dover race —when I thought our chances were pretty much wiped out. . . . I think it may have been misinterpreted. People thought I'd given up or quit. I didn't. I just thought that realistically we got too far behind to catch up. But some of the adversity that struck us in that race went on to catch up with the other competitors, and now we're right back in the thick of things."

The car Kulwicki had in Atlanta had been good to him. He had first raced the No. 8 chassis at Atlanta in March 1989 and had won the pole. In 27 previous qualifying attempts in the car, Kulwicki had won eight poles—including the one at Charlotte just a month earlier—and had started worse than eighth only three times. No. 8 was also the car Kulwicki's team trucked to Dover on Friday night for the spring race after he'd crashed two cars in practice. He started 37th and finished 12th that day.

While Kulwicki's disastrous result in the second Dover race put him in a hole he didn't think he could crawl out of, it was on that same day that Allison believed things started turning back in his favor in what had been a season-long battle with Elliott.

"Bill had a dominant car that day," Allison said. "I think he should have won, had everything gone smoothly. It was sort of a sign to us, even though we finished fourth and he finished second, that his fortune had turned around and gone the other way."

Allison had overcome so much—the death of his grandfather and his brother and the crashes at Bristol and Pocono and in The Winston. The win at Phoenix that gave him the points lead again made it easy to believe he was destined to be champion.

Allison, however, was taking nothing for granted.

"Our focus is to run the best race we can possibly run and to try to finish as high as we can," Allison said. "If we finish fifth, we win the championship no matter what. But we can't start thinking about that. We have to run a smart race, finish as high as we can and be satisfied with it when it's all over."

Allison and McReynolds had been working on running smart races all season. Allison's nature was to go as hard as he could for as long as he could, but the Pocono crash had been an example of when his lack of patience proved costly. Allison had plenty of time to get back to the lead in that race without trying a daring move in Pocono's treacherous second turn, but the opportunity was there and his instincts were to take it.

"Davey was a race driver," Wayne Estes said. "You could not talk him into going slow intentionally. He and [car owner] Robert [Yates] would go down to Daytona and Ford would be lobbying NASCAR officials at the track that day saying, 'We need help, we need help.'"

Manufacturers are always asking NASCAR to make changes in their cars' spoiler sizes or other aerodynamic characteristics to help them go as fast as the other manufacturers. Or faster.

"You could tell Robert and Davey, 'You guys have to understand that we can get you more unless you come down here and run 192 mph when we say you can only run 189,'" Estes said. "One day in the middle of one of those meetings, Bill France picks up a phone. He hangs up and looks at the Ford officials and says, 'The 28 car just ran 193 [mph], I think you guys have all the help you need.'"

Throughout 1992 season, McReynolds had used a simple mantra to remind Allison that the team's focus was the championship. "Remember the big picture, Davey," McReynolds said repeatedly. "Remember the big picture."

The big picture had come into focus by Nov. 14, the final day of practice and qualifying before the Hooters 500.

Brian VanDercook had worked with Bob Latford, one of the men who had designed the points system two decades earlier, to produce a detailed chart showing what Allison needed to do to stay out front. At a glance the team could look at where all of the contenders were running and what that meant for Allison. If, for example, Allison were 10th and Elliott were fourth, the team would know instantly what that would mean points-wise if the race finished with the cars in those positions.

Kulwicki, meanwhile, had done a little figuring on his own.

"In this particular race, we've beaten Davey an average of 35 points over the past three years," Kulwicki said. "We've beaten Bill Elliott by an average of about 10 points and Junior's [Johnson] cars by an average of 13 to 15 points. It's an interesting angle to look at. Our record in this race over that period of time has been better than those other guys, better than Kyle's [Petty], better than Harry Gant's."

Kulwicki had also looked over the history of the late-season points races to find inspiration going into Phoenix. He had noticed that in 1990, Dale Earnhardt had trailed Mark Martin by 49 points with three races to go, but rallied to win by 26. Earnhardt had done that despite the fact that Martin did not run into any great disaster—Martin finished 11th, 10th and sixth in the final three races and still lost the title.

"I was looking for a positive angle to work on," Kulwicki said, "something that said, 'It's not over yet.'"

As the contenders thought about what might happen to their title hopes on Sunday, Saturday was still a full day.

After the morning practice, second-round qualifying saw Jeff Gordon improve on his speed of 176.521 mph from Friday with a lap at 177.735 mph. That was fastest among second-day qualifiers, earning him the 21st spot for Sunday.

Gant stood on his speed of 176.657 mph and wound up with the 29th starting spot. Richard Petty stood at 175.318 mph and got the 39th spot alongside Eddie Bierschwale's Olds on Row 20. Dave Marcis took the provisional spot to start 41st.

The field was set. It included 16 Fords, 15 Chevrolets, five Pontiacs and five Oldsmobiles. Four drivers were the sons of former Winston Cup champions—Richard and Kyle Petty, Davey Allison and Dale Jarrett. Jarrett would start 32nd in the No. 18 Chevrolet owned by Washington Redskins coach Joe Gibbs, whose entry into the sport at the start of the 1992 season had drawn national headlines. Jimmy Hensley, on his way to winning the rookie of the year award, qualified 34th fastest at 176.140 mph.

For the drivers qualified in the top 20, Saturday provided the opportunity to hone their cars' setups in racing trim, allowing them to get a feel for how they might react the following day.

For Allison and his team, it provided an opportunity for a little gamesmanship.

Racing for a championship was a new experience for most of the people at Robert Yates Racing. Yates had been around championship-level teams as an engine builder, and Allison could rely on his father's experiences. But McReynolds had never been this close before.

"We tried not to panic," McReynolds said. "We did some extra things with the car. We got that car ready Tuesday night and put it in the middle of the shop. We were going to take a day on Wednesday to do a race morning checklist on the car. We wanted to check every bolt, every terminal and every wire.

"We just wanted to make sure all of the I's were dotted and the T's were crossed. We didn't want to go beat ourselves because of some crazy mechanical problem."

After the morning practice, McReynolds and Allison started playing mind games.

"You know what we're going to do?" Allison said to McReynolds.

"What?" McReynolds said.

"We're going to cover this car up and go over here and eat lunch," Allison said. "Think that will blow their minds?"

Allison wanted to skip the midday practice, figuring it would make his challengers think he was completely satisfied with how his car was running.

It wasn't the most daring gamble—the team wasn't likely to reinvent the wheel in a one-hour practice for the final race of the season —but it also didn't scare anybody, either. While Allison skipped the midday session and made only a few laps in the final practice that afternoon, Kulwicki and Elliott went about their business.

Elliott's crew chief, Tim Brewer, waved off questions about the mechanical troubles that had bedeviled his team.

"The things that took us out at Charlotte and at Phoenix, throw those out the window and we've been a pretty solid race team," Brewer said.

"I'm not going to go off the deep end and start changing and second-guessing or some of that weird stuff."

Kulwicki wasn't in the mood to make predictions.

"When you race, if you make predictions you have to eat your words a lot of times," he said. "I don't predict and I don't gamble.

"If I had to bet, Davey's edge is that he's 30 points ahead. As far as who's going to perform best in this race, it's a flip of the coin. So many things can happen with lapped traffic, pit stops, mechanical failures, there's really no telling. . . . It's just a fine line between what happens and what might happen. My chances are pretty good, but I'm not making any predictions. I just can't."

Kulwicki also said he hadn't thought much about how his life might change if he wound up as the season's champion.

"It's probably a good thing I haven't," he said. "The pressure really hasn't gotten to me. Pressure, the way you react to it, is the way you perceive it. What is a pressure situation to one person may not be to another person.

"The guy going out there to kick a field goal with five seconds left in the game—how much pressure he feels largely depends on the way he perceives it. If he can block everything out, it's just another kick. If he looks out and sees the 50,000 people in the stands, he might choke. I'm really just trying to not let that happen, to focus on preparing the car and running my best race.

"Winning the championship would change my career, probably change my life. But I've been too busy trying to prepare for this race to contemplate how many interviews I might be doing down the road. I will deal with that if it comes."

Even if Kulwicki won the championship, however, he knew it was unlikely he'd ever face down the kind of fame that had come to be second nature for Richard Petty.

Petty could have filled a warehouse with the going-away gifts he received from tracks and sponsors and fans that season. There had been a statue of Petty dedicated just outside the Atlanta track's offices that weekend. Other tracks had named grandstands in his honor and relabeled streets near tracks as Petty Boulevard or Petty Avenue.

On the night before Petty's final race, there was one last party, the biggest of the entire Fan Appreciation Tour. Held at the Georgia Dome, it featured a star-studded country music lineup including singers Lorrie

Morgan, Ricky Van Shelton and Joe Diffie. The headline act was the group Alabama, which also would sing the national anthem before the race on Sunday and which had written a special song in Petty's honor about his career-long love affair with race fans.

The show ran three hours, beginning at 7 p.m., and was carried live on cable television and a network of nearly 300 radio stations.

Petty handled the evening the way he handled everything else, with grace and a great big smile. But his wife, Lynda, knew he was beginning to feel the emotions of the reality that faced them. Richard's racing career would be over in 24 hours.

"We were standing on the stage and he said, 'You know, I feel like a politician,'" Lynda said the next day. "You get up in front of that many people and they're yelling and yelling and, you know, whether they ever wanted you to win or cared if you won, they supported you as a person.

"For your values or for your character or whatever it is, they loved you and they supported you, and that's a humble feeling."

McReynolds skipped the soirée.

He left the track and went back to a hotel in Morrow, Ga., where he was staying that weekend with his wife, Linda, and their two young children, 3-year-old Brooke and 17-month-old Brandon.

"How are you doing?" Linda McReynolds asked when her husband came in. She knew the pressure he was under and that he had a million things going on in his mind.

"I think we're okay," Larry said, using "we" in the common racing vernacular to mean his race team.

All McReynolds wanted was a chance to sit and gather his thoughts. The family ate dinner and Larry sat with his charts and notes until about 11 p.m., thinking things through one more time. He slept better than Linda ever thought he would have.

He was up well before sunrise on Sunday to drive to the track before traffic began to swell. McReynolds would be there along with every other crew chief and crew member in the sport when the gates to the garage swung open.

By mid-morning the garage would be swarmed by fans and sponsors' guests taking pit tours. Long before they arrived, however, the teams began going through their final checklists to make sure they had not overlooked a simple problem that might spell disaster once the green flag flew.

Shortly after the garage opened, Estes was standing atop a transporter talking to someone. He looked down to see Kulwicki walking to his garage stall, carrying eight shock absorbers toward the car with one looped between the fingers of each hand. Even in the final hours before the biggest race of the season, there was still time to think about making last-minute changes that could prove to be the difference between being the champion and falling short of winning the year's ultimate prize.

Petty arrived in a helicopter belonging to Felix Sabates, Kyle's car owner, landing at about 7:45 a.m. at a private airport adjacent to the track. He went straight to a luxury bus he and the family had used as a base at the track all year long.

This day, the bus wasn't as crowded as it had been at previous races. Lynda had asked people to give the family a little more room this time. There were some exceptions. A few people from the various sponsors connected with Petty and the Farewell Tour came in for an audience. A woman who'd been waiting outside the bus for most of two days also got her autograph.

Deb Williams, associate editor of *Winston Cup Scene,* a weekly newspaper widely circulated among NASCAR fans and in the garage area, spent the morning with the family, too.

As the hours passed, Petty grew reflective.

"She is the one who made it work," Petty said of Lynda. "She let me do what I wanted to do and she took up the gap; a lot of my responsibilities I didn't do. I just kept on racing. I don't know if I'll be able to handle the responsibilities now. After 55 years, I'm going to have to grow up. I can't play no more. . . . It's going to be different. So far, we've been lucky. We've adapted to everything else. I think we can adapt to this, too. I've sort of gone with the flow my whole life."

Petty comforted himself with the knowledge that he wasn't leaving the sport, just retiring as a driver. He would still be a team owner. He would still have a son racing and would still have racing in his life.

"There is life after driving," he told Williams. ". . . There is no event so important that it couldn't be done without you. No matter how big you are or how important, it will go on without you. The world will keep turning; everybody will go do their thing. The good Lord fixed it like that so things could continue."

Just before 10 a.m., Lynda asked everyone except family to leave the bus. Kyle came to join the group. At 10:15, they came out and Petty, with three security guards running interference, walked to his final drivers' meeting.

The typical drivers' meeting is a short and fairly perfunctory session. A NASCAR official reminds the competitors about the pit road speed and recites a litany of reminders that, after a few times of hearing it, becomes almost as rote as a flight attendant's pre-takeoff safety spiel. A visiting dignitary or two—a local Congressman or a governor some weeks, a race sponsor's company CEO others—is introduced and a short prayer is said.

On Nov. 15, 1992, however, there was other business.

First of all, it was the final drivers' meeting over which Winston Cup director Dick Beaty would preside as chief of the inspectors and rules officials for NASCAR. Beaty was highly regarded in the garage area as a man who was both fair and reasonable in a job that in many ways made it nearly impossible for its holder to be considered either.

When a particular manufacturer's cars are winning more often than any other, every other manufacturer instantly blames NASCAR rules and starts lobbying for change. When a racer is caught trying to slip something by that doesn't conform to the rules, his first response is to blame the person who discovered the violation. The cheater claims either that the same kind of cheating is being perpetrated by all other teams and is being overtly allowed by the inspectors, or that the inspection process is thwarting a legitimate bid to be innovative in improving a car's performance. It is never the driver's fault.

Beaty was also racing's referee, the man who watched the action and was the final arbiter on whether an action was out of bounds or just good, hard racing. On this day, he offered a stern warning to the drivers in his final race.

"If you hit one of those guys in the running for the championship," Beaty said, "you'd better find the rest of them and hit them, too. If you don't, there's going to be some serious trouble when I come after you."

The man who would step into Beaty's shoes the following year had been on the other side of NASCAR's pointed finger many times in his career.

Gary Nelson had been one of the sport's most "creative" crew chiefs in his long tenure with several top teams. Before the start of the 1992 season, Nelson had been hired to spend that year as Beaty's replacement in training.

His selection had raised eyebrows—and some blood pressures—around the garage. It was as though one of the world's best magicians had been hired to investigate and reveal the secrets of pulling a rabbit out of a hat or sawing an assistant in half.

This would also be the last drivers' meeting Kirk Shelmerdine would be required to attend as crew chief on the No. 3 Chevrolets driven by five-time champion Dale Earnhardt, who was closing out his least productive season in more than a decade.

On the Tuesday after the Phoenix race Shelmerdine, just 34, told the members of his team that he was retiring as a Winston Cup crew chief. He had told Earnhardt and car owner Richard Childress of his plans just two weeks earlier, saying he felt tired and spent after winning championships with the team in 1986, '87, '90 and '91.

"After 16 years of this, I don't have the desire, and that's a must," said Shelmerdine, who had left home in Philadelphia at age 16 to come South and go racing. "I want to relax with my wife and son for a while."

Shelmerdine's departure fueled rumors that Earnhardt and Childress were about to part ways after eight remarkably successful seasons, in which Earnhardt had won 43 races and four titles. Earnhardt and Childress quashed those rumors a week later by announcing an extension of their contract, but talk about Shelmerdine's departure continued in light of the team's unexpected struggles during the '92 season.

Earnhardt had won only one race all season, the Coca-Cola 600 at Charlotte, and was in danger of finishing outside the top 10 in points after being the champion the past two seasons and no worse than third since 1986. Earnhardt won 11 times in '87 and nine times in '90, but had only six top-fives in the '92 season after 28 races.

Petty also was part of the program at this drivers' meeting. After a year in which he had received gifts everywhere he went, this time he wanted to hand some out.

To each of the other 40 drivers qualified for his final race he presented a commemorative money clip bearing the name and date of the race, the driver's name and starting position and the phrase "Thanks for the Memories, Richard Petty." Petty, who also gave belt buckles to the officials working the race, called each driver up and presented him the clip, an item only 40 men would ever be able to say they earned.

Ty Norris, who would later go to work for Dale Earnhardt, noticed his future boss was up to some mischief once the money clips had been handed out and the more mundane parts of the drivers' meeting had begun.

"It was Jeff Gordon's first race and he was sitting next to Dale," Norris said. "Jeff was wide-eyed, in awe. He was sitting next to one hero and another was giving him this money clip.

"They were sitting there telling him about the rules of the road for that event. They're going through all the procedures and Gordon's focused in on whoever was talking. He was just staring at them, not like a lot of the drivers who are looking around or staring at their watches. He was staring at them like a kid in class."

With Gordon paying rapt attention to the parts of the meeting Earnhardt had heard hundreds of times before, Earnhardt swiped Gordon's money clip. Gordon never saw a thing.

"Everybody was finished and they were walking up to Richard shaking his hand and thanking him," Norris said. "Jeff walked out of the meeting and suddenly remembered he'd forgotten something. He went back to his seat to look for the money clip but it wasn't there. He was running around looking for it.

"Dale was about to fall on the floor laughing. Finally, he walked over to Gordon and said, 'You need to pay attention, kid, this is a pretty big deal.' It was hilarious to stand there and watch the whole thing happen."

After the meeting Petty and his family went to a stage on the frontstretch to get one last round of gifts. Among them was a bald eagle to be released in Petty's honor at a Tennessee sanctuary. R.J. Reynolds arranged for the release and Petty was allowed to name the bird, with the limitation that it could not be named for a person. So Petty chose "Traveler," the name of Civil War general Robert E. Lee's horse.

Driver introductions followed, beginning with Marcis and ending with Rick Mast, the pole-sitter. Drivers climbed into their cars and their crews lined up along pit road as Alabama sang the national anthem.

Skies were blue and the sun was shining brilliantly, but a freshening breeze added a chill to the midday air.

ESPN began its national telecast with anchor Bob Jenkins setting the stage for Petty's final race and for the championship battle to be decided that afternoon. With the song "Wild-Eyed Southern Boys" playing in the background, video clips of the six men still in the championship hunt flashed across the screen. The song and the pictures ended with the words "It All Ends Here" on the screen.

Petty was sitting in the seat of his No. 43 Pontiac, fumbling with his earplugs, when pit reporter Jerry Punch stuck his microphone through the window.

"It has just been a great year," Petty said. "Our racing has not been too good, but everything else has been great. I started out to say thank you to the fans, but the fans have turned it around and said, 'Thank you, Richard.' I've enjoyed all 35 years and I hope the fans have, too."

Punch asked Petty if there might be any chance he'd give the fans a victory to remember him by.

"That would be asking a little bit much to tell you the truth," Petty admitted. "We're going to try to go out there and do the very best we can. The good Lord willing, we'll be right there with them at the end."

Next came John Kernan, squatting next to Allison's Ford.

"Right now, I am just incredibly nervous," Allison admitted. "I don't think I've ever been this nervous in my life. We think we're in pretty good shape, we just want to have an event-free race, stay out of trouble and hope we'll be around at the end."

The plan was for Petty's children to give a special command for Richard to start the No. 43 Pontiac's engine first. Kyle and his three sisters delivered the command, but Richard did not hear it. Neither did virtually anybody else, thanks to the ever-excitable public address announcer Bill Connell's incessant commands—"Let's clear pit road! Let's clear pit road, please!"

A few moments later, track owner Bruton Smith gave the general command to fire engines. Petty and the rest of the field flipped the ignition switches on their cars. As the field rolled off pit road, Petty took his position behind the pace car to lead the first parade lap, as he had done all season.

Four Apache helicopters swooped down over the field and began circling the track along with the field. As the pace laps continued, the choppers seemed to get closer and closer to the cars on the track, and lower and lower beneath the bowl of grandstands surrounding it. As the cars came down the frontstretch, the choppers swept by the press box and control towers at what seemed like eye level.

Speedway president Ed Clark, in his first race in that position, could feel Bill France Jr.'s eyes burning into the side of his face from the box next to his. When Clark could no longer resist the urge to look over at France, he could offer only shrugged shoulders by way of explanation.

Finally the choppers peeled off. Petty slowed and allowed the field to slip past him as he fell back to his 39th-place starting position.

The cars completed their pace laps and a crowd estimated by track officials at 165,000—although it was probably closer to 125,000 —rose to its feet.

Forty-one cars came off the 24-degree banking of Turn 4 and the pace car swerved onto pit road.

As Mast and Brett Bodine, the front-row starters, paced the field the championship contenders took one last deep breath. All of the distractions, all of the discussions leading up to the season finale were gone now. For 328 laps, their entire world would be what was going on inside the cockpit and around them on the track.

About 150 yards short of the start-finish line, Mast and Bodine approached a red line painted on the outside wall. Spotters perched atop the press box stood poised.

One final moment of relative calm passed.

Mast and Bodine reached the red line.

A flagman perched in a stand above the start-finish line cocked his wrist.

"Green flag!" the spotters yelled. "Green flag!"

Buddy Parrott (left) was among the many NASCAR veterans whose careers crossed paths with Richard Petty.

Junior Johnson (left) won three of his six championships as a car owner with Darrell Waltrip behind the wheel of his cars.

Donnie (left) and his nephew Davey (right), were part of NASCAR's Allison family tradition.

Not everything went right for Bill Elliott and his team in their magical 1985 season—it just seemed that way.

Bill Elliott climbs into his No. 9 Ford for the 1985 Southern 500 at Darlington Raceway. Elliott's victory in that race allowed him to collect a $1 million bonus from R.J. Reynolds Tobacco Co.

Bobby and Davey Allison, the father-son combination who finished first and second in the 1988 Daytona 500.

Alan Kulwicki's attention to detail was legendary—he even had a small glove box put in each of his cars to hold a comb, a handkerchief and a stick of lip balm.

Bill Elliott's path to Winston Cup stardom began when he raced his brothers around the junkyard their father owned.

Davey Allison's face never did do a good job of hiding his mischievous nature.

Bill Elliott found it difficult to adjust to the crush or media attention that came after he reached stardom in Winston Cup racing.

Alan Kulwicki celebrates his first career Winston Cup victory at Phoenix International Raceway in 1988. It was after that win that Kulwicki debuted his "Polish Victory Lap."

Davey and Liz Allison with their son, Robby.

Emergency workers surround the remains of Davey Allison's Ford after Allison's savage crash at Pocono International Raceway during the 1992 season.

Davey Allison and crew chief Larry McReynolds nervously wait out qualifying at Charlotte Motor Speedway, with their No. 28 still on top of the list

Richard and Lynda Petty offer their condolences to Gerald Kulwicki, Alan's father, after the driver's death in 1993.

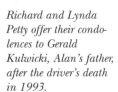

Alan Kulwicki celebrates winning the 1992 Winston Cup championship after the Hooters 500 at Atlanta Motor Speedway. Tom Roberts, Kulwicki's friend and public relations agent, is standing beside the driver.

Race fans came to the Robert Yates Racing shop in Charlotte, N.C., to leave signs and other remembrances after Davey Allison's death in a helicopter crash in 1993.

All Blaze, No Glory

ick Mast hadn't led a lap in the entire 1992 season. He could change that by making it around the 1.522-mile Atlanta track ahead of the field at the start of the Hooters 500.

Mast and Brett Bodine ran side by side into the first two turns. Most tracks of 1.5 miles or more have bends in their frontstretches, making them into what is commonly called a trioval. Atlanta Motor Speedway is like that today, but in 1992 it was a true oval. Each straightaway was just that, straight, and a quarter-mile long. Each pair of turns at the ends of those straightaways ran for a half-mile, meaning that the cars were turning twice as much as they were going straight on any given lap.

Mast had the nose of his Oldsmobile in front of Bodine's Ford coming of the second turn of the first lap and led going down the backstretch. In Turn 3, however, his car drifted up the banking enough to allow Bodine to cross to the low lane behind him, giving Bodine the shorter path through that end of the speedway.

As the cars came off Turn 4, Bodine was ahead. Dale Earnhardt, who'd started third, was right behind him. Mast was trapped on the high side of the track, hugging close to the right-hand side of the two cars racing underneath him.

Less than 40 seconds into the race, the day took its first dramatic turn.

As Bodine went into the first turn on Lap 2, the presence of Mast's car just to his outside and Earnhardt's right behind him began to conspire against him.

Bodine's Ford was punching a hole through the air as it raced along, with the stream of air being pushed over its nose and roof exerting downward force to help hold the car's tires onto the track. This downforce is the key to how a car handles at racing speed.

As Bodine's car moved into Turn 1, the air passing over the right side of its nose was being deflected away from that side and the right rear of his No. 26 Ford by the presence of Mast's car just to its outside. When Earnhardt moved his Chevrolet to the low side in an effort to pass Bodine for the lead, his car took the air off Bodine's left rear.

This combination took away so much of the downforce on the No. 26 Ford that Bodine couldn't control the rear end of his car. It snapped around on him, sending him sideways up the banking and into Mast.

Bodine slammed the outside wall, rear end first. Mast spun and whacked the wall, too. Earnhardt dove quickly to his left and barely missed Bodine's spinning car. Mark Martin nearly spun, too, but also saved his car.

Just over a lap into the race, the entire field was still tightly bunched. Elliott and Kulwicki went to the low side, racing past by a whisker before Bodine's car washed back down across the track toward the apron. Kulwicki, in fact, had to swerve dramatically to miss Bodine and almost got hit from behind by Ricky Rudd.

Allison, who'd started three spots behind Kulwicki, went high. He slowed as Bodine's car slid down the track in front of him, but Hut Stricklin didn't slow as quickly and clipped the left rear of Allison's car as Stricklin tried to go low to miss Allison's Ford. Stricklin's car continued toward the low side of the track and got there just as Bodine's reached the same spot. They collided violently; an impact that would send both drivers to the hospital once the wreck was done.

Wally Dallenbach, Rich Bickle and Bob Schact also wound up spinning and wrecking back in the pack as traffic stacked up behind the incident. Earnhardt won the race back to the start-finish line to lead Lap 2 as the yellow flag flew.

As the cars came around, everyone tried to locate the championship contenders. Elliott and Kulwicki had made it through, just barely. From the stands, Allison's Ford appeared to be all right. From pit road, however, his crew could see that Stricklin's hit had shoved sheet metal on the left rear of Allison's car outward and upward.

The crew asked Jimmy Spencer's crew to have Spencer ride beside Allison's car and see if the sheet metal had been pushed in enough to make it rub against the left-rear tire, creating a danger the tire would blow out. It had not.

But the metal had been pulled away from a crush panel that lines the space behind the tire opening. This panel keeps air from racing up the inside of the wheel well into the trunk area, where the fuel cell is located. The hole between the sheet metal and this crush panel meant that air could now get into that trunk area, acting as an aerodynamic parachute that would keep the car from running at its best until the problem was fixed.

McReynolds faced his first important decision of the afternoon.

He could bring Allison to pit road under the yellow, have the crew push the sheet metal back in and hope that the added drag from the hole in the crush panel wouldn't hurt the team too much until he could figure out what more to do.

If Allison came in, however, he would go back onto the track behind all of the cars that did not pit under this first yellow. Only a few had come in, most notably Martin, who'd run through debris from the Mast-Bodine accident and was worried he'd cut a tire. Richard Petty also came in for tires and a chassis adjustment. McReynolds decided to keep the track position and wait until the first scheduled pit stop to work on repairing the car.

The green flew to begin Lap 12. Earnhardt had beaten Ernie Irvan and Martin back to the yellow on Lap 2 and was just ahead of Irvan and Geoffrey Bodine for the restart.

Having already dodged disaster once running in traffic, Kulwicki wasted no time in trying to get closer to the front. He went three-wide in Turn 2 on the first lap after green, racing Elliott and Sterling Marlin doggedly for position. They were still bunched together on Lap 16 when Morgan Shepherd and Derrike Cope nearly wrecked right in front of them. Elliott, running in the high line, had to back quickly off his throttle to keep from hitting Cope. Kulwicki slowed too, allowing Marlin and Rusty Wallace to dive to the low side and move past him.

Irvan passed Earnhardt for the lead at almost the same moment, and Geoffrey Bodine began closing in on them to make it a three-way race for the lead.

Back in the pack, Allison's car was losing ground. As his crew had feared, the punched-out crush panel was affecting the car's handling.

On pit road, members of Allison's crew began discussing what they might do to remedy the situation. There was concern, but no panic. The race had barely begun. There was a long, long way to go and the crew had been through so much together all season. Compared to some of the obstacles that had been cleared just to get this far, a little bent-up sheet metal was not much of a challenge at all.

Earnhardt pushed his way back into the lead on Lap 31 after discovering that his Chevrolet ran better if he took an exceptionally high line around the track.

Sometimes a car handles better low; down near the white line marking the spot where the banking begins and the flat apron begins. That's the shortest way around, of course, but there are also times when a car just won't run as well in that groove. The driver has to feel this and search for a line where he's able to roll into the corner without losing momentum and jump back on the gas as soon as possible for the run down the straightaway. On a track with two-thirds of its distance made up in the turns like Atlanta, finding that right line is vital.

Earnhardt initially pulled 20 car-lengths ahead of Irvan, but once Irvan saw Earnhardt pulling away he, too, moved up the track and began to cut into Earnhardt's advantage using the higher line. Geoffrey Bodine, meanwhile, stayed in the low line and began to catch up rapidly, too, with his car working well down low. He passed Irvan for second and began challenging Earnhardt for the top spot.

Earnhardt, who had put Richard Petty a lap down on Lap 40, held Bodine off and maintained the lead. But the high line began to take a toll on his car's engine.

By staying high on the banking, he was running his engine at high rpm and putting a strain on its parts. By Lap 55, Earnhardt radioed to his crew and said he thought there might be a problem developing. Bodine closed in further.

To this point, none of the championship contenders had been around the lead. Elliott was running just outside the top five. Kulwicki had moved up steadily to a spot just behind Elliott. Allison wasn't gaining any ground, but he wasn't losing any more, either. McReynolds kept telling him to be patient, to hold on until the first pit stop when the crew could begin repairing the damage Allison had suffered in the Lap 2 incident.

ESPN, naturally, was following the championship story closely.

Producer Neil Goldberg, the man in charge of the telecast, had assigned cameras to isolate on Elliott, Allison and Kulwicki, following each of those cars every inch of the way. That decision paid off early, since Goldberg had been able to show his viewers replays of how each made his way through the crash on Lap 2.

The first replay of Allison's car failed to pick up on the smack from behind by Stricklin, but once Punch learned from the crew that there was a problem Goldberg's production team found a series of replay angles showing what had happened.

The announcers were genuinely excited about the race they'd been given to call.

Bob Jenkins, the play-by-play voice of the three-man crew, had set the scene eloquently in the moments leading up to the green flag. His analysts were a pair of former Winston Cup champions, Benny Parsons and Ned Jarrett. Jarrett had a case of laryngitis that had rendered him almost incapable of uttering a sound on Saturday. By race day his voice was better, but still raspy. Parsons kidded Jarrett in the prerace that he'd lost his voice because he was so excited.

Having won championships themselves, Jarrett and Parsons knew the race they were calling was something special. They knew even the top three contenders could not afford to run conservatively in an effort to win the title.

"Davey Allison has to finish fifth or better to clinch the title," Jarrett said. "If he can run fifth, he'll have a car that's good enough to win the race."

As the announcers ran down the lineup just before the green flag, Parsons commented on the fact that Gordon's car had been fast in testing, and that after some trouble on Friday Gordon had been fastest in second-round qualifying. "I think it's fantastic that Jeff Gordon's first race is coming in Richard Petty's last race," Parsons said.

In addition to all of the camera operators and other technical personnel working behind the scenes, Jenkins, Parsons and Jarrett were also supported by a group of statisticians for whom this day would provide perhaps their greatest challenge.

Ken Martin had been working in the booth for 10 years, spotting for the announcers and charting the progress of the race. He worked for the Lingner Group, an Indianapolis-based production company that supplied personnel and equipment for ESPN racing telecasts. That year, the company also began producing a show called *Checkered Flag,* that aired on Mondays and reviewed the weekend's racing action. So Martin had stopped going to the track each week to stay back in Indianapolis and get that show ready for air.

Knowing how important the Atlanta race would be, Goldberg called in extra help. Martin had been asked to come help the announcers follow the championship race.

It wasn't until 1998 that NASCAR began using transponders as the basis for its primary scoring system. Transponders are located in the right-rear wheel well of each car and send a signal to a scoring computer every time they cross a trip wire dug into the track at the start-finish line.

In 1992, races were scored by hand, with scorers writing down the elapsed time into the race each lap the car they were responsible for crossed the scoring line.

Ken Martin had a radio link from the ESPN booth to the scoring stand, and at various points in the race he would verify the position of each of the championship contenders. Len Thacher, another member of the team, would then key those positions into a spreadsheet set up to calculate what points a finish in that position would be worth, then add that to the total each contender had coming into the race.

The resulting total would be displayed for viewers under the heading "Points as of Now" going into or coming out of commercial breaks.

Some race fans still find this statistic useless, and even somewhat annoying. A car's position 75 miles into a 500-mile race has nothing to do with where it's going to be at the end of the day. Points are not awarded until after the race, so a driver on Lap 50 in reality has the same number of points he started the day with.

But on this day, even this statistic's most strident critic had to admit its relevance. On Lap 25, will Allison running 11th, Elliott sixth and Kulwicki ninth, the graphic showed Allison 20 points ahead of Elliott and 22 up on Kulwicki. On Lap 44, Allison had dropped to 13th, Elliott was up to fifth and Kulwicki was sixth. At that point, Thacher's numbers showed that if the race ended that way Allison would have 4,052 points, Kulwicki 4,048 and Elliott 4,043.

As Bodine closed in on Earnhardt's bumper as Lap 60 approached, ESPN took a commercial break. When the race came back on, the first image on the screen was of Earnhardt's Chevrolet heading onto pit road. The speed limit was 55 mph, but Earnhardt was barely rolling. His engine was not running. He was out of gas. His high line had been the long way around the track, and he hadn't been able to get back around after seeing his fuel pressure gauge flutter as he came off Turn 2.

As Earnhardt crawled toward pit road, Bodine crossed the line to complete Lap 61 and officially took over the lead. He pitted the next time around. Irvan came in on the same lap, meaning that the top four cars had all made pit stops and that Elliott, who'd been running fifth, took over the lead when he completed Lap 62.

That was important, since leading a lap means five bonus points. With the championship battle as close as this one, getting that bonus was crucial to the top contenders. Elliott now had his.

Danny "Chocolate" Myers, the gas man on Earnhardt's team, hurriedly emptied two 11-gallon cans of fuel into Earnhardt's car. The engine had died and the crew knew it would have to push the car down pit road to get it refired. One crewman had a small bottle of ether to squirt into the intake manifold as they pushed, a perfectly legal trick used to help restart the engine under such circumstances.

Earnhardt's crew pushed him all the way past the exit line off pit road before the motor finally roared back to life. Wallace, Bodine and Irvan were already back on the track, getting back up to racing speed.

At almost the exact moment that Earnhardt's engine started again, however, Michael Waltrip's yellow No. 30 Pontiac went spinning into the outside wall in Turn 4. Waltrip had a flat left-front tire as his car slid back across the track toward the opening to pit road. NASCAR officials had no choice but to put out a yellow flag.

It was a terrible break for Earnhardt, Wallace, Irvan, Bodine and other cars that had already made pit stops under green.

They had slowed to the speed limits for their trips onto and off of pit road and had sat for 16 to 18 seconds while their crews worked on their cars. Meanwhile, the cars that had not pitted had been racing around the track at nearly 180 mph—basically at around 30 seconds per lap. Earnhardt was now two laps down. Irvan, Bodine and Wallace were just one down and would have made that up if the other cars had to come in for stops under green. Waltrip's spin came at the worst possible time for them.

The caution was timed perfectly, on the other hand, for Elliott, Kulwicki, Allison and the other drivers who'd yet to stop.

Elliott got the best of the deal, taking over the lead and getting his bonus points. It was a big break for Allison, too, who was beginning to feel that the damage to his car wasn't anything that the crew couldn't fix on the upcoming pit stop.

The circumstances had moved Kulwicki all the way up to second, too, but his heart jumped into his throat as he headed in for his stop under the yellow flag. As Kulwicki downshifted to head into his pit stall, he heard a sound he didn't like.

"Something just popped!" he yelled over the radio.

The car had popped out of gear as he shifted into first. Kulwicki had suffered a similar problem at Charlotte in October. As the crew dropped the jack after a pit stop in that race, he went to shift up to pull out and the car wouldn't move.

This time, Kulwicki was able to pull away, but he had to do it in second gear. NASCAR allows the crew of a car that has lost first gear to push it out of the pit stall, but that meant every pit stop would take a few moments longer, a critical disadvantage especially under green-flag conditions.

There was a lot going on after the pit stops as the cars rode around behind the pace car.

When the yellow flag comes out, the pace car pulls in front of the race leader, Elliott in this case. When Elliott and the other cars that had not made their pit stops pulled off the track, the cars that had pitted earlier pulled up right behind the pace car.

When Elliott and the others returned to the track, they tried to get back behind the pace car and in front of the other cars. But passing is not allowed under the yellow. In effect, Irvan, Wallace and Bodine had made up their lap, but were now trapped behind the pace car at the tail end of the lead lap, with the leaders right behind them.

As NASCAR officials tried to get the field back in line properly for the restart, Kulwicki's team was trying to figure out just what had happened to his "Underbird."

"Do you think maybe I just didn't have it in gear good, or is there really something wrong with it?" Kulwicki asked over the radio.

Neither crew chief Paul Andrews nor team manager Cal Lawson had an answer. As they gave each other a puzzled look, Joey Knuckles came over into the Kulwicki team's pit box from the stall where Allison was pitting just in front of them. Knuckles knew a Winston Cup transmission as well as anybody on pit road—that was part of his job on Allison's team. Kulwicki's smaller team had no such transmission specialist with knowledge rivaling Knuckles' expertise.

"Don't you dare let Alan put that thing into first gear!" Knuckles yelled into Lawson's headphones. "If he does he's liable to tear out everything but high gear and that's all you will have all day."

Everybody involved in the championship chase knew that the other contending teams would be listening in on each other's radio communications. This time, eavesdropping turned into one competitor helping out another, trying to prevent a mistake that might have turned into a huge advantage for his own team. Knuckles knew that Allison wanted to earn the championship, and the act of sportsmanship was second nature to most of those competing up and down pit road.

The field finally got back into shape for a restart on Lap 72, with Elliott first and Kulwicki second in the official running order but well back in traffic behind the group of cars trapped on the tail end of the lead lap.

Elliott led the first lap after green, but on the second trip around Kulwicki got a run to Elliott's low side off Turn 4. Kulwicki pulled alongside Elliott as they came to the start-finish line, and nosed barely into the lead as they crossed it.

Perhaps half of Kulwicki's hood was in front of the nose of Elliott's Ford, but it was enough for Kulwicki to be scored as the leader and to pick up his five bonus points.

Elliott surged back ahead of Kulwicki on the next lap and stayed there for the next six circuits. Once again on Lap 80, Kulwicki went low off Turn 4 and barely beat Elliott to the line, leading his second lap of the day. Once again, Elliott surged back on the following lap and regained the lead.

Another player, however, was coming into the battle for the lead. Martin, who'd made the early pit stop after running through the debris from the Lap 2 crash, had been slicing his way through the field.

Waltrip's problem had allowed Martin to make his second pit stop under the yellow and now he was back in the picture.

On Lap 82, he sped past Kulwicki into second place. Coming off Turn 2 on the following lap, Martin went to the inside while Elliott and Kulwicki got side by side, making a daring three-wide move to take the lead.

Seconds later, Schact's car slowed on the apron going into Turn 1. He had lost power and there was no way he could make it back to pit road. The yellow flag came out once again, allowing Irvan, Wallace, Bodine and the others who'd stayed ahead of Martin after the restart to come all the way back around and make up their lap. Earnhardt also made up a lap, leaving him just one down.

Under yellow, only cars on the lead lap can come in for stops on the first lap that pit road is open. Cars one or more laps down must wait until at least the second lap to stop.

When the lead lap cars came in this time, McReynolds quickly ordered his crew to change only right-side tires, saving time since only one side of the car has to be jacked up and then let down by the one jack-man who's allowed over the wall during a pit stop.

It had only been about 20 laps since the previous yellow and the previous pit stop, and Allison's tires hadn't worn that much. His car had burned less than half of its fuel load, so Allison's tank could be filled again in the amount of time it took to change only two tires. The benefit? A two-tire stop would allow Allison to get off pit road before everybody else, giving him the race lead and the five-point bonus that Elliott and Kulwicki had already collected.

Elliott was fifth on the restart, Kulwicki sixth. Martin lined up third, right behind Jimmy Means, who had also taken on two tires on his stop to gain track position. It took Martin five laps to work his way through lapped traffic, which had been on the inside line below the leaders on the restart, and get by Allison for the lead. Harry Gant, one of those with an outside shot at the championship, had been feeling ill all weekend, but now was up to third.

Richard Petty was well back in the field. He'd lost a lap early, and had been fighting the car's handling all day. The crew had made a major chassis adjustment on the second stop and changed four tires again on the third stop. But the King would never get a chance to see how those changes would affect his car.

There would have been a storybook quality to it had Petty's final race ended in victory lane. But nobody believed there was any chance to see that happen. Petty hadn't won a race in eight years. He hadn't finished second since 1987 and had only two top-10 finishes over his final four seasons.

The more realistic goal for Petty was to finish the 500-mile race without incident, then to take his final bows in postrace ceremonies and be done with it.

On Lap 95, however, that goal became unattainable, too.

The wreck started just before the start-finish line on the frontstretch. Ken Schrader made a move to the inside as he tried to pass Dale Jarrett. Dick Trickle's car was running on the inside, too, and when Schrader went that way there wasn't enough room for all three cars. Trickle and Schrader made contact and began to spin.

The leaders, including all of the points contenders, were already into Turn 1 and well ahead of the wreck. The front end of Schrader's car hit the inside wall, a concrete barrier three feet high and nearly a foot thick, that separates the racing surface from pit road. The hood was knocked off and flew high into the air before raining back onto the track.

The flying hood caught Benny Parsons' eye. He shifted his focus from the leaders and back toward the frontstretch, alerting his colleagues in the booth and the viewers at home that a crash was taking place. The image on the screen switched in time to see Schrader and Trickle spinning, almost in formation, back into the inside wall.

Traffic coming behind them quickly began to stack up. Wally Dallenbach Jr. got hit as he tried to slow down and went sideways right in a pack of traffic. Darrell Waltrip's car got hit and then so did Rich Bickle's.

Running in that pack right behind Bickle's Ford was the red and blue No. 43 Pontiac of Richard Petty.

"Halfway down the frontstretch everything just went blank," Petty said. "All those cars were everywhere."

A replay from Petty's in-car camera showed his view. Smoke from the tires of the Schrader and Trickle cars cloaked the track. Petty slowed, but in an instant he was being hit from all sides, by Bickle's car and then by Waltrip's, which had been hit by Dallenbach's and shot across toward the outside wall and into the left side of Petty's car.

Within a second, flames were visible from underneath Petty's Pontiac. The impact from Waltrip's car had knocked off the oil cooler, and oil from inside the engine was leaking down onto the car's hot exhaust pipes, igniting bright orange flames.

Petty knew where the fire was coming from. Even at age 55, his instincts kicked in. By this point, his car was already to the end of the frontstretch, clear of the inside wall near the entrance to Turn 1. He kept the car rolling and turned sharply to his left, driving right up to where he knew safety trucks equipped with fire extinguishers were parked beyond the exit of pit road.

Dale Inman, who was spotting for Petty, had first thought the flames were about to burn out on their own. As Petty kept moving, however, the blaze flared up again to a point where the whole undercarriage of the car seemed to be on fire.

"Richard, it's big," Inman said. "Get out of there."

Petty had reached the trucks, but he had been thinking much more quickly than the safety workers. On the replay from Petty's in-car camera, one of the workers could be seen taking out a camera and snapping a few photos of the King's car.

"Bring the fire extinguisher!" Petty yelled as one safety worker approached. "Bring the fucking fire extinguisher!"

Finally, the workers got the fire out.

"I figured I'd better find me a fire truck," Petty said later. "I think all of those cats wanted to get an autograph. I sent them back to get the fire extinguisher."

Petty climbed out of his battered car. The hood was bent virtually in half. The nose was shattered. He knew that the only way the car was going to get back to the garage would be hooked to a wrecker. Petty, with his driving helmet in his right hand, walked around the front of a wrecker and waved to the crowd. His gesture, actually partly a wave and partly a shrug of his shoulders, seemed to say, "Well, that's not exactly how I wanted to end it, folks, but there it is."

Petty rode back to the garage in the wrecker towing his car. When he got there, more than 100 people—reporters, fans and his own crew—were waiting. Petty took a walk around the car, then met the media.

"I went out in a blaze," Petty said, "but I forgot the glory part."

Petty then talked for a moment with Inman and crew chief Robbie

Loomis, trying to decide if the car could be put back together well enough for Petty to make at least a few laps toward the end of the race.

"Can you do it?" Petty asked. The crew was determined to make it happen. "Then let's do it."

Petty went back to his bus, where Lynda and their daughters came to find their father.

"They were all crying," Petty said. "It really took a load off me because I saw, through them, how glad they were that it was over with."

Lynda Petty managed a smile.

"Anyone could have run 328 laps and parked the car in the garage," she said. "Not him. He goes out in smoke and flames and fire. Always spectacular."

There Will Be Other Years

As Richard Petty's crew began repairing his car, the championship contenders were asserting themselves in the Hooters 500. None made pit stops on the yellow after the big wreck involving Petty, so Mark Martin kept the lead. Davey Allison was second, with Harry Gant third, Bill Elliott fourth and Alan Kulwicki fifth.

One hundred laps into the 328-lap race, five of the six drivers who came into the day with a mathematical shot at the championship were in the top five positions. Only Kyle Petty, unable to make up the lap he'd lost on the early pit stop, wasn't in the picture.

Fourteen cars were on the lead lap at the restart on Lap 104. Dale Earnhardt was 15th, the first car a lap down, and he jumped ahead of Martin trying to get back on the lead lap. Earnhardt then pulled away, showing that he had a good car and might get back into contention if caution flags fell his way.

Kulwicki moved up to challenge Elliott for fourth, and the two cars ran side by side for almost two laps. Their Fords nearly made contact twice. With a championship on the line every position was important, and neither was giving an inch.

Allison, meanwhile, began to feel the effects of changing only two tires on the prior pit stop. He lost second to Gant and by Lap 122 had dropped back to sixth, with Geoffrey Bodine and Jimmy Spencer closing from behind.

Elliott passed Gant for second and was closing on Martin, whose car was getting looser with every passing lap. Kulwicki was right with Elliott, running third. Martin held the lead until Lap 134, but Elliott drove around him in turns 3 and 4. Kulwicki swept past Martin, too, taking second. Allison, meanwhile, lost sixth place to Bodine.

Every change in positions changed the points situation, and by Lap 143 it was suffocatingly close. According to Len Thacher's spreadsheet, at that point Allison would have won the championship by six points over Kulwicki and by 11 over Elliott. If Kulwicki could pass Elliott and take the lead, he'd be one point off Allison's pace. If Allison fell to eighth with Kulwicki in the lead, Kulwicki would have a three-point edge.

It was that close. One pass, one position, one lap could wind up making a difference.

None of the leaders had stopped since the caution for Bob Schact's stalled car on Lap 85, so the window for another stop was approaching. Martin was the first of the front-runners to come in on Lap 148. Earnhardt, who hadn't got the yellow flag he needed to catch back up to the leaders, pitted on Lap 150 instead of taking the risk of running out of fuel again.

Kulwicki and Allison came in on Lap 155, with Kulwicki's team pushing his car off pit road past Allison's car, which was being serviced in the next pit box. Just before Allison left a second later, a member of his crew delivered a swift kick to the still-protruding metal on the left rear of the Ford, hoping to push it back in just a little.

Elliott completed Lap 157 as the leader, meaning he'd led 42 laps to that point, then came in the next time by.

Irvan, who unlike the other leaders had stopped following Petty's crash, inherited the lead and stayed there until Lap 167, collecting a $10,000 prize for being the leader at the halfway point on Lap 164.

As Irvan reached the halfway mark, Martin's Ford was heading to the garage. A few laps after Martin's pit stop, crew chief Steve Hmiel had noticed puffs of white smoke coming out of Martin's exhaust pipes as the car went into Turn 1. It was not a good sign.

A lap or two later, Martin radioed in that he'd felt the car shudder badly as he sped down the backstretch. He took the car down onto the apron and limped around with the engine running at around 4,000 rpm, half of what it should have been turning.

He came down pit road once, but thought the trouble might be going away. He drove on through the pit lane and tried to make another lap but the engine would not go any faster. Martin came back around and pulled behind the wall. His day was done, and Martin became the first of the six possible championship winners to fall out of the race.

Gordon had been complaining that his car was too tight—meaning he was having trouble making it turn through the corners. On each pit stop, crew chief Ray Evernham had made slight changes to loosen it. Still, Gordon wasn't happy.

So when Gordon stopped just before the halfway point, Evernham called for a bigger change. This one worked—too well. A few laps later Gordon came off Turn 2 and got loose, smacking the wall and crumpling the sheet metal on his Chevrolet.

Gordon came back to pit road and his crew went to work, changing tires and trying to pull the sheet metal away. He went back out but came right back in. The impact with the wall had ruined the car's alignment. It would do Gordon and his brand new team no good to run the rest of the day with the car that badly damaged.

Gordon completed 164 laps—exactly half of the scheduled distance. He would wind up 31st in his first career Winston Cup start, one spot ahead of Martin, earning $6,285.

Not long after Gordon's departure, Allison got yet another scare.

"Guys," Allison said over his radio. "I think I ran over something and cut a tire."

Team members immediately began preparing for Allison to come in, grabbing new tires and lining them up against the wall and making sure the air guns used to get the lug nuts off and back on were ready to go.

"Hold on, maybe it's not going down," Allison said. "Maybe we're all right."

Crew members climbed up on the wall on the inside of pit road to get a look as Allison's Ford went by. The tire didn't seem to be going down, but there was evidence that something had happened. There was a dent in the left-front valence, the piece of the car extending downward from the front grille along the bottom of the car. The valence was actually pushed in on the left corner, the driver's side, just in front of the wheel.

It would later be determined that the bump Allison felt came when a piece fell off of a car running in front of him and thumped the nose of his car, causing the damage.

Not knowing what had happened, Allison backed off the throttle for only a moment, but it was enough time for Rusty Wallace to pass him and drop Allison into eighth place.

Elliott, meanwhile, was holding the lead. He caught and passed Gant, who had been running so well just a little while earlier, leaving only 11 cars on the lead lap. Elliott also had to work his way around Dave Marcis, putting Marcis another lap down, and in the process Kulwicki began closing in from behind, a few feet each lap.

Up in the booth, Ken Martin checked the positions after Lap 186. With Allison in eighth and Elliott and Kulwicki running first and second, he knew the points race was close. Still, he could barely believe what he saw when Thacher gave him the numbers.

If the race had ended at that point, Elliott would have earned the bonus for leading the most laps and would have gained 10 points on Kulwicki—the other five for finishing first to second for Kulwicki. They would have, therefore, had 4,073 points. Allison's total, for an eighth-place finish after having led a lap in the race, would have been 4,075. Allison would be the champion by two points over Elliott, who would have won the tiebreaker with Kulwicki for second because Elliott had won more races that season.

The race was approaching the 300-mile mark and little had been settled.

Martin was out and Gant and Petty were both one lap down, so their chances to come from behind to win the title were virtually gone. Richard Petty was out, at least for now, but his crew was working to get his car ready to come back for one last curtain call.

The championship race, though, was still a jumble.

Allison's team knew how the math was adding up. The situation was growing critical. Every time the No. 28 Ford went into the corner, air swept into the opening in the crush panel, shoving the car to the side. Sterling Marling and Geoffrey Bodine closed in, trying to get past Allison and take away eighth place.

Bodine eventually passed Marlin and was clearly running faster than

Allison. It was only a matter of time before Allison would drop to ninth, and maybe lose more spots, unless his team came up with a solution for his problem.

As Allison fought to hold his ground, his crew huddled behind pit wall with several pieces of aluminum, trying to figure out how to fashion a patch that could be applied quickly during an upcoming pit stop. They batted around ideas, leaning into each other's ears and yelling to be heard through their headphones above the noise from the track.

Earnhardt, the two-time defending champion who this year was just trying to fight his way back into the top 10 in the final standings, was meanwhile losing his battle to stay on the lead lap.

He began losing the handle on his Chevrolet, drifting dangerously close to the outside wall as Elliott closed in from behind. On Lap 203, two laps after Elliott had passed him to put him a lap down again, Earnhardt lost the battle. His car got out from under him in Turn 2 and he slid it, rear-end first, into the outside wall. Earnhardt held the car against the wall until the traffic cleared, then limped back to pit road.

The yellow was out for the first time in more than 100 laps. Only 10 cars were on the lead lap, meaning Allison could make several stops under the caution to make repairs on his car and still not lose more than two positions. It was the opportunity the team needed.

Kulwicki's crew was nearly halfway through its stop by the time Allison got his Ford to his spot on pit road. Kulwicki and Elliott both were heading back onto the track by the time Allison's crew finished changing his right-side tires and swung around to the left side of the car, where all the trouble was.

Once the tires were changed, the work began. Joey Knuckles and Ryan Pemberton were taking care of the damage to the front valence, pulling the dented slice of metal back out to something close to its original form to try to smooth out the aerodynamics affecting the nose of Allison's Thunderbird. They then took long strips of tape and placed them along the valence to hold the repair into the shape they had restored.

The discussions about how to fashion a patch for the popped-out sheet metal behind the left-rear wheel had been cut short by Earnhardt's spin and the yellow flag. Nobody had been able to figure out quite how to make it or how to attach it anyway.

Another, less artful method was devised. As Knuckles and Pemberton worked on the front end, another crewman grabbed a sledgehammer and began slamming the punched-out sheet metal. One swing to the side, another with a downward angle to push the whole quarterpanel down. If the hole couldn't be plugged, it could be pounded back in to where less air would be gulped as Allison ran into the corners.

As the pace car brought the field back around toward the frontstretch, Allison's crew gave him the signal to pull out. He went down pit road at 55 mph and then raced back around to make another trip down pit road for more work on the front and the rear.

This time, a crew member took time to carefully clean Allison's windshield so he could see through it as the car went into Turn 3, where the setting sun was shining right into the eyes of the drivers, a situation that would get worse as the race went along.

Allison went back out and caught up to the rear of the pack as the field was signaled there would be one lap to go before green. He was now 10th, the final car on the lead lap. Elliott was still first and Kulwicki second, meaning that as of that point, Elliott and Kulwicki were dead even in points with Allison six points back.

Still, Allison and his team felt fortunate. They had survived two major scares already and were still in there fighting. The caution flag came in time to make the repairs without losing a lap. If they had done their work well, Allison's car would now be good to go.

Elliott got the jump on the restart, with Kulwicki having to battle Kyle Petty's lapped car through the first two turns. Kulwicki pulled clear of Petty at the end of the backstretch, however, and set off after Elliott while Ernie Irvan and Jimmy Spencer battled for third on Lap 209.

Kulwicki caught Elliott in turns 1 and 2 on Lap 210. Kulwicki went to the low side off Turn 2 and nosed ahead. Elliott fought back on the outside and was in front by a few feet as they raced into Turn 3. Kulwicki got his car through that end of the track an instant faster, however, and roared off Turn 4 with a slight advantage. He held it to the line and was credited with the lead on Lap 210.

Elliott had led from Lap 167 to Lap 209, a stretch of 43 laps, bringing his total for the day to 85 laps—more laps led than anyone else in the field to that point.

Kulwicki had just led his third lap, and if the margins by which he led all three were added together it would not have equaled one car-length. Each time he'd been only a nose in front, and each time it had been Elliott with whom he had been dueling.

The duel was far from over.

Elliott was back in front by the time the cars reached Turn 1 on Lap 211, but Kulwicki made the low line work for him again and he was the leader off Turn 2. Once again, Elliott had enough momentum to lead at the end of the backstretch. Once again, Kulwicki fought back off Turn 4. This time, his lead at the start-finish line was less than half the length of Elliott's hood.

"Outside!" spotter Danny Cameron told Kulwicki every time Elliott was alongside him. "Still outside!"

Kulwicki remained ahead through Turn 1 on Lap 212, but Elliott pushed back in front off Turn 2. Irvan, who had cleared Spencer to move into third, was lined up behind Elliott in that end of the speed-way and had provided a slight push in the draft. But Irvan cut to the low side, going even lower than Kulwicki and threatening to make it a three-wide battle for the lead in turns 3 and 4.

Irvan backed off slightly, however, thinking better of it, and Kulwicki kept his momentum off the fourth turn. This time, the nose of Elliott's car was even with Kulwicki's right-front wheel when they crossed the line.

"Still there!" Cameron said.

As the cars roared toward Turn 1, the two men racing for the season's championship rubbed fenders like they were racing for a trophy and a $500 check on a Saturday night at a dirt track in Wisconsin or Georgia.

Elliott had his nose back out in front in Turn 1, but Irvan got behind Kulwicki this time and gave Kulwicki some drafting help. Finally, as the cars raced off Turn 4 to complete Lap 214, Kulwicki got far enough ahead of Elliott to pull in front of him.

"Clear!" Cameron was finally able to yell to his driver.

Given the circumstances, the crowd had just seen one of the most breathtaking sequences of racing in Winston Cup history. Although lead changes are only official at the start-finish line, Kulwicki and Elliott had swapped the top spot at least a dozen times between Lap 210 and Lap 214.

The hard racing seemed to take a toll on Elliott's Ford, which clearly wasn't handling as well on the new set of tires as it had been before the yellow for Earnhardt's spin. By Lap 216, Elliott had not only lost second to Irvan but had fallen behind Spencer into fourth as well.

Allison, meanwhile, was beginning to think his team's work was going to pay off. Soon after Elliott had dropped to fourth, he moved around Sterling Marlin to take seventh place. McReynolds had Brian VanDercook check the points chart to confirm that that would put Allison one point ahead of Kulwicki if things remained the same.

Unless.

There is absolutely no way to determine who the first person at Atlanta Motor Speedway was that day to think about how important the five-point bonus for leading the most laps in the race might become. Most likely, it occurred to different people at roughly the same time, as soon as Kulwicki began to pull away from Irvan, Spencer and Elliott to take charge of the lead.

All day on long green-flag runs, the car with the lead had been able to stay there. Kulwicki had led only two laps before taking command this time, but there were still plenty of laps left for him to catch and pass Elliott's total of 85.

On ESPN, Ned Jarrett mentioned the bonus for leading the most laps without knowing that Ken Martin and his team were already figuring that into the totals they were providing. Perhaps that mention jarred the memories of people monitoring the broadcast, spurring questions about how that issue stood. Perhaps someone from NASCAR scoring mentioned something over the radio and it was overheard along pit road.

It would be hard to imagine anybody thinking that far ahead during the five laps of riveting side-by-side racing between the two leaders and two of the top points contenders. But after Kulwicki got clear of Elliott and began to pull away, the race settled down.

And all over the property, the wheels began to turn.

Richard "Chip" Williams, NASCAR's media relations director, and Ty Norris from R.J. Reynolds were working in the press box when reporters started asking questions about which driver was going to lead the most laps.

"I don't know," said Williams, who never lets a chance to make a smart-aleck remark slip by. "The race isn't over yet."

Williams and Norris, in fact, had already been talking about how close the championship race still was with the laps winding down. Just as they began to consider the implications of the bonus for leading the most laps, Williams got called over NASCAR's radio frequency.

"Who is going to lead the most laps?" came the question.

This time, Williams resisted the smart-aleck answer.

"We were just looking at that," Williams said. "Let me check on it."

Not since Petty had topped Waltrip by 11 points to win the 1979 championship had things been this complicated on the final day of the season. In many years the championship had been clinched a race or two before the finale. Even when the title battle went down to the final day, there was only one challenger with an outside chance of catching the leader. The calculus was relatively simple in those cases.

Not today. This time, the calculations had to be exact and they couldn't wait until after the race. There were thousands in the stands who wanted to know how the championship race was shaking out. ESPN's viewers wanted correct information, too.

Most importantly, however, the teams involved in the championship battle had to know what was going on.

Imagine the consequences if the calculations were five points off, or one lap off. Late-race pit strategies still had to be planned. Decisions needed to be based on solid information, not educated guesses.

There is a great deal of teamwork involved in Winston Cup racing, but ultimately the pressure of a team's performance comes down on the driver and his crew chief. They get the glory when things go well. They take the blame when things do not.

Now, the pressure was spreading. The 1992 Winston Cup championship race was coming down toward its final moments, and the drivers weren't carrying calculators in the cars. The decisions that might make the difference between winning and losing would have to be made by somebody else and relayed to them.

Williams couldn't do the math and answer a question every 30 seconds. There was a small closet in the back of the press box, where supplies and equipment were deposited during race weekends. Williams walked in and pulled the door shut behind him, trying to get a minute's peace to make sure he knew where things stood and where they might go.

On the track, Kulwicki was clicking off laps and holding onto his lead. Elliott's car began to handle better after its tires got a little heat in them. He passed Spencer for third and then swept by Irvan to take second.

Potentially the most important pass in that portion of the race, however, was the easiest one Allison made all day. After Elliott had passed Spencer, Spencer brought his car—which was owned by Davey's father, Bobby —to pit road for an unscheduled pit stop.

A piece of paper, perhaps a wrapper off one of the thousands of hot dogs consumed by fans that afternoon, had blown out onto the race track and stuck to Spencer's front grille. The paper blocked enough of the area left open to allow air to get in and cool Spencer's engine that his car began to overheat. Not wanting to risk a good finish by blowing the engine, Spencer's team brought him to pit road to get the paper pulled away.

Spencer's unscheduled stop allowed Allison to move from seventh to sixth position. He'd come in needing a top-five finish to clinch the championship, but because he had led a lap and picked up the five points, he could now clinch with a sixth-place finish.

There was a palpable sense of relief in Allison's pit as Davey moved into the position he needed to walk away the winner.

"Remember the big picture," McReynolds urged one more time. "Hold what you've got right there and we'll be fine."

When Kulwicki crossed the line to lead Lap 242, he had led his 35th lap. One lap later, he took the yellow flag as the leader after Bobby Hillin's car lost an engine and dropped fluid into the racing groove. Pit road was about to become very busy once again, and as close as the championship race was every second would count.

Kulwicki paced the lead-lap cars down pit road with Elliott right behind him. Kulwicki's pit stall was just past the start-finish line, meaning he was credited with leading Lap 244. Elliott's crew was waiting for him a few more stalls down toward the Turn 1 end of pit lane.

As the crew finished its work on Kulwicki's car, they gave him a shove to help him get going without first gear. It took perhaps an extra tenth of a second for Elliott's crew to get the left-rear tire bolted on. Kulwicki was rolling as the team finished work on the right side of Elliott's car.

When Elliott's No. 11 Ford was dropped off the jack, he hit the gas and pulled out. Kulwicki was already alongside of him, however, and Kulwicki won the race to the line at the end of pit road by, once again, less than half the length of his car. That meant he would hold the lead at least until the green flag flew again.

The green came back out to begin Lap 250, leaving 79 laps until the checkered flag. Nobody would be able to make the rest of the way on fuel, meaning that there would be at least one more round of pit stops. If the race stayed green, those would almost certainly come in the form of gas-and-go stops sometime during the final 20 laps.

One more factor was added to the building drama. Who would pit when?

Allison came out in the same place he had been running when he came in—sixth. That meant he would win the championship if he didn't lose any ground. If he finished sixth and Kulwicki won the race and led the most laps, they would tie with 4,073 points. Allison would win the title because, like Elliott, he had more victories that Kulwicki.

The championship was still Allison's to win.

Or to lose.

Coming into Turn 4 on Lap 253, Irvan's Chevrolet drifted high. As Irvan came through the turn, the back end of his car suddenly shot sideways. He tried to jerk it back under control, brushing Terry Labonte's car running just inside of it.

Irvan's car shot back across the track, with Rusty Wallace sliding clear by an eyelash.

Allison was running right behind Wallace. There was barely enough room for Irvan's car to miss Wallace's rear end and yet get directly in front of Allison's, at a 90-degree angle to the line Allison was running.

Allison had only enough time to begin to turn his wheel sharply to the left, altering his Ford just enough so that the right front took the brunt of the impact with Irvan's car.

Allison's car shoved Irvan's nose first into the outside wall. Irvan's Chevy bounced off and skidded back across the frontstretch in front of Allison's Ford, which made a slow, counterclockwise loop with smoke boiling off the tires. The left rear smacked the inside wall just where the logo for Atlanta's spring race, the Motorcraft 500, was painted.

"Oh, no!" Parsons yelled. "Davey Allison is in the crash!"

Allison's car came to rest just short of the start-finish line, between Irvan's car and the inside wall. He tried to get it going again in the vain hope he could somehow cross the line before the leaders got back around, allowing him to stay on the lead lap. Allison backed up to drive around Irvan, but when he tried to go forward, the car would not steer.

Allison had broken the tie rod, a part in the suspension system that links the steering mechanism to the wheel. As he tried to move forward, the car went right back to where it had been before he backed it up.

"It won't turn!" he said over the radio.

His crew, looking on helplessly from just a few yards away along pit lane, could see that for themselves.

Allison tried to back it up once again, but he saw the car wasn't going anywhere. The leaders flashed by, with Kyle Petty getting his lap back by beating Kulwicki to the line.

Allison knew what had happened.

"Boys, we're done," he said.

VanDercook, mainly to settle his nerves, had been shuttling back and forth between the team's pit stall and the media center. He was on his way back up a set of stairs toward the pits when he heard word of the crash over his headset. He knew the cars had come to rest just in front of where he was emerging from the stairs leading up from the media center. He went and jumped up on the pit wall.

"I don't know why," he said. "But I thought for sure Davey was going to get out of the car and try to beat the stuffing out of Ernie, if for nothing other than frustration."

Allison did get out and head toward Irvan's car, but only to see if Irvan was okay. Before Allison got there, a safety worker grabbed him and steered him toward the back of an ambulance for a ride to the infield care center.

Allison gave one half wave to the crowd as he took off his gloves, then reached up and unstrapped his helmet. He took the helmet off, stuffed the gloves inside and paused at the back door of the ambulance to give the crowd another wave. Allison climbed in the ambulance and noticed that as Irvan approached he seemed a little wobbly. He stuck out his hand and helped Irvan steady himself as he climbed in to share the ride to the infield.

"There will be other years," Jenkins said on ESPN as Allison disappeared into the ambulance, speaking of the young star's championship hopes. "There's no question about that."

VanDercook found Davey's wife, Liz, and they headed for care center.

McReynolds, meanwhile, got on the radio to his crew.

"Listen guys, we're not going to win this championship," he said. "But we're going to go back in there in the garage and fix that car.

We're going to get back in this race and fight to get second or third or whatever we can get, but we are not going to quit."

Allison reached the infield care center and was examined. Physically, he was fine. He, Liz and VanDercook began to leave when Allison turned around and went back inside. He wanted to make sure that Irvan was okay, too.

"I don't know if it knocked me out or not," Irvan said of the impact of his car with Allison's. "I was conscious enough to walk in [the infield care center], but I don't remember doing it. The first thing I remember is Davey Allison coming in to find out if I was all right. I didn't even know who else was in the accident until Davey came in.

"I just don't remember much about it. I know we had a fast car most of the day, and I think I remember it being a little loose going into the fourth turn but that's it."

A phalanx of reporters was waiting at the exit of the care center. According to the unwritten pecking order of NASCAR media, television gets the first shot. John Kernan was there with the microphone when Allison walked out, holding Liz's hand.

This situation provides a perfect illustration of how immediate the media access is in NASCAR. Imagine a pitcher who had just given up a grand slam in the World Series stopping on his way to the showers to be asked about what happened, or a quarterback running off the field after throwing an interception in the Super Bowl being surrounded by reporters wanting instant reaction.

Allison could not have been more gracious.

"That's just the way it goes sometimes," he said. Behind them, the camera picked up Liz, leaning against VanDercook, wiping away tears. "We'd had some troubles and we were trying to work our way back up there. We were just trying to run a smart race.

"We ran over something in Turn 3 earlier in the race and then caught a lucky caution. I thought we'd be okay. Then I saw Ernie get loose over there in [Turn] 4 and we just ran out of room. I just hate it for all of those guys over there in the garage, all of the guys at Robert Yates Racing. They deserved better than this; they deserved to win this championship. But we just didn't get it. It just wasn't meant to be."

Allison thanked the fans for their letters of support during the trying year. He turned and talked to radio's Motor Racing Network then answered a few questions from the other reporters who'd reached the scene.

Irvan was not apologetic about his role in eliminating Allison from title contention.

"I hate what happened to Davey," Irvan said. "[But] as far as I am concerned, I had just as much right to be out there racing as anyone else. I could have been the points leader if some things hadn't happened through the year. That's the way it goes. What goes around comes around. We were out there racing our race. If you get tangled up, then you get tangled up."

Allison's Ford had been hooked to a wrecker with a belt looped around the engine block, lifting the front end of the car off the track. The wrecker came around on the frontstretch and headed back down toward Turn 4, going the wrong way, to reach the end of pit road and the garage entrance. The crew was waiting when the wrecker got there.

After leaving the care center and dealing with the media, Allison went to the trailer he'd been using as a base of operations all weekend to wait for the car to be repaired.

As he and VanDercook walked in, Allison plopped back on a bed and sighed.

After everything he had endured all season, didn't he deserve just one break?

"Brian, why me?" Allison said. "I can't believe it. Why me?"

End Game

Davey Allison's wreck simplified matters for Alan Kulwicki and Bill Elliott.

One of them was going to be the 1992 Winston Cup champion. One also was most likely going to win the season's final race, but it was rapidly becoming apparent that the race winner and the champion might not necessarily be the same driver.

Neither Kulwicki nor Elliott pitted on the caution after Allison's crash. Terry Labonte, who had nearly collided with Irvan before Irvan went back across the track and hit Allison, did come in to make sure his car was okay. That meant Labonte had a few more laps of fuel that the leaders—but still not enough to go the rest of the way.

Just before Allison's wreck, ESPN pit reporter Jerry Punch and a NASCAR official approached Cal Lawson in Kulwicki's pit to check their figures about how many laps Elliott and Kulwicki had led.

By the time the cleanup from Allison's wreck was done, the leaders had completed 258 laps. Kulwicki had led every lap since 210, giving him 49 in that stretch and a total of 51 for the race. Elliott's total stood at 85.

There were 70 laps remaining. If Kulwicki could lead the next 52 laps, he would have led 103 laps with only 18 laps left in the race. If Elliott led the final 18, he would wind up with 103 laps led also.

In the event two drivers tie for the most laps led in a race, each driver gets the five-point bonus. Such a tie has happened less than a handful of times in the current points system's history, but the way things were going anything seemed possible.

If they tied with 103 laps led and Elliott won the race with Kulwicki second, Kulwicki would beat Elliott for the championship by five points.

If that seems a little difficult to follow, imagine trying to figure all of that out on the fly with the Winston Cup championship hanging in the balance.

Then add in the other factor in the equation. Fuel mileage.

Kulwicki's last pit stop had come as he concluded Lap 244 and began Lap 245. To clinch the bonus for leading the most laps, he needed to lead Lap 310 and pit on Lap 311. That's 67 laps.

Earnhardt had run out of fuel in 55 laps on the day's first run, but he had been running a much higher line in a Chevrolet. Kulwicki was sticking mainly to the low groove, a shorter distance than Earnhardt covered in the high line. Kulwicki was also driving a Ford.

What Paul Andrews and Cal Lawson had to do was figure Kulwicki's fuel mileage and determine whether the No. 7 "Underbird" had enough to lead the race through Lap 310. If Kulwicki could make it that far, he could finish second in the race and still win the championship.

Lawson and Andrews weren't being pessimistic about losing the race to Elliott. They were simply facing reality. Because of the problem in their car's transmission, they knew it would take Kulwicki longer to come in, get enough fuel to go the distance and then get back up to speed. Two seconds longer than it would take Elliott, maybe three. Translated onto the track, that time lost on pit road would be more than enough for Elliott to take over the race lead.

There is no computer on board a Winston Cup car telling the crew how many miles per gallon the car is getting or how much fuel is left in the tank. There isn't even a fuel gauge; at least not one with a scale from F to E. There is only a fuel pressure gauge, which shows the driver at a glance one possible reason that his car might be slowing if he doesn't know why.

Mileage is figured based on the weight of the fuel. A fuel can holds 11 gallons. It is weighed empty and weighed again when full. A gallon is measured out and the can is weighed again to double-check the weight of a single gallon.

When a driver makes a pit stop, two full cans are used to fill the fuel cell, which holds a NASCAR-mandated maximum of 22 gallons. A catch can is placed into an overflow valve to collect any amount that washes out as the load is poured in.

Once a pit stop is over, the gas in the catch can is poured back into the fuel can, which is then weighed. That weight is subtracted from the weight of a full can to determine how many gallons of fuel were actually poured into the car.

By dividing that amount into the number of miles traveled since the previous stop, miles per gallon can be computed.

Approximately, that is.

Lawson and chief mechanic Danny Glad checked the figures. According to their calculations, Kulwicki's car would run out of gas on Lap 310. Under any other circumstance, they would have called for a stop by Lap 307 to ensure a two-lap cushion, and would still be holding their breath hoping they weren't pushing things too far.

But Lap 307 wouldn't be enough. Kulwicki would have led only 100 laps, and would be leaving Elliott up to 21 more to lead to the end of the race. That would give Elliott 106 laps led and the now-pivotal five-point bonus. He and Kulwicki would tie for the points lead, giving the title to Elliott on the tiebreaker of more wins that season.

As Lawson and Glad did their calculations, Andrews waited to hear the result.

"When you figure it out," Andrews said to Lawson, "don't tell him. Everybody's listening."

Andrews was right, of course. With Allison gone, Kulwicki's crew was watching every move Elliott's team made, and Elliott's team was watching Kulwicki's. Both teams were tuned into each other's radio frequencies as well.

There was nothing for Lawson to tell Kulwicki anyway. He couldn't advise his driver to slow down and try to conserve fuel to increase his chances of making it to Lap 310, because Elliott was just a few seconds behind. The whole point of staying out was to lead laps and it would do no good to conserve fuel if Elliott passed Kulwicki.

Elliott's team didn't need to be told what was going on anyway. Crew chief Tim Brewer knew exactly what was happening. "You need to try to get up there and lead as many laps as you can," Brewer told Elliott.

"I'm trying," Elliott said.

He certainly was. After the green flew on Lap 259, Kulwicki found himself fighting to clear the lapped car of Morgan Shepherd, who was three laps down but for some reason seemed determined to get one of those back.

Shepherd held the inside line for three laps, with Kulwicki struggling to get past him. Once, entering Turn 1, their cars nearly bumped. Kulwicki could have let Shepherd go, but he knew his car would be faster if he could just clear Shepherd and run in line in front of the lapped car, giving Kulwicki's car a little push in the draft.

Eventually, Kulwicki pulled ahead. Elliott ran alongside Shepherd for a lap or so, too, before finally lining up behind Kulwicki to challenge him for the top spot. But Elliott just didn't have enough to get around the No. 7 Ford.

In the ESPN booth, Ken Martin was working feverishly on the same calculations as Kulwicki's crew. He needed to make sure the announcers understood the situation clearly so they could in turn relay it to the viewers.

Kulwicki's lead stabilized at about 15 car lengths. Geoffrey Bodine was third, with Rusty Wallace fourth. Jimmy Spencer, Ricky Rudd and Kyle Petty were racing for fifth. Rudd, driving for Hendrick Motorsports, was beginning to feel ill and had inquired about getting a relief driver. The team wanted to put Jeff Gordon in the car, but NASCAR wouldn't allow that because Gordon was a rookie.

Allison's car, minus its front quarterpanels, came back on the track as the leaders completed the 294th lap. He had lost nearly 40 laps, but his team was determined that it was going to be running when this season ended. The No. 28 Ford looked more like a car that should be racing in NASCAR's modified division than a stock car, and Allison wasn't running nearly as fast as he had been before the crash. But he was running.

Rudd's car slowed dramatically on the backstretch on the 300th lap. His engine had given way, costing him a top-10 finish. But Rudd's car had not dropped any fluid on the track, so there was no yellow.

Bodine elected to give up fifth place to short-pit, coming in early to get enough fuel to go the distance and take on left-side tires in hopes he could make up ground on the others who would pit later and not change tires. If a caution came out, Bodine would also have the option of staying out and inheriting the lead as the other lead-lap cars made stops.

Meanwhile, back in the garage, Richard Petty was getting ready to go back to work. He was strapping himself back into the No. 43 Pontiac, or at least what was left of it after the crew had done its work following the fiery early-race crash. Petty planned to drive up the ramp from the garage area to pit road and to wait until two laps remained in the race. Petty would then pull out and be on the track for his final checkered flag.

There had been no communication about pit strategy over the Kulwicki team's radios; just the routine of calling out lap times and intervals as Kulwicki passed the start-finish line. As the driver worked lapped traffic, spotter Danny Cameron made sure his driver knew when he was clear. This was no time for a mistake.

Lawson's stomach was churning.

He knew that the team's only chance to win the championship was to keep Kulwicki on the track and in the lead until after Lap 310. What he didn't know was whether the car would still have enough fuel to still be running by then.

"When are we going to pit?"

Lawson's thinking was interrupted by Kulwicki's voice over the radio.

"When are we going to pit?" Kulwicki asked again.

"Alan," Lawson said. "We've got that figured out. We will let you know in a minute."

Lawson could almost hear Kulwicki's mind racing to figure out the hidden meaning behind his response. After another lap, maybe two, Kulwicki had the answer.

"Does this mean I am going to have to lead the most laps?" Kulwicki asked.

"Yes," Lawson said. "Yes, Alan, you're going to lead the most laps if you do what I tell you."

Kulwicki waited another lap.

"When are we going to pit?" he asked again.

Lawson knew that Kulwicki realized it was going to be close. The driver knew how long it had been since the previous pit stop.

As Kulwicki came around to complete Lap 307, Lawson pressed the button on the ear of his headset.

"We're going to pit you in three more laps," Lawson said.

Elliott's team wasn't as worried about staying out longer than Kulwicki. Brewer and Junior Johnson had every reason to be confident their car was getting better gas mileage than Kulwicki's, or anybody else's for that matter. In March of that year, they had stolen a victory at Atlanta by stretching fuel and staying out longer than the other contenders had.

The laps counted off. For a few moments, ESPN's announcers couldn't figure out why Kulwicki would risk staying out beyond Lap 307, the lap they had been told he needed to come in.

"Why would he risk it if he has to stop anyway?" Ned Jarrett wondered.

Ken Martin knew why. He had figured out that Kulwicki needed to lead until Lap 310 to clinch the bonus, but he had to make absolutely sure he was right before he gave the information to the announcers.

He checked with scoring one more time. He looked at the numbers one more time. Finally, just as Kulwicki was about to stop, he wrote a note and handed it to Jenkins.

Jenkins looked at the note quickly, then handed it to Parsons and then to Jarrett.

"Are you sure?" Jenkins mouthed to Martin.

Martin nodded, knowing the consequences if he was wrong.

"I had worked more than 300 races," Martin would later say. "I knew the ramifications. I knew that if I was wrong, Bob Jenkins was going to kill me."

Jimmy Spencer pitted on Lap 308. Rusty Wallace came in the next time around and stalled his car leaving pit road. He, too, had lost first gear. Kulwicki would have to be careful to not have the same thing happen to him when he finally came in.

Kulwicki came around after having led Lap 309.

"Pit now?" he asked.

"No!" Lawson said. "Go around one more time. One more time! Do you understand?"

Radio transmissions can break up. Lawson wanted to make sure Kulwicki heard him clearly. Only the entire season hung in the balance.

Kulwicki drove by the entrance to pit road. Elliott had closed the distance between him and the leader to about three car-lengths, but when Kulwicki crossed the line to lead Lap 310, he had led his 103rd lap. Elliott could lead the final 18 and reach the same number, but Kulwicki would still win the championship by finishing second.

If, of course, Kulwicki had enough gas to get back around the track.

On the backstretch, Kulwicki moved to the low side of the track. He used a hand-signal, an up-and-down wave, to show Elliott that he was planning to slow down and head to pit road. There are no brake lights on a Winston Cup car.

Kulwicki rolled down off the banking in Turn 4 and started down pit road. His crew waited impatiently.

"Okay, Alan," Andrews said, "nice and easy. Don't let it stall on you. Here we are, right here!"

Kulwicki had gone 67 laps around a 1.522-mile track—nearly 102 miles—on the previous load of fuel. With 22 gallons on board, that worked out to just over 4.6 miles per gallon. With 18 laps left, about 27 miles, the crew figured it needed to give Kulwicki six gallons to go the distance.

From experience, they knew it took about six seconds to empty an 11-gallon can into the fuel cell. Kulwicki slid to a stop and the can went in. One second. Two seconds. The crew began to start pushing him off, but the gas can still stayed in the valve. Three seconds. Kulwicki slammed the car into second gear and peeled away.

Everyone glanced at stopwatches. The fuel can had been in the car for 3.4 seconds. If six seconds equals 11 gallons, then 3.4 seconds equals just more than six gallons. A few drops had spilled out of the overflow valve, but there obviously had been some left in the tank, too.

Would it be enough?

Elliott was still on the race track. Kulwicki came out just ahead of him after his stop, meaning he was almost a full lap down. At that moment, Elliott was first and Terry Labonte, who had topped off his fuel tank on the caution after Allison's crash, was second. Kulwicki was the only other car still in the lead lap. Bodine, who had short-pitted, was just behind Elliott, one lap down in fourth place.

Elliott led until he crossed the scoring line on pit road to complete Lap 314. This time, unlike the late pit stop at Dover that cost the team that victory and seemed to turn the season's momentum, Elliott made sure there would be no debate about strategy.

"We ain't changing nothing," Elliott said to Brewer over the radio. "We're going to put gas in it and we're going to go."

Like Kulwicki, Elliott was in his pit stall for 3.4 seconds. He got back on the track about half a straightaway ahead of Kulwicki.

Labonte stayed out when Elliott came in and was scored as the leader on Lap 315, then came in for his final stop. Nobody had really factored Labonte into the picture when working out the five-point bonus, but by leading one of the laps Elliott needed to tie Kulwicki with 103 laps led, Labonte made it a 10-point cushion for Kulwicki.

Kulwicki could now actually win the championship even if Bodine somehow managed to catch up and take away second. All Kulwicki really had to do was finish without incident. But there was no guarantee that was possible.

After putting the 3.4 seconds worth of fuel into the car on the final pit stop, Kulwicki's crew could have weighed the fuel can to get a better picture of how much fuel they'd managed to get into the car. Instead, the can was placed back on the rack behind pit wall.

"We felt like we had enough," Lawson said later. Besides, nothing could be done about it now.

Just to be safe, though, Andrews radioed Kulwicki and told him not to burn up fuel in an unnecessary effort to chase down Elliott to win the race.

Kulwicki said nothing. A couple of laps later, however, Kulwicki came back across the radio.

"What are you saying, Paul?" Kulwicki asked. "Does this mean we don't have enough gas?"

Andrews said only that it was going to be close, and the only prudent course of action was to conserve whenever possible.

Winning the race was no longer important.

"Just hold what you've got and we'll win this thing," Lawson finally told Kulwicki.

As the laps counted down, Ken Martin glanced up at the monitor in the ESPN booth and saw for one last time the "Points as of Now" graphic he had been working on all day. Instantly, his heart jumped. The graphic showed Kulwicki with 4,083 points and a 15-point edge on Elliott. It was wrong. Kulwicki was going to finish with 4,078 and a 10-point margin over Elliott's final total of 4,068.

Kyle Petty's car had been riding around on the apron with smoke boiling from its pipes for several laps. Petty had kept the car out of the racing groove, but was trying to salvage a decent finish. With five laps to go, however, NASCAR gave him a black flag, ordering him to pit road. He would finish 16th, eight laps down. Harry Gant would finish 13th and edge Petty by 10 points for fourth in the final standings.

As Elliott came across to complete Lap 326, a great roar went up from the crowd as Richard Petty's car started rolling down pit road. From the front windshield forward, all that remained of it were the wheels, frame rails and engine. All of the sheet metal had been cut away, but The King would be on the track when his final race ended.

As Petty rode slowly off Turn 2, Elliott took the white flag indicating one lap to go. Kulwicki came by about eight seconds later. He'd allowed Elliott to pull away knowing that he was winning the championship right where he was.

Allison completed 285 laps to finish 27th—two spots ahead of Irvan and one behind Earnhardt. He wound up with 4,015 points, finishing third, 50 points ahead of Gant.

Elliott came through Turn 3 one last time, squinting against the setting sun. As he came off the fourth turn, he moved to the outside to get around Petty's car. Elliott passed Petty just before they crossed the finish line, meaning their cars were the first two to see the checkered flag.

Kulwicki was 8.06 seconds behind Elliott. But the championship was his.

Three hours, 44 minutes and 20 seconds after Rick Mast and Brett Bodine had led the field to the green flag, the Hooters 500 was over.

But the party was just beginning.

Party Time

Did we win?"

Alan Kulwicki had been virtually silent since the late-race exchange with Paul Andrews and Cal Lawson about conserving fuel. The driver had the information he needed and his focus had shifted to the task—completing the final laps as efficiently as possible, nursing every drop of fuel to make sure his championship dreams didn't die a cruel death just a few miles short.

As he crossed under the final checkered flag of the 1992 Winston Cup season, Kulwicki now had one more question.

He already knew the answer but he wanted it confirmed one more time.

"Did we win?" he asked.

"Yeah, we won it," Andrews said from pit road, where Kulwicki's team had erupted in celebration.

Kulwicki knew exactly what to do. He had kept his promise that he wouldn't repeat the reverse victory lap—the "Polish Victory Lap," as it had been dubbed after its debut at Phoenix—until he won a championship. Now that moment had arrived and Kulwicki was ready for a reprise.

He spun his car around on the frontstretch and headed back toward the fourth turn, driving in a clockwise direction opposite the traditional path taken on an oval track. This put the driver's side window on the grandstand side, allowing the sport's new champion to see those standing to cheer him and the historic race they had just witnessed.

As Kulwicki's celebration began, two others were simultaneously starting as well. By getting Richard Petty's car back on the track in time for the final two laps, The King's team had assured that a postrace send-off would take place as planned. There was also the matter of Bill Elliott, who had earned his fifth win of the season, and what now seemed like a hollow trip to victory lane.

ESPN couldn't show three celebrations at once. So, as usually is the case in such matters, television dictated the flow of the postrace activities.

First came Kulwicki.

Cameras followed his backward lap. He then rolled all the way down the frontstretch again before turning on to the pit road in the Turn 4 end of the track. Pit lane was awash with people—crew members, NASCAR officials, photographers, reporters and fans—all wanting to be part of what was happening.

Kulwicki finally pulled his car to a stop.

ESPN's cameraman adjusted his lens to compensate for the shadows being cast by the grandstands and gave viewers their first view of Kulwicki as champion. Public relations operatives shoved baseball caps into the window, each hoping Kulwicki would put theirs on as he climbed from the car.

It was bedlam. But one person was in command of himself through it all.

Kulwicki pulled off his helmet and glanced at the camera once, then again, fighting a grin. He fumbled with the adjustable strap on one of the caps, preparing to put it on.

Kulwicki reached down on the inside the door and came up with a black plastic pocket comb. He'd retrieved it from a "glove box" built into each one of his cars, a place that held a comb, a stick of lip balm and a handkerchief whenever he raced.

Before putting on Winston Cup champion cap, Kulwicki cut his glance to his rear-view mirror and ran the comb through his black hair. He was the champion and wanted to look like one.

"C'mon, Alan!" Benny Parsons said as he saw Kulwicki's grooming regimen.

Finally, Kulwicki put on the cap and ducked his head through the open driver's side. He stood on the window opening and climbed to the top of his Ford "Underbird," thrusting his index finger upward in a No. 1 signal to salute the crowd.

He was the first owner/driver to win a Winston Cup title since 1979 —the last of Petty's seven championships. He was the first Winston Cup champion with a college degree.

In his seventh Winston Cup season, Kulwicki climbed down off the No. 7 car and spoke to ESPN's Jerry Punch.

"I'll tell you, man, this is like living a dream here," Kulwicki began. "The car ran great. Our engine was fantastic all day and the car handled real well. The Goodyear tires, this is the fastest we've ever run at this track and the longest the tires have ever lasted."

Kulwicki then ticked off a list of his sponsors and kept right on talking.

"We ran great. I led the most laps, I knew how far I had to go in the race to lead the most laps and at that point there was no way that he could beat me," he said. "I was a little bit safe coming down pit road. We lost first gear in the transmission on the first pit stop so I had trouble getting out of the pits all day long. I think that's probably where he [Elliott] made up a little bit of time on me was getting in and out of the pits because we were having transmission trouble.

"At that point, I knew where we were. I wanted to win the race, because we had led quite a while, but there will be other races. This championship is what I wanted.

"Thank God for the fortune to be here and be in America and compete on the Winston Cup circuit. Man, when I moved down South years ago this was my dream. I came with a pickup truck and a trailer and I want to thank all of the people that along the way in ASA and everywhere in my career have helped me. You know I said that . . . We nicknamed this car the Underbird today, we were going into this race the underdog and we ran good. I am really proud of the whole team."

Kulwicki then called off the names of his team members, apologizing for any he left out in the excitement of the moment.

"It was a team effort," he said. "We've got a great team and I am really proud of them, I couldn't have done it without them."

Kulwicki then realized that Punch had barely asked him one question.

"This is a long answer to one question," Kulwicki said. "Just cut me off whenever."

Punch did, but only to offer congratulations to the champion, who had just become the 21st man to earn stock-car racing's top prize.

"Thank you," Kulwicki said. "This is just a storybook ending having Hooters sponsor the race. My dad's here. It's just really wonderful."

Next came Petty's valedictory moment.

During the Kulwicki interview, Petty was still sitting in the driver's seat of his Pontiac, shaking hands with well wishers as he waited for a signal to refire the engine on his battered machine to take one last lap around a race track.

At the signal, Petty flipped the ignition and headed off pit road. The song written for the weekend by the country music group Alabama wailed over the track's public address system as Petty drove slowly around the track. He came off Turn 4 and rode down pit road, slapping hands with dozens of crew members and others lined up to greet him there. As he passed by the flag stand, the checkered flag waved one last time.

Punch, fighting to keep his own emotions in check, was there when Petty stopped.

"It has been wonderful," Petty said. "Thirty-five years and the good Lord has looked after us all of these years and I am still walking around. I hated I got into a wreck and disappointed me and some of the fans, but the big deal is we're here talking to you when it's over with. I wouldn't change none of it. I wouldn't trade nothing for nothing else."

That left only Elliott's victory to be documented for the television audience.

"We lost but we won," Elliott said. "I gave it everything I had. Regardless of what happened, it's been a long season. I'm just glad it's over with. This team has done a fantastic job all year long. To go out winning the race—that last race Richard Petty will ever run in—I guess that says something. But we didn't win the championship."

At least Elliott and his team had something to celebrate. Allison's team had lost the points lead on the season's final day and now faced a long winter to think about what they might have done differently.

"I was jealous and I was mad watching Kulwicki and Elliott battle and watching us ride around with no front end," Larry McReynolds said. "That made a statement about the whole season."

But Allison wasn't about to let his crew chief and his race team kick itself for long.

"Guys, we gave it everything we had," Allison told the team. "We had a good season, we won five races, and they'd better look out next year."

McReynolds, once again, was impressed with his young driver.

"He was my inspiration," McReynolds said later. "I am the worst loser God ever put on this Earth, but Davey always looked at things from a positive standpoint and had that way of picking you back up.

"He had a little saying, and it's on a little bookmark in my desk, he used it privately and publicly. 'There's nothing that can come my way today that God and I can't handle together.' He lived by that—he had to, with all that he had to go through, and it taught me to live by that motto."

As the postrace interviews began, Petty made it clear that his career was, absolutely and once and for all, over.

"Lynda's going to bury my helmet," Petty said. "She said she was going to bury it so I could never race again. I won't ever step into the car again for a race, but I never said I wouldn't test the thing."

Earlier in the weekend, ESPN had announced a series of races for retired driving legends that amounted to a combination of the International Race of Champions series, where drivers from different forms of auto racing compete in equally prepared cars, and professional golf's senior tour. The series, called the "Fast Masters," would begin in 1993 and would feature Bobby Allison's return to competition, a prospect that excited Davey immensely.

Petty wanted no part of it.

"They're getting all these legends races started and they wanted to know if I was going to come back and run these old-timer races," Petty said. "I said, 'If I'm going to run, I'm going to run with the big boys.' That means I am not going to run anymore."

And so, after 35 years, one of the greatest individual careers in the history of American professional sports was over.

"It has been a heck of a week and a heck of a year and a heck of a 35 years," Petty said. "God doesn't put many people on Earth and let them do and accomplish and go and play their own game as much as I have.

"We want to thank you all [the media] and thank all the fans. It's beyond words. I can't really describe my feelings on that. It has just been a wonderful life for Richard Petty if he just falls over right here.

"To pull out on the race track and see everybody jumping and hollering making that final lap when the race was over was something special. The funny thing about it was that after the race nobody went anywhere. They had the winner of the race, a champion and somebody leaving the sport. People just hung around. It was great. You'd like to see all of the races have this much enthusiasm."

Petty said he didn't know how he felt about the fact that his career was over.

He had talked to Banjo Matthews, a veteran car builder and former driver, the previous day. Matthews had told Petty it would take a few weeks for reality to set in.

"He said I'd wake up one morning in a couple of weeks and say, 'What have I done?'" Petty said.

But Petty knew what he was doing.

"My daughters, my wife, [crew chief] Robbie [Loomis] and all of the boys in the crew have been uptight all week," Petty said. "They were uptight before the race started and I think they were sort of halfway glad that we crashed the car and I could walk away from it. Otherwise, I would have had to run another 300 laps and they would have had to stand there and hold their breath. It's a relief for them probably more than it is me."

ESPN's broadcast of the Hooters 500 was to be followed by a special tribute to Petty. While the body of the special had been taped earlier, Dave Despain was at the track to introduce it live. As the day's story had unfolded, Despain had been furiously writing and rewriting the words he would use.

"What a race weekend," Despain began as video footage shot that weekend rolled. "Like so many others, and yet, like no other. The familiar crowds, everyone seeking an autograph. An endless chain of ceremonies . . . and finally, the big race itself, starring The King, Richard Petty."

The show included interviews with Petty's family and his competitors, but its best moments came when Petty talked about the motivation that had fueled the brilliant career ending that day.

"I never started out to set records, never thought about setting records," he said. "I just went out and did what I wanted to do and was real fortunate to be able to do what I did. In the meantime, the records came along. If I set a goal and got to it I didn't set it high enough. If I set one and never did get it I was always going to be disappointed. I always looked at the situation and said, let's just do better today than we did yesterday."

Elliott had won the race, the 39th victory of his Winston Cup career and his fifth career win at Atlanta Motor Speedway. It had been a good track for him, but also one at which he had suffered a personal tragedy in 1990 when Mike Rich, a member of his crew, died in a pit road incident that led to the use of speed limits on pit lane.

"I want to congratulate Alan Kulwicki," Elliott said. "He did what he had to do and came out on top. Tim [Brewer] had tried to tell me on the radio to lead every lap I could and man, I was doing everything I could. . . . I knew that if Kulwicki finished one place behind me I wasn't going to beat him. I knew.

"With the points spread we had, if I could have led all the laps then maybe, but we didn't. We won the race and that's that."

Although Elliott had been driving a car owned by Harry Melling for most of his career before joining the Junior Johnson team, Elliott was in a particularly good position to appreciate what Kulwicki had accomplished. Under Melling's ownership, Elliott's team had remained a largely family-run operation. Especially early in Bill's career, Bill and his brothers Dan and Ernie were calling all the competitive shots for their race team.

"I envy him because of what he can do," Elliott said of Kulwicki. "All this year he could do things and he didn't really have to deal with things. If you've been around racing you can understand what I am saying.

"He could come in and work on his car and he could be the type of person that if he didn't want to do something, he didn't. I would love to be able to do what I did in 1985, '86, and '87—just work on the race car, do my thing and forget about the other stuff."

After Elliott's championship season in 1988, he had won only five races over the next three seasons and finished no better than fourth in points before coming to Johnson's team in '92.

"There comes a point where you've got to be able to do it all," said Elliott, alluding to the sponsor commitments and all the off-track activities that tugged at a driver's time. "That will determine where he goes from this point on. I'm not taking anything away from him, but this comes to the point where there's a lot of things that can pull you away from what you love to do. Driving a race car and working on it is what he loves to do. It's the same for me, but there were just several things that kept pulling me away from it."

The echoes of the post-race cheers for Kulwicki's championship had barely begun to fade when the unlikely champion faced the questions about how the challenge of serving as champion might make it harder for him to keep running his own ship in the manner of which Elliott seemed so envious.

"I realize it happens," Kulwicki said of the potential distractions. "A certain amount of that goes with the territory. You can't be all things to all people. I'm going to do my best to accommodate as many people as possible and try not to let it get in the way of running the race team."

As the celebrations and interviews progressed, there were a couple of moments when the key players in that day's drama crossed paths.

Petty and Kulwicki got within earshot of each other once, not long after the race had ended.

"Congratulations," Petty said. "You've got six more to go to catch me."

Kulwicki chuckled at the thought of trying to win seven championships the way Petty had in his career that had just ended.

"I ain't going to catch you, Richard," Kulwicki said.

After the interview on pit road, Kulwicki and his team worked their way through a crush of media and well-wishers toward victory lane, where Elliott's celebration and the tedious task of taking a series of photographs with the winner wearing every different sponsor's baseball cap were just wrapping up.

"I will never forget it," Tom Roberts said of the moment when the two men who'd just waged the greatest championship finish in the sport's history met. "It was heartfelt and not with any animosity intended, but Bill shook Alan's hand and said, in that voice of his, 'Con-grad-u-lay-shuns, ass-hole.' I got a kick out of that."

Elliott insists he never said anything of the sort, but Roberts maintains that he heard the remark. Like so many great stories in NASCAR lore, the definition of "truth" depends on the memories of those telling the tale.

It is impossible to overstate how atypical Kulwicki was as Winston Cup champion. Kulwicki became the third non-Southerner to win the title, joining 1989 champion Rusty Wallace, who was from Missouri, and Bill Rexford, a New Yorker who won the title in 1950, the second year of NASCAR's competitive history. Kulwicki certainly was the first champion to say he could sure use a massage and a bratwurst after his title-clinching race.

"We were talking earlier," Kulwicki said. "We were joking, 'Kulwicki can't win it. He doesn't have an airplane or a motor home or anything. Whoever heard of a good ol' boy named Kulwicki?' Well, now maybe they have."

As the interviews continued, workers were making final preparations for a party Ford was hosting that night at the Airport Hilton.

Ford had finished first, second and third in the points standings with Mark Martin sixth behind Harry Gant and Kyle Petty. It had also won the manufacturer's title for the first time since 1969, breaking a 16-year run by General Motors.

"GM had won it largely because we didn't really have any contenders for six or seven years," said Michael Kranefuss, who as director of Ford's Special Vehicle Operations program was the point man for Ford racing at the track. "GM started to make a big point out of it and it got carried over into the papers in Detroit. The Chevy guys were making a big splash about it and that irked the Ford people and it became much more important."

With the manufacturer's championship already sewed up before the final race and the prospects good that a Ford driver would win the points title, a planeload of Ford executives flew in for the Hooters 500 and for the big party scheduled afterward.

Each of the four Ford teams with a shot at winning the championship had brought along one of its "show cars." A show car is a glorified replica of the team's race car, painted and decaled in the same scheme the team uses on the track, that is hauled around to grocery stores and car dealerships to draw potential customers. Many show cars are one- or two-year-old cars that had actually been raced and then retired, while others were built specifically for display purposes.

The show cars from the Kulwicki, Elliott, Allison and Martin teams were staged in an area near the ballroom of the Hilton, with the champion's car to be pushed in once the results were in to serve as the centerpiece of the celebration.

Allison's car owner, Robert Yates, had arranged for all of the members of his team to stay the night in Atlanta on Sunday to attend the party. With Allison leading the points coming in, it's safe to assume they weren't planning to be there to salute Kulwicki as champion.

Yates and his team still made an appearance at the celebration, but Junior Johnson did not. He had an appointment he had no intentions of missing.

Johnson had met his first wife, Flossie, when he was 13. They set up house together in Wilkes County and eventually got married in Las Vegas in 1975. In 1991, however, Johnson started divorce proceedings. He had fallen for Lisa Day, a much younger woman who'd grown up nearby the Johnsons' home and whom Junior had known most all of her life. What had begun as a friendship had grown into more.

Johnson understood that his split with Flossie would cause much gossip in the NASCAR community and much enmity within his family. He also knew the divorce would carry a heavy financial cost. But he also knew what he wanted.

After the required year of separation, the divorce became final on Oct. 27, 1992, two days after the race at Rockingham. Flossie got the house and one of the shops adjoining it. Johnson got the chance to marry Day. Their wedding was scheduled for Tuesday, Nov. 17.

The Sunday night Ford party produced some legendary moments.

Carolyn Yates, Robert's wife, came wearing a black fur coat. At one point during the evening, Kranefuss had it on—much to the delight of all in attendance.

"It was a great party, a great party," Kranefuss said. "That night, I had a good time."

Kulwicki arrived late after finishing up at the track. Wayne Estes, the Ford PR man, and Kulwicki had entertained each other all season with their own imitations of Kranefuss's thick German accent. Estes convinced Kulwicki to perform the imitation for the crowd, which roared with laughter.

When Estes left the ballroom to find a bathroom, he felt the carpet near the doorway squish under his feet. There had been that much beer and champagne spilled in celebration as people had walked in.

Kranefuss' wife, Immy, went up to her room long before her husband. She had an early flight back to their home in Michigan the following morning. She gave Estes a key and told him to make sure Michael got there when the party was over. Many hours later, Estes helped Kranefuss to the door, propped him against it, inserted the key and basically allowed Kranefuss to fall inside.

Cal Lawson, Kulwicki's close friend and the team's manager, remembers only part of that party, too, but not because he celebrated himself into a state of oblivion. He was almost in a state of shock from the day's incredible events.

"What if we had been wrong?" Lawson remembers thinking to himself. "What if we had figured it wrong and Alan hadn't led the most laps or didn't have enough points? What if we had been wrong?"

Kulwicki stayed at the party into the early morning hours, too, but remained in control of himself in the process.

"Alan stayed a long time, but he didn't get wild," Estes said. "He was already aware he wanted to be a good champion and I don't think he wanted to see pictures of himself later. He was very aware of the image."

While Kulwicki might have left with his dignity intact, he didn't leave the party that night with everything he arrived with.

As the weather turned colder toward the end of the 1992 season, Kulwicki had begun wearing a specially made leather jacket. It was in the style of a military pilot's "bomber" jacket with Hooters Racing insignia over the left breast. On the sleeves, the insignias read "Top Wing" instead of "Top Gun," a play on words with the restaurant chain's signature food offering.

Immy Kranefuss had seen Kulwicki in the jacket and she liked it. She and Kulwicki had struck up an unusual friendship along the way, with Kulwicki sometimes turning to her for advice about what gifts he should buy the particular lady friend that had caught his fancy at various times.

Playfully, Mrs. Kranefuss began asking Kulwicki to give her the jacket. Kulwicki was in no way inclined to do that, since it was a one-of-a-kind item that he clearly enjoyed wearing. Mrs. Kranefuss persisted in her request, however, and one day Kulwicki had finally heard it enough.

"I will give you this jacket," he said, "if I win the championship."

Kulwicki had no doubt dismissed the promise from his mind as soon as he had made it. Immy Kranefuss, however, had not.

Before she went to her room that Sunday night, she walked up to Kulwicki and put her hand on the jacket.

"Alan," she said. "Give me my jacket."

Kulwicki's eyes popped open. He remembered the promise, but never thought he would have to make good on it. But now, he took off the jacket.

A deal was a deal.

New York, New York

When Darrell Waltrip won the 1981 title with Junior Johnson's team, he became the first Winston Cup champion to be honored by NASCAR and R.J. Reynolds Tobacco Company at a banquet in New York City.

In its desire to bring stock-car racing into the mainstream of American sports, NASCAR and RJR believed that by taking its champion to the nation's largest media market it could get the kind of attention it had never been able to win before. There was also, they believed, a cachet in getting everyone all dressed up for a ceremony at New York's famous Waldorf-Astoria Hotel.

In the first few years in New York, the banquet was held in the Starlight Roof, a meeting room on the 18th floor of the Waldorf that holds about 250 people. Soon, however, the soirée outgrew that hall and moved to the hotel's Grand Ballroom, which can hold more than 1,500 people at tables on its expansive floor and in two levels of balconies surrounding it.

By 1992, the banquet was a full-blown spectacle. Dress was black-tie for the gentlemen and formal evening gowns for ladies. ESPN was airing the banquet live, placing increased pressure on teams to finish in the top 10 so the driver would appear on stage to thank his sponsors in front of a national television audience.

At Alan Kulwicki Racing's shop in North Carolina, preparations for the new champion's crowning moment began the morning after the Hooters 500 and that evening's party.

Cal Lawson soon found himself wondering if it wouldn't be more efficient to simply have a telephone receiver surgically attached to the side of his head.

The team's secretary had left her job on Sept. 30 and no replacement had been hired. That meant there was nobody there to answer the phone, let alone help handle the details that needed to be worked out for the team to travel to New York for the Dec. 4 banquet.

"It was wearing me out," Lawson recalls. He was handling everything from planning the team members' traveling itineraries to arranging tuxedo rentals.

He spent the better part of one afternoon on the phone with an artist commissioned by Goodyear to create a 24-karat gold replica of the champion's car, a trophy that is particularly treasured by every champion who wins it. The trophy is crafted with such detail that Lawson spent several minutes describing the exact location and configuration of the glove box the team put into every one of Kulwicki's cars to hold his comb, handkerchief and lip balm. The glove box would be part of the intricately prepared interior of the car on the trophy Kulwicki would receive.

Wayne Estes called early in the busy week to offer assistance, but since Lawson was flying by the seat of his pants he really didn't know what Estes might do to help.

Things eventually worked themselves out.

"One guy on the team was from New Jersey," Lawson said. "He was going to stay at the Waldorf with us, but he wanted to drive up and take his kids and let them stay with his parents during that weekend. So I told him he could drive up in the team's van.

"As it turned out, one thing that I'd overlooked was how we were going to get all of the trophies and stuff home from the banquet. They had these big signs and things and we wanted to keep them all. We loaded it all in the van and he wound up bringing it back."

While Lawson worked on banquet plans, crew chief Paul Andrews kept the team working on preparations for the 1993 season and a defense of the championship. The team would work right up until the day they left for New York. After the banquet, on a Friday night, they would spend Saturday in New York and return home on Sunday. On Monday, they'd be back in the shop working.

From Winston-Salem, N.C., the home of R.J. Reynolds Tobacco and its marketing arm, Sports Marketing Enterprises, Ty Norris and the SME staff were also hard at work trying to line up media opportunities for Kulwicki for banquet week in New York.

It was a tough sell. NASCAR had been coming to New York for more than a decade. Every columnist predisposed to write a "Bubba in the Big City" piece on stock-car racing had already done so. Besides, as the champion himself had said in Atlanta, who had ever heard of a good ol' boy named Kulwicki?

"I was talking to a guy from one of the New York papers and said we'd be bringing the champion up there," Norris said. "I said he was coming to pick up his money at the banquet. He said who is it? I said Alan Kulwicki. They said, 'Alan who?'

"Then I said, 'He's getting a $1.2 million check.' The guy said that [baseball player] Bobby Bonilla had signed with the Mets the year before for five years at $29 million, so we weren't much of a story. They really blew us off.

"So we decided we were going to get what we could get in New York and just have fun. We ended up having a decent amount of exposure up there. But we had a blast."

Kulwicki was determined to make sure that happened. The festivities surrounding Rusty Wallace's championship celebration in 1989 had been particularly memorable—Kulwicki himself had been seen sipping champagne from a lady's slipper that night at the champion's party following the banquet. Kulwicki was determined to do his best to top that party with his own.

He also was determined to give a memorable speech. Some were dreading Kulwicki's remarks because they remembered a long, rambling speech he gave when he won rookie of the year in 1986. Kulwicki knew better this time and as the days between the final race and the trip to New York passed he began thinking about what he wanted to say. He wanted to his championship speech to leave an equally lasting but much more positive impression than had his rookie of the year remarks.

In Indianapolis, meanwhile, the staff at the Lingner Group was pulling together elements it needed to produce the banquet for the live audience in the Waldorf's Grand Ballroom and for the telecast.

When Tom Roberts asked Kulwicki to pick a song on the Thursday before the Hooters 500, he was doing so at the request of Jenny Nickell, who was in charge of getting the video/music montage of the champion's life and season prepared for the broadcast.

The first step in that process was already proving to be problematic.

On the Monday after the final race, Nickell called Roberts.

"I don't know if I can get permission to use the Frank Sinatra version of 'My Way' in time," Nickell said. "I am pretty sure I can get the Elvis [Presley] version."

Roberts knew that wouldn't sit well with Kulwicki.

"He says it has got to be Sinatra," Roberts said.

Most television networks have blanket agreements with music licensing agencies allowing them the rights to use a piece of music in a broadcast. Royalties to the particular artists and songwriters are paid from the fees the networks pay under the agreement. ESPN, however, had no such blanket agreement. It paid for rights on an as-needed basis—every time ESPN wanted to use a piece of music it cleared the use of that particular song and paid only for those rights.

"It takes a while to get permission," Nickell said. She ultimately would get the okay by early the following week. "The fact we got the song cleared that fast was a miracle."

Ken Martin, who had been feverishly figuring the points standings in the booth during the Hooters 500, had returned to Indianapolis. While Nickell handled the music side of the Kulwicki piece, Martin was in charge of getting the right images to match the music and tell the story of NASCAR's new unlikely champion.

"My goal was to make Alan cry," Martin said. "I knew people saw him as a cold guy, and I wanted to see him show emotion."

Martin called Gerald Kulwicki in Wisconsin and arranged to drive up to look through the family's scrapbooks.

"We were kind of desperate for photos of Alan as a boy," Martin said.

Once he had arrived at Gerald Kulwicki's house and started going through the family's photo albums, it didn't take Martin long to find the picture he had come to get.

It was a photo of two young boys, no more than 7 years old, sitting in a small, black "tin lizzy" type car. The two lads in the photo were

Alan Kulwicki and his brother, Kenny, the one who had died when Alan was in eighth grade.

"I knew that was it," Martin said. "I never asked Alan about it, but I always sort of believed that his whole Mighty Mouse thing was his way of remembering Kenny. When I saw the picture of Alan and Kenny in the little car I knew that was it."

Martin shot footage of Gerald Kulwicki talking about Alan. He shot the photo of Alan and Kenny and dozens of others from the photo albums. He finished up late on Friday and started driving back toward Indianapolis. About 4 a.m. he pulled over at a rest stop and caught a couple hours of sleep. He was back in Indianapolis by 9 a.m. Saturday.

Next came the process of editing the footage he'd shot in Wisconsin and other footage from Kulwicki's earlier days in racing, including film of him racing in ASA events in car No. 28, the same number that Allison was now using in Winston Cup.

Nickell was still cutting through the red tape, but felt sure enough about ultimately getting clearance to use the Sinatra version of "My Way" that Martin went to marrying the visual images with the lyrics.

"You know," Martin said, "the first verse of that song is kind of a downer."

Indeed it is:

And now, the end is near, and so I face, the final curtain.
My friends, I'll say it clear; I'll state my case of which I'm certain
I've lived a life that's full—I've traveled each and every highway.
And more, much more than this, I did it my way.

That was no way to start a video celebrating Kulwicki's championship. It sounded, in fact, more like something appropriate for a retirement tribute. Or even for a funeral.

The weekend after Thanksgiving, Kulwicki and Ty Norris met at the Charlotte airport to travel to New York. During the flight, Kulwicki pulled a sheaf of papers from his briefcase.

"What's that?" Norris asked.

"I've been looking into buying a plane," Kulwicki said.

Kulwicki and his team still drove to a lot of races and flew commercially when they had to travel by air. He knew, however, that being champion would demand much more of his time in 1993, and was considering buying a plane that would allow him to cover more ground and have more control of his schedule.

"Do you know how much it costs to have a plane?" Kulwicki asked Norris. "After you buy it, you've got to have pilots and a hangar to put it in and pay for the fuel and all of that stuff."

There was an option, Kulwicki said.

Bob Brooks, the chief executive officer of Hooters, had told Kulwicki that his company had two airplanes based in Atlanta and that Kulwicki could use them as needed. Kulwicki knew there might be times when company business would make it hard for him to get one of the planes, but the pragmatist in him made that option sound appealing.

The champion is traditionally quartered for his week in New York in the Waldorf-Astoria's presidential suite, which has among its furnishings a desk used by Gen. Douglas MacArthur and a rocking chair brought in for the comfort of President John F. Kennedy's bad back.

Kulwicki spent the week with Norris doing what RJR and NASCAR had managed to line up—newspaper interviews, radio shows and photo opportunities at the New York Stock Exchange and with his car in Times Square.

His team members came up in the middle of the week and were feted by Ford at a luncheon on Thursday at the Four Seasons.

"I wish I could stand here and say that I was with Alan when he turned down Junior Johnson," Michael Kranefuss said at that gathering. "But I was the one who told him I thought he was a complete idiot."

Mark Brooks, the sometimes overly exuberant son of the Hooters CEO who had been through some difficult times as he tried to gain the team's acceptance, made up a lot of ground with a simple gesture that week. Brooks had lapel pins made for each member of Kulwicki's team and entourage—gold rectangular pins featuring the Mighty Mouse character against a pearl-white background. Over the course of the weekend the pins became a coveted indicator that the wearer was part of the new champion's inner circle.

Kulwicki and Norris talked several times that week about what Kulwicki should include in his banquet speech and about its overall tone and message.

Kulwicki recounted the story about the electrical short and fire that delayed his trip to the South. "It was like somebody was saying, 'Don't go down there,'" he said.

"You have to tell that story," Norris said. "That's the kind of stuff people want to hear."

"No, they don't," Kulwicki said. "They've all heard it and I don't want to sound like I'm trying to talk about how bad I had it."

"Alan," Norris said, "this is going to be your night. You've got to tell those stories. That's what this is about."

Kulwicki and Norris were still arguing during a cab ride on Friday morning, less than 12 hours before the banquet.

In the afternoon, Kulwicki put on his tuxedo and stepped outside of the hotel for one last photo opportunity. He posed under the Park Avenue entranceway of the Waldorf with a Winston show car and with the Miss Winston model who would be assisting with the trophy presentations on stage that evening—Brooke Sealy, the woman who would eventually marry Jeff Gordon.

Kulwicki's duties continued with a round of pre-banquet receptions in various rooms scattered around the hotel. From there, he ducked into a small room just off the Grand Ballroom and stooped to one knee, finishing the notes for the speech he'd finally written. Minutes later, he was introduced to the crowd and brought out to sit at the head table.

The Winston Cup banquet sounds like an elegant affair, and in many ways it is exactly that. It is also tedious.

Each of the drivers in the top 10 is brought to the stage and presented his portion of the season's points fund. The manufacturer's championship trophy also is presented and the rookie of the year is honored. More than a dozen season-long contingency awards also must be presented, although after 1998 many of these were thankfully moved to a Friday breakfast sponsored by the National Motorsports Press Association.

Some of the awards were presented before dinner, nearly two hours before ESPN's telecast. After the meal, the parade of the top 10 drivers was ready to begin. But there was a problem. T. Wayne Robertson, the affable senior vice president of Sports Marketing Enterprises and the man who had the checks to present to the 10th-place through second-place drivers, was not in position.

Martin had finished his work on the "My Way" video just in time on Monday to get it to Nickell, who had left a spot for it on the master tape that would be used in the banquet hall and on the telecast.

Now, he was backstage in the Waldorf helping run the show, and his immediate problem was finding Robertson. He found him the men's room.

"You're on, buddy," Martin said.

Robertson hurried onto the stage, but not before his tardiness had been noticed.

"The 1992 Winston Cup championship was competitive," Robertson joked, "but not as competitive as going to the bathroom in this place."

Darrell Waltrip, the ninth-place finisher in points, one-upped Robertson's quip.

"Wayne would have been here on time," Waltrip said when he came to accept his check, "but Dale [Earnhardt] had him pinned up out there trying to find out where his check was."

Earnhardt had finished 12th in points and, for the only time between 1983 and 2000, would not be among those coming to the stage that night.

Later in the evening, NASCAR president Bill France Jr. rose to pay tribute one more time to the sport's all-time winningest driver.

"We all watched with enthusiasm and, quite frankly, with some sadness as Richard Petty completed his last year as a driver," France said. "Throughout the 1992 season, the sport expressed more emotion toward Richard than any other individual in our history.

". . . We salute Richard for all you have done to move this sport along to where it is today, the finest motorsports series in the world. . . . Tomorrow, Richard becomes a car owner and a team manager. Before tomorrow comes, let's give Richard and Lynda one more standing ovation, and let it be the best they've ever had."

Dick Beaty, who had retired as Winston Cup Director at season's end, also got a standing ovation as he accepted an award of excellence for his years of service.

Mark Martin, the first of the six drivers who'd been in the championship hunt on the last day to make the stage, got a laugh when he said he'd found Jimmy Hensley's check for being named rookie of the year on the podium.

"I know he's looking for it," Martin said.

Kyle Petty, fifth in the points, followed Martin and ignored the time limit he'd been given for his remarks. Petty had the audience in stitches.

"Alan," he said to Kulwicki, "you better marry this girl."

Kulwicki had a date for the evening sitting beside him at the head table.

"If you don't, and you marry another girl, you're not going to be able to enjoy your videotape of this banquet," Petty said.

Petty also talked seriously about his father and about what a thrill it had been for him to race against The King.

"Richard Petty has meant everything in the world to me," he said. "Lynda Petty has probably meant more to me than Richard has. I don't know why he gets all the awards, she should get two-thirds of them. If I could have chosen my parents, I would have chosen those two people sitting right over there."

Harry Gant, who finished fourth in the standings, didn't attend the banquet. He was in a North Carolina hospital with pneumonia, and team owner Leo Jackson accepted on Gant's behalf.

Allison was next, thanking his parents as well as Jimmy Hensley, Bobby Hillin and Dorsey Schroeder, the drivers who had filled in for him after his injuries during the season.

Then came Elliott, who accepted his second-place share of the points fund and then produced a "trophy" of his own to present to the champion.

Elliott pulled out a gold comb, about six inches long, engraved with the words "1992 Winston Cup Champion Designer Comb." As champion, Elliott reasoned, Kulwicki couldn't afford to be seen combing his hair with a 39-cent plastic comb any more.

The champion's portion of the program began with a video introduction Ken Martin had prepared while in Wisconsin the previous week rummaging through Kulwicki's past.

In it, Gerald Kulwicki, who was sitting with Alan at the head table as the tape rolled on the big screen, introduced his son and said of the championship season, "I can't believe this happened in my lifetime."

When the piece ended, a technician running the video machines feeding the tape to the hall and the broadcast accidentally hit a fast-forward button.

Scenes from the 1992 season blipped across the screen for a few seconds until the screen went black. There was an awkward few seconds where nothing happened, mainly because nobody knew what to do. ESPN viewers then saw banquet host Barney Hall, the long-time voice of NASCAR on Motor Racing Network radio, who had no idea what to do next.

"We'll just stand by a second," Hall said.

Gerald Kulwicki's introduction was supposed to be followed by a brief review of Kulwicki's season, ending with an announcer calling Kulwicki to the stage. As the crew backstage scrambled to get things back into position, Kulwicki decided the thing for him to do would be to come on stage and allow the proceedings to go on.

France had the first presentation—a championship ring.

"I am sure," France said, "that you will win another one."

Kulwicki thanked France and NASCAR for "giving me a fair shake," when he came South to compete.

By this time the video had been re-racked and it rolled, bringing R.J. Reynolds chairman and chief executive officer James W. Johnston to the stage.

"My job here tonight is to make sure he can pay for the party he has planned," said Johnston, who paid his own tribute to Richard Petty and Dick Beaty before standing aside to allow Ken Martin's "My Way" video to begin.

Martin had cut the first portion of the song and began the video with the next stanza.

Regrets? I've had a few, Sinatra's voice began. *But then again, too few to mention.*

I did what I had to do, and saw it through without exemption.

Images of Kulwicki's car smoking after engine problems or one of the season's accidents flickered across the screen. As the music continued, the song that had become a Sinatra signature seemed more and more like it had been written especially for the new Winston Cup champion.

I planned each charted course—each careful step along the byway.

And more, much more than this, I did it my way.

The photo of Alan and Kenny with the little black car came early. There was a picture of Alan as a young boy in church carrying a prayer book and another photo of him and his brother, this time at Christmas.

Yes, there were times I'm sure you knew,

When I bit off more than I could chew.

But through it all, when there was doubt, I ate it up and spit it out.

I faced it all and I stood tall. And did it my way.

Pictures of Kulwicki and his earliest race cars came on the screen and faded away. There was a clipping of the story Tom Roberts had written that prompted the phone call and their friendship, with the headline "Kulwicki Soon to be a Household Word."

I've loved, I've laughed and cried, I've had my fill—my share of losing.
And now as tears subside, I find it all so amusing.
To think I did all that, and may I say, not in a shy way,
Oh no. Oh no, not me. I did it my way.

More images of Kulwicki's rise through the Winston Cup ranks were shown, including the first victory at Phoenix and the Army-themed car he'd driven at Daytona in 1991 before landing Hooters as his sponsor.

The song then built toward its crescendo. The scene on the screen shifted to Atlanta and the climactic race.

For what is a man? What has he got?
If not himself—then he has naught.
To say the things he truly feels and not the words of one who kneels.
The record shows I took the blows. And did it my way.

Kulwicki was shown combing his hair, then climbing onto the roof of his car after winning the championship. As Sinatra reprised the final line of the song, the final shot of the video was taken from below; looking up at Kulwicki silhouetted against the early evening sky accepting the cheers of the Atlanta crowd.

When Martin had finished the video earlier in the week, he thought it was pretty good.

"It was short on the bells and whistles," Martin said. "We didn't put a lot of effects in there. The music and the photos, that was it."

That was enough, although Martin failed to get his wish—Kulwicki had a definite lump in his throat when the song was over but he was not crying. Many others in the audience were, however.

The last bit of business before the champion's speech was the presentation of the championship check.

Johnston presented Kulwicki with $1,125,551.

When the ovation died, it was finally Kulwicki's turn.

He began by thanking RJR and its staff, including a special thanks for Norris, who, Kulwicki said, "has become a pretty good friend of mine over the past couple of weeks."

Next came thank yous to the sponsors—Hooters, Naturally Fresh Salad Dressings and Classic Mixers—and to Ford Motor Company.

"My career has taken a lot of different turns along the way," Kulwicki said. "One of them, about two years ago, was starting the season without a sponsor. I raced a camouflage car with 'Army' on it at Daytona, which was sponsored by R.J. Reynolds. I ran an unsponsored car for a few races and then finally Hooters came along.

"At the time I thought it was maybe going to be a one-race deal. They stayed on for a few more races, eventually the rest of the season and then a multiyear sponsorship. They've turned out to be a bigger, better sponsor than I ever thought they could have when we first got together. I want to thank them for all of their support. I feel it has been a mutually beneficial relationship and maybe there are more good things for both of us.

"I want to thank my team. I don't think much has been said about them tonight. We acknowledged them briefly before. A lot of things have been said about what I stand for, my determination and work ethic and everything like that. We're still one of the smallest teams on the NASCAR circuit and these guys work really hard and they deserve a lot of the credit. Everything that I stand for they stand for also. I wouldn't be here without them.

"Paul Andrews my crew chief . . . we started years ago and we've had a lot of trying times to get to this point but he stuck in there and did an excellent job and really matured the past couple of years."

Kulwicki then ticked off a list of his team members' names, all the way down to the team scorer.

"My dad here, Gerry Kulwicki, my [step]mom, without them I would-n't be here either. It was a pretty touching moment . . . my dad's not a real emotional kind of guy, and to some people I'm not, that's about as emotional as I get. I want to thank them a lot and I'm glad that he got to experience something like this in his lifetime. I'm sure it means a lot to him.

"The wives of all the team members who've put up with a lot of the sacrifices that go into winning a championship like this. Believe me there's a lot of hard work to it. Some of my team members are seated down there and some are up in the balcony. That's only appropriate because I surely do look up to you. Let's have a round of applause for them."

With all of those expressions of gratitude on the record, Kulwicki then progressed into the truly memorable part of his remarks.

"I woke up this morning and asked myself, 'How did this happen? How did I get here?'" he said. "All of the interviews that you go through after winning something like this make you reflect back on all of the things you had to do to get to this point. You really start to reflect back on your whole life and it brings back a lot of memories.

"Six years ago I was just a little guy with a dream who moved down South with a pickup truck and a trailer. After running a few NASCAR races and dreaming about it for 10 years, I thought maybe I was ready to take a stab at it.

"I sold my short-track equipment, some of which you saw there in pictures from ASA competition. I gave a notice on my apartment, closed the checking account and took everything I had. I really had to leave my whole life behind to move down South. They were having a going-away party for me, and the only thing was I didn't know where I was going. There were some opportunities, some rides and some potential sponsors. I decided to take a gamble that one of them would come through.

"When it came time to go I wasn't sure where I was going. I had the trailer loaded half full with household equipment. I had a bed in there and a welder, all kinds of stuff. A couple of days before I was ready to go the truck had an electrical fire and burned down. I stopped and asked myself if someone was trying to tell me something. It would have been real easy to quit, turn back or say, 'It just wasn't meant to be,' or, 'I can't do it.'

"But I kept on and when I first came down South, I've got to be honest, I was really scared. I was swimming for my life. Fear of failure is a good motivator and I think that's what drove me in the early years. Through a lot of hard work on the part of my team, I don't want to take all the credit for this, they really deserve a lot of it, there's a lot of people who've helped me over the years. I just eventually worked my way up little by little.

"My team has done a lot to get me to this point. I have been the underdog a lot of my career. I didn't start out choosing to do it this way, it just sort of happened. I started my own team out of necessity when there weren't any other offers. I kept building it up and it got to the point where I just had too much invested in it, emotionally and financially, to give up on it.

"You know, there are more things to life than just money and getting paid money to win races and drive cars. The goal was to win races and a championship and there's a lot of satisfaction in doing it this way. If I've been an underdog or if I've been an example to a lot of the little guys out there then I am proud to fill that role. There are a lot of short-track drivers and guys in Busch Grand National racing and people all across the country coming into the sport making it bigger and better day by day. Hopefully some of them will look at it and say, 'Well, if he did it maybe I can do it, too.' I hope I continue to be an example in the future, a good example."

Kulwicki thanked the drivers with whom he had waged the tight championship battle for keeping their competition clean and honorable.

"I really am a fortunate person to be here tonight and I really count my blessings," he said. "We've got a lot to the thankful for here. I hope that in the year to come I will be a good representative. I hope that when 1993 is over that Winston and the people at NASCAR and the competitors all look back and say, 'We were proud to have him represent us as our champion.' Thank you."

They were simple words straight from the heart, but they were words that in many ways told more about the man who'd said them than a hundred newspaper stories or magazine features could have revealed.

As the banquet ended, Kulwicki stood center stage and allowed the cheers to wash over him.

He had, indeed, done it all and stood tall.

The banquet was over but the evening was not. There was still the champion's party, set up in a room just off the main lobby of the Waldorf. With help from R.J. Reynolds, Kulwicki had arranged for a Los Angeles-based party band known as Jack Mack and Heart Attack to provide the entertainment.

"We knew it was a kick-ass band when we looked up and Richard Petty was leading a Conga line," Norris said. "I've never seen people have more fun in my life."

The party began shortly after 11 p.m. and was rocking by midnight. Hooters girls were at the door checking invitations, and their level of security was decidedly lax. The room got extremely crowded extremely quickly.

About 2:30 a.m., the band finished a song and said, "Good night, everybody!" They'd been paid to play that long and they were finished.

Kulwicki immediately found Norris in the crowd.

"They can't quit!" Kulwicki said. "I told you when we were coming up here that I don't care what else happens, I want people to walk out saying that's the best party they've ever been to. They've got to keep playing!"

Norris went up to talk to the band. "Guys, we need you to play another hour," he said.

No way. The gig was over.

"We really need another hour, guys," Norris pleaded.

The band held an impromptu meeting. They'd stay another hour for $1,000—in cash.

"We're all there in tuxedos and nobody had $1,000 on them," Norris said. "I thought we could have rounded it up, but we talked them into letting us add it to the bill."

An RJR official actually drew up an addendum to the band's contract on a napkin, agreeing to pay the band $1,000 for the additional hour. He drew lines for the signatures and the band signed off.

There were, however, a few more details.

"The band said, 'Well, we've got to pay the lighting guy to stay if we're staying,'" Norris said. So Norris pulled $200 out of his pocket to pay the lighting guy.

Next came the man on the soundboard. Kulwicki provided the cash to satisfy him. Before it was over, the $1,000 for an additional hour turned into nearly twice that.

But in the end, the band played on.

New Season,
New Hurdles

he idea that there is a NASCAR "off-season" is ridiculous to those who make a living in the sport.

From the time the season ends in mid-November until testing begins in January the pace is only marginally less chaotic than the nine-month grind of the season itself. There is no long holiday break —crew members might get an extra day or two off around Christmas.

Winston Cup cars are built from the ground up, beginning with a skeleton of steel bars welded together to give the car its basic shape. All of the mechanical elements of the vehicle are married to this framework, piece by piece, from the suspension system to the engine compartment and from the fuel cell to the front valence.

As the end of a year approaches, each team takes inventory of its cars and decides how well they've stood up to the rigors of the season. Some may have been wrecked beyond repair. Some may be too old to keep using and are eventually turned into show cars or sold off to some team running in a lower division. New cars must be prepared to replace those rotated out of the team's fleet.

Even holdover cars must sometimes be reworked down to the chassis. If a manufacturer changes the model it's racing—if Chevrolet decides it wants Monte Carlos instead of Luminas, for example—all of the bodies must be converted to the new style.

Even when there's no model change, NASCAR frequently makes new rules for a new season, requiring changes to the bodies that, in turn, demand the teams make other changes to compensate for the effects of the new mandates.

The "off-season" is also the time where drivers change rides and crew members load up their tool boxes and go down the road to another shop in pursuit of better money or better opportunities.

Tim Brewer was among those looking for a new employer in December 1992. His relationship with team owner Junior Johnson had deteriorated profoundly over the final weeks of the season as Bill Elliott lost his grip on the championship. So Brewer and Johnson parted ways, with Brewer being "released" from his duties as crew chief on the No. 11 Fords. Was Brewer fired or did he quit? Ultimately that didn't matter. What mattered was that Brewer needed a new job and Johnson needed a new crew chief for Elliott.

Neither had to look very far.

Johnson moved Mike Beam over from his other Winston Cup team and made him Elliott's crew chief. Beam had been with Sterling Marlin the previous two seasons on the cars backed by Maxwell House, the sponsor Kulwicki felt Johnson had spirited away from him prior to the 1991 campaign. Before that, Beam had been Elliott's crew chief at Melling Racing in 1990, so the two had worked together before.

Maxwell House was leaving Johnson's team at the end of the 1992 season to become the sponsor for Bill Davis' new team—the one with which Bobby Labonte would make his move from Busch Grand National to Winston Cup. Brewer was hired as Labonte's crew chief.

Budweiser was staying on as Elliott's sponsor and Johnson had landed McDonald's to back his other team. He had hired Hut Stricklin, who'd spent most of the three previous seasons driving for Bobby Allison's team, to drive the McDonald's car. Johnson hired Mike Hill to serve as Stricklin's crew chief.

While Johnson was restructuring his teams, the new champion was adjusting to that role. Alan Kulwicki expected things to be different. As he said in his speech at the banquet, he was determined to find a way to incorporate those demands into his life so he could properly represent the sport.

There had been a few changes in Kulwicki's team in the off-season. Engine builder Ron Vicarro left to go to work for the Richard Jackson-owned team that would field Fords for Rick Mast in the '93 season. Jackson's team was switching from Oldsmobiles and needed a Ford engine expert to help with the transition.

Kulwicki took the defection in relative stride, giving engine-room loyalists Danny Glad and Randy Clary more responsibilities and beginning to look for a specialist in working with cylinder heads to fill the position Vicarro vacated.

Kulwicki's January schedule was filling up.

He would have to meet with the media during the annual preseason "media tour" conducted by Charlotte Motor Speedway and go to Daytona for test sessions leading up to the Daytona 500. He went back to his high school in Greenfield, Wis., to talk to the students there. He was also scheduled to go to Marietta, Ga., with the car for a test in a wind tunnel, then travel to Detroit for a drivers' seminar with Ford officials and for an appearance at a large auto show held there every year.

Kulwicki wanted to make sure he was fulfilling all of the duties expected of him by series sponsor R.J. Reynolds as the circuit's champion.

So he called Ty Norris.

"What do you need me to do?" Kulwicki asked.

"Nothing now," Norris said.

Kulwicki had already participated in the Winston Cup Preview, an annual race season kickoff in Winston-Salem where drivers sign autographs for fans who buy tickets to get in, with the proceeds from the event going to charity.

"You just keep working on your cars and getting ready," Norris told Kulwicki. "When we get to Daytona, you will have plenty to do."

"Okay," Kulwicki said. "I guess I just thought I would be doing more for you guys before the season."

"No, we're okay now," Norris said. "But you will be slammed at Daytona and you just need to get ready for that."

Kulwicki went to Marietta for the wind tunnel test. Wayne Estes lived in that Atlanta suburb and arranged to fly to Detroit with Kulwicki on the Hooters-owned plane the champion had been given permission to use. Kulwicki spent the night before the trip at Estes' home.

The plane Kulwicki and Estes took from Atlanta to Detroit for the drivers' seminar and auto show was a Merlin 300, a 10-passenger plane with twin turbo-propeller engines. It was one of two owned by Hooters —the other was a larger jet used for longer trips.

Dick Trickle, who had been a star in American Speed Association competition in the Midwest as Kulwicki was coming along, had arranged to fly back from Detroit on the Hooters plane with Kulwicki and Estes. The plane would fly first to Charlotte to drop off Kulwicki and Trickle, then return to its base in Atlanta with Estes getting off there.

As they prepared to leave Detroit, however, wintry weather began to grip the city. Charlie Campbell, the company pilot for Hooters, looked at the conditions and the forecast and told Kulwicki the weather was marginal.

"We can go if you want to, but if it was up to me we wouldn't fly," Campbell said.

Kulwicki trusted the veteran pilot's judgment.

"If you don't want to go, I don't want to go," he said.

Estes was relieved.

"There was always these stories about these guys being cowboys and taking all kinds of risks," he said. "I felt good knowing these guys were being safety-conscious."

Kulwicki, Trickle and Estes went to a Comfort Inn near the airport to spend the night. After checking in, they went to a Denny's restaurant to have dinner. Kulwicki and Trickle began swapping stories from their days in ASA.

"They had raced each other many, many times and it was fun to hear them talking," Estes says. "Up there, it had always been Trickle out front and Alan trying to get there, and now in NASCAR the roles were reversed. But they were absolute equals sitting in that Denny's talking."

Denny's had a special meaning for the racers.

"They only used to go to Denny's if they won the race," Estes said. "If they lost it was cheese crackers and a soda. But if you won and you got a check, you could take the crew guys to Denny's."

Kulwicki's pace picked up quickly after that, however, and within a matter of a few days Winston Cup teams were back in Daytona getting ready for the season's first—and most important—race.

Kulwicki badly wanted to win the Daytona 500.

After winning the championship, he told friends that the next time he did the "Polish victory lap" would be after winning the circuit's most prestigious event. He told a friend that, with a championship now on his résumé, he now had only two major goals he really wanted to accomplish in the sport.

"I want to win the Daytona 500," he said, "and I want to take the Budweiser sponsorship away from Junior Johnson."

Two years earlier in February, when Kulwicki came to Daytona without a sponsor for the year and with only the one-race Army deal from R.J. Reynolds, Johnson had held court at dinner with a group of sportswriters. Asked about Kulwicki's rejection of his overtures to join his team, Johnson told the reporters that he thought Kulwicki was wasting his career and that the driver was "ignorant" to continue trying to drive and own his team when other options had been there for the taking. Kulwicki had not forgotten.

Stock-car racing takes over Daytona Beach, Fla., for nearly two weeks in February.

Teams begin arriving on the Wednesday or Thursday a week prior to the running of the 500. The season's first day of official practice is on that Friday, with qualifying for the Daytona 500 on Saturday.

Daytona 500 qualifying is different from every other qualifying format all season. Only the front-row starting positions are determined in Saturday's first round, and in 1993 those spots went to Kyle Petty and Dale Jarrett.

Petty, making sure the family name remained in the headlines, ran 189.426 mph around the 2.5-mile trioval to win the pole over Jarrett, who was beginning a second season as driver of the Chevrolets owned by Washington Redskins head coach Joe Gibbs.

Elliott just missed a front-row spot, running 189.024 mph for the day's third fastest speed. All that did for him, however, was give him the No. 2 starting spot for the first of two 125-mile qualifying races on the following Thursday. His starting spot in the Daytona 500 would depend on his finish in that race, as would the rest of the field for the main event of Speedweeks.

Davey Allison ran 188.523 on his qualifying lap, 15th fastest, while Kulwicki's speed was 187.445 mph, 24th best. Jeff Gordon, officially beginning his rookie season, was faster than Allison and Kulwicki with a lap at 188.726 mph, the 11th best speed.

Although Norris and others had warned him, Kulwicki soon realized he was not ready for the crush he faced at Daytona as the reigning champion. During the first practice day on Friday, photographers and cameramen walked right into his garage stall, poking their equipment in as he and Andrews tried to talk about their car.

Most of the regular NASCAR press knew that Kulwicki didn't like being distracted while he was working. They had learned that it was best to pick their spots carefully, interviewing Kulwicki only as opportunities presented themselves.

Now, though, the situation was different. He was the champion, and therefore his movements were now inherently more newsworthy than they had been when he was merely the fierce independent owner/driver succeeding modestly in spite of the odds.

Kulwicki's patience with his new notoriety didn't last 24 hours into the new season. On Saturday, he had his crew put up a pair of stanchions and attach a rope of pennants to each to create a boundary around his garage stall. People not there to work on the car were told to stay behind these barriers.

By 2000, NASCAR inspectors would spend time on their first day at the track putting a similar banner of pennants around the entire garage area. This provides a walkway behind the team transporters for fans while roping off an area for the cars to come in and out of the garage and for the teams to work. Some fans ignore these barriers completely, but they do reduce the number of people walking right up to a driver or a crew chief at the car to ask for an autograph.

In 1993, however, nobody roped off his garage stall. NASCAR boasted about the access it offered fans, and it would never do to have its new champion appear so standoffish. Kulwicki was ordered to take down the stanchions and the pennants.

The champion was ready to blow his stack when Norris walked by.

"You can call me the worst Winston Cup champion ever if you want to!" Kulwicki said. "That's it! I am done! No more! I am not doing anything else. These people are walking all over me! I am done!"

Norris let Kulwicki blow off steam. He said very little—Kulwicki gave him little chance to—and eventually walked away with the driver still fuming.

A while later, Norris returned.

"Alan, I tried to tell you it was going to be overwhelming," Norris said. "If you let it get to you like this, it's going to be a very long year. Now tell me what it is you want and I will try to see if I can get it done for you."

Kulwicki wanted his barriers, but Norris knew NASCAR would never go for that. He tried to spread the word for the media to give Kulwicki's some room, but knew the only real solution would be time for Kulwicki to get used to the reality of his new status.

Kulwicki also vented his rage to Tom Roberts in the team's transporter lounge.

"I can't take it anymore!" Kulwicki said.

Roberts knew his friend was genuinely agitated because he was grabbing at his hair, a habit Kulwicki had when he was upset or nervous. This time, Roberts thought Kulwicki might actually start pulling out clumps of the hair as he grabbed at it.

"I can't take it anymore!" Kulwicki said.

Roberts empathized. But he also knew his job.

"Alan, it's part of your responsibility now," Roberts said. "Trust me, this will be as bad as it gets all year. Once we get through Speedweeks, you'll still have things to do but they won't be coming at you from all sides like they are here. You've got to trust me."

Reporters had expected the pressure to get to Kulwicki, but maybe not so soon. When the eruption came, it was news. So when Kulwicki did take time to answer questions, that was the topic.

"If I refuse to do stuff, to go to the drivers' seminar, do the media tour, go to Winston-Salem, and stay to work on the car, then everyone would say, 'He isn't cooperative and he wasn't a good champion,'" Kulwicki said. "So I am sacrificing to a certain extent. I am doing the best I can up to a certain point. At some point, I am going to have to say, 'I've got to work on the car so I can't do that interview now.'

"The key will be to balance it, to know when it is time to say no. I hope when that comes that all of the guys in the media will understand.

". . . Whatever the demands are now, they probably have doubled from five years ago. I've never walked away from the car in the past like I am doing now. It's good the crew has acquired enough experience in the last few years, that we've been through enough things together that I trust them.

"It's not enough to work hard, you've got to work smart, and not just me. They've got to manage their time. If I walk away and they mismanage their time, then I come back and expect the cars to be done for me to set them up and they aren't. . . . Then we're all going to be in trouble."

The first racing of the season comes on the Sunday after Daytona 500 pole qualifying, one week before the season's first points race. It's a special non-points event for the previous year's pole-winners originally called the Busch Clash and since renamed the Budweiser Shootout at Daytona.

Dale Earnhardt used the 1993 Clash to signal that his struggles of the previous year were behind him. Earnhardt drew the 13th starting position for the race, which at that time consisted of two 10-lap segments. He roared to the front in his black No. 3 Chevrolet in the first segment, and then was relegated to the rear of the field when the finishing order of the first segment was inverted for the start of the second. Again, Earnhardt sliced his way through the traffic and blitzed the field to win the second segment as well.

Chevrolets, in fact, finished first, second and third in the final segment.

Immediately, Ford teams began to smell a rat.

"It's obvious to me that the Chevrolets did the best job of politicking over the winter," said Allison, who finished sixth in his Ford. "NASCAR has completely eliminated us from the week. We don't have a chance."

NASCAR had changed the rules to allow each make of car to use a larger rear spoiler during the off-season. The Ford teams' main complaint after the Shootout was that the Chevrolets had been given too much leeway in fitting the templates—metal pieces shaped in the legal silhouette of each make of car used in inspection to see if the cars comply.

Elliott finished last in the first segment of the Clash and eighth overall.

His Ford started leaking oil onto the track during the warm-up laps before the first 10-lap portion of the event. The leak was so bad that NASCAR officials put out the black flag before the first segment started, ordering all of the cars onto pit road to see which one was causing the trouble. As Elliott's crew tried to repair his car, the other 14 crews worked on getting his oil off their cars' windshields.

Drivers dissatisfied with their qualifying times in the first round on Saturday had the option of making a second-round run on Monday or a third-round run on Tuesday. Doing so would drop them in the starting order for the qualifying races behind drivers standing on their first-round speeds, but could improve their chances for making the field for 500 depending on the outcome of the 125-milers.

Petty, the fastest driver, and Elliott, third fastest, would be joined in Thursday's first 125-mile race by the rest of the drivers whose qualifying speeds put them at odd numbers in the final order—including Gordon at 11th and Allison in 15th. Jarrett, second best, and Kulwicki, 24th, would be in the second 125-mile race with the others at even numbers on the speeds list.

The results of the first 125-miler fill the spots on the inside of rows two through 15 in the Daytona 500. The top finisher aside from the pole-winner, in this case Petty, who was guaranteed starting first in the main event, gets the No. 3 spot for the 500, followed by the next best finisher in the No. 5 spot and so on. The outside spots on the same rows are filled by the finishing order of the second race.

After that, drivers not already in the field get starting spots based on their qualifying speed from earlier in the week. Provisional starters then complete the field.

Kulwicki refused to join the debate over Chevrolet's purported advantage over the Fords. "I'm not going to be a complainer," he said. "I don't want to be a cry-baby."

But the complaints were renewed after the qualifying races, each won by a Chevy.

Gordon signaled his potential by beating Petty and Elliott, among others, in the day's first 125-miler. "Oh my God!" he said as his car came to stop after he was guided to Victory Lane with instructions from his crew over the radio. "I could get used to this!"

Perhaps the thrill of victory hit him a bit too hard—Gordon caught a 24-hour bug and was barely able to practice on Friday before canceling autograph sessions that night. Thanks to chicken soup and lots of sleep, however, he was back at the track on Saturday.

Earnhardt won the second qualifier, the fourth straight year he'd won his 125-miler. Elliott's second-place finish in the first race gave him the fifth starting position in the 500. Allison was fifth in that race, putting him 11th for Sunday. Kulwicki was fourth in the second race, giving him the 10th starting spot.

None of them would be a factor, however.

"It's just about better to have a bad Chevy than a good Ford," lamented Mike Beam, Elliott's crew chief.

Earnhardt, who also won the Busch Grand National race on Saturday, went into Sunday's Daytona 500 with a wave of momentum. Despite his demonstrated skill in the Daytona draft, though, he had not won the 500 in 14 previous tries—and every year that he added to the streak the number of questions about it multiplied exponentially.

They wouldn't go away in 1993, either.

Earnhardt led more than half of the laps in the 500, but with three to go he had the precocious Gordon riding on his rear bumper. Jarrett, also in a Chevrolet, pulled up, passed Gordon and then pulled even with Earnhardt with less than two laps remaining.

Jarrett had the momentum and, despite a bump from Earnhardt, swept into the lead thanks in part to push in the draft from Geoffrey Bodine.

With his father, Ned, calling the action from the CBS broadcast booth in one of the most memorable moments in racing television history, Dale Jarrett won the Daytona 500. Earnhardt finished second, with Bodine third. Gordon came in fifth, behind Stricklin, Junior Johnson's new driver.

Elliott blew an engine after completing just 99 laps and finished 39th in the 41-car field. Allison fought an ill-handling car all day and finished 28th. Kulwicki finished on the same lap as Allison, three laps down to the leaders, in 26th.

Things got a little better for Kulwicki the following week at Rockingham, on the track and off it. After the media crush at Daytona, the season's second race at the track in the Sandhills region of North Carolina seemed like a vacation. Kulwicki qualified only 20th, but finished fourth in a race won by Rusty Wallace.

Elliott qualified well again, starting third, but finished 11th. His team's season was to get a jolt a few days later after Junior Johnson went to the doctor to see about his indigestion. Johnson had been diagnosed with arterial blockages several years earlier and doctors at Duke University Hospital in Durham decided to do an angioplasty. They were unable to successfully complete the procedure, however, and recommended surgery. So on March 3, Johnson had a triple bypass.

Allison had started an abysmal 39th and finished 14th at Rockingham, but he righted his team's ship the following weekend at Richmond with a victory after starting 14th. Elliott blew another engine and finished 33rd at Richmond, but Kulwicki seemed to be settling in, starting sixth and finishing third. He and Norris went to dinner together on Thursday, the night before qualifying, and Kulwicki was reluctant to let the evening end.

Cal Lawson, Paul Andrews and anybody else with whom Kulwicki had been close knew the pattern—after the Daytona blow-up Kulwicki wanted his friend Norris to know that he was sorry for what had happened. Instead of apologizing directly, however, Kulwicki's habit was to try to rewind the friendship back to the point before the problem and pick things up from there.

The fourth race of the 1993 season was supposed to take place on March 14 at Atlanta Motor Speedway, but a ferocious storm hit the Southeast and blanketed the area with snow. The race was postponed until the following Saturday, on what would have been the season's first off weekend.

On the original race day there was one lone figure in the garage working on his car. Kulwicki wore his driver's helmet as he worked, protecting his head from the cold.

Kulwicki started the postponed Motorcraft 500 from the 29th position in the same car he'd used to clinch the 1992 championship. He finished 36th after a crash in Turn 4 as he tried to pass Geoffrey Bodine, but it wasn't Bodine with whom Kulwicki was angry.

"Earnhardt drove right into the side of me on the straightaway," Kulwicki said. "Twice."

Morgan Shepherd won the Atlanta race. Elliott ran ninth for his best finish of the young season. Allison was 13th after another poor qualifying effort—he has started 31st. Allison qualified better the next week at Darlington, starting ninth, and finished 11th. Elliott started 28th and finished 14th in a race won by Earnhardt.

Kulwicki finished sixth at Darlington, the third time in five races he'd finished sixth or better. His winnings that day pushed him past the $5 million for his Winston Cup career. After the poor showing at Daytona and the wreck at Atlanta, Kulwicki's team seemed to be rounding into shape.

The next race was at Bristol, where Kulwicki had won in each of the past two years. It seemed like a perfect opportunity for the reigning champion to get some momentum for the long season ahead.

The Final Curtain

month into the 1993 season, Alan Kulwicki was coming to terms with the demands being placed on him as champion. He was, however, still irritated with the number of personal appearances he was being asked to make by his sponsor.

He had been at a Hooters restaurant in Columbia, S.C., the night before qualifying at Darlington and was scheduled for a similar appearance the next week in Knoxville, Tenn., before going to Bristol.

Kulwicki had hired a business manager, Don Hawk, before the season to help sort through the various business opportunities that might come his way after winning the 1992 title. Hooters CEO Bob Brooks had also hired a marketing director, Dan Duncan, to help Mark Brooks run the racing program and capitalize on the championship.

Tom Roberts lived in Alabama, and under normal circumstances he would have flown commercially from Huntsville, Ala., to Knoxville to meet Kulwicki at the appearance that Thursday. He then would have ridden in the Hooters plane from Knoxville to Bristol later that night.

In this case, however, Roberts elected to fly directly to the Tri-Cities Airport that Bristol shares with Kingsport and Johnson City.

"Alan had a lot of questions, problems and bones to pick with how things were going with Hooters," Roberts said. "He felt maybe that they were trying to take too much of his time. That had gotten to the point where I felt like those guys needed to hash it out and didn't need me in there as a referee."

Kulwicki started his Thursday—April Fool's Day—with morning prayers at St. Thomas Aquinas Church in Charlotte, a regular part of his routine. Later, as he was leaving to meet the Hooters plane and the Concord airport, he went by the shop to get Cal Lawson to make the trip with him.

The team planned to drive to Bristol after practicing pit stops that afternoon. One of Lawson's jobs with the team was tire specialist, and part of that role was to apply a bead of glue to the lug nuts used to hold the tires in place on the car. When Kulwicki found him, Lawson was in the middle of gluing up lug nuts for the pit practice. Lawson told Kulwicki he would just ride up with the team later that day.

Lawson and his girlfriend, whom he would later marry, were to meet Dan Duncan and his wife for a late dinner that evening. Clark and Terry Mosley, friends of Kulwicki and Lawson, had lined up a blind date for Kulwicki for that night as well.

Kulwicki got to the airport in Concord before pilot Charlie Campbell arrived from Atlanta in the Merlin turbo-prop. The other Hooters plane, the larger jet, had been slated for the trip to Knoxville but that changed when members of the company's sales staff needed it to fly to a meeting in New York, a longer trip.

While he waited, Kulwicki talked to a pilot who flew Rusty Wallace's plane. Wallace had a King Air, a much larger plane than the Merlin that would carry Kulwicki that day. Several Winston Cup drivers and teams had bought the King Air model, and Kulwicki was once again thinking about buying his own plane for his team.

Kulwicki was wearing the duplicate leather jacket he had ordered to replace the one he'd given to Immy Kranefuss at the Ford championship celebration in Atlanta.

Kulwicki had borrowed back the original in January for a photo shoot because the duplicate was not yet ready. When the photo session was over, Kulwicki packed the jacket in a box and shipped it back to Kranefuss in Michigan. When the box arrived, however, it was empty. The original "Top Wing" jacket had been stolen. Its whereabouts remain a mystery to this day.

In Knoxville that evening, Kulwicki signed autographs at the Hooters restaurant on Kingston Pike and then headed for McGhee Tyson

Airport. He, Mark Brooks and Dan Duncan boarded the plane, with Campbell at the controls, and took off at 8:45 p.m. for the 112-mile flight to the Tri-Cities Airport.

At about 9:15 p.m., Kulwicki used a telephone in the airplane to call the airport and make sure Clark and Terry Mosley were there to pick him up.

Campbell was in contact with the traffic control tower, approaching from the west. He had requested that the airport's flight services operation supply him with an auxiliary power unit to keep the engines warm and a quick turnaround on fuel, indicating he planned to drop off his passengers and take off again quickly to head back to Georgia.

A plane carrying Dale Earnhardt was coming in from the opposite direction at almost the same time, with pilot Mike Colyer at the controls.

Colyer was given clearance to land his plane first, with Campbell following instructions to turn and line up a safe distance behind the Earnhardt plane for his final approach.

Colyer and Campbell were both flying on instruments. There was some light rain and a ceiling at 4,000 feet, but no lightning. Visibility was at least 6 miles, but Colyer could already make out the lights of the airport ahead of him about 15 miles away. Campbell's plane was about two miles behind, descending through 1,500 feet.

Colyer heard the Tri-Cities tower tell Campbell that he was number two for landing. It was 9:27 p.m. Everything appeared normal.

About 30 seconds later, Colyer heard the radio microphone being keyed from the cockpit of the Hooters plane.

There was a grunt and then a scream.

Then there was the sound of an impact.

And then, nothing.

The tower called for Campbell to respond. It tried again. Still nothing.

The next call was for emergency crews to scramble. The tower believed a plane was down.

Six miles northeast of the airport, just off Interstate 81 near the town of Blountville, Tenn., Wanda Lambert heard a loud noise. She ran out to the top of a hill and heard an explosion, one she said sounded like a gas tank blowing up, about a quarter-mile from her house.

Colyer landed safely. Shaken, he told the passengers on his plane what he'd heard over the radio. When he walked into the flight services office, he saw people who he knew were waiting for Kulwicki's plane to come in right behind them.

Earnhardt saw Mike Bales, president of Appalachian Flight Services. "Did the Hooters plane go down?" Earnhardt asked.

Tom Roberts had checked into his hotel in Johnson City and went to the lounge in the lobby. He knew that when Kulwicki got to town, he would eventually wind up there. Roberts would ask him if he got the chance to talk to Duncan and Brooks about the demands on his time.

Wayne Estes was in his hotel room watching television. Just before 10 p.m., the local NBC affiliate broke in with a bulletin saying a Level 3 emergency had been declared at the Tri-Cities Airport, and that a Level 3 emergency involved a plane with more than one engine.

"I knew I was going to know somebody on that plane," Estes said. "I had to. It was the night before practice started at Bristol. If it was a plane with more than a single engine and it was flying in, it had to be a commercial commuter flight from Charlotte or a team plane. I knew it, I just had to wait and see."

Cal Lawson arrived at his hotel and was handed a note telling him to come to the airport. He hadn't heard the reports of the airplane crash, now spreading across the region's radio and television outlets, and didn't see the note as a cause for alarm. He figured Kulwicki and Duncan were running late and, instead of meeting for dinner as planned they would meet at the airport and decide what to do from there.

Within an hour of the first bulletin on television, crews had made their way to the scene and shot footage of the wreckage. By 11 p.m. it was on the air and Estes saw it. The plane had nosed into on open field, blown apart and caught fire, but there was enough of the fuselage left for Estes to see it was orange and white. The reports said it was registered to Hooters.

Estes reached for the telephone and dialed Don Hawk's number.

Only when the phone started ringing on the other end did it occur to him that Hawk might have been on the plane and that Hawk's wife might not know about the accident. Estes was relieved when Hawk picked up the phone.

Hooters CEO Bob Brooks had been to the home of another executive in the company that evening. They had talked about how good things were going with the business.

When Brooks got home, the calls had already started to come in.

Brooks turned on the television and saw the same footage Estes had been seeing. He, too, recognized the colors of the plane. He knew his son Mark had been on board.

Larry McReynolds and Davey Allison were staying in the same hotel. They wound up sitting in McReynolds' room watching the television and listening to the radio to find out what they could about what had happened.

Roberts was still at the hotel when Rusty Wallace entered. Wallace had heard the news that a plane had crashed and that it was thought to be Kulwicki's.

Ty Norris was checking in about the same time. He'd heard about a crash near Blountville on the local radio news as he drove in, but didn't really know where the town was and hadn't associated the accident with racing. Now he made the connection. He saw Roberts and asked him if he wanted to go out to the airport.

When they arrived, Paul Andrews, Cal Lawson and Danny Glad were already there. Wallace came, too. Nobody had anything official to say but it was clear by now that the Hooters plane had indeed gone down.

The initial investigation was complicated by the fact that workers on the scene were searching for a fifth body—everyone thought Roberts was on board. In most newspapers the following morning, in fact, it was reported that Kulwicki and four others had perished in the crash. When Roberts was accounted for, some believed a second pilot had been on board.

Finally, after 2 a.m. on Friday, the group waiting back at the airport was taken into a small office and provided with the details that had become available in the hours after the crash. The plane had carried four people—Kulwicki, 38; Duncan, 44; Mark Brooks, 26, and Campbell, 45—and all had been killed.

As Friday morning dawned, the few people in the racing community who had somehow avoided it the night before awoke to learn the horrible news.

The weather reflected the pall that had fallen over the racing world, cold with dense fog and a chilling mist that dampened everyone venturing out into it.

Estes arrived at the Bristol track and walked up a long, steep hill leading from the parking lot to the gate. From there, he would walk down the steps of the frontstretch grandstands through a small open-

174

ing right under the flagstand at the start-finish line, then across the track and into the infield to go to work.

As Estes came inside the track gate, he saw the Hooters team transporter sitting on the front straightaway, looming like a ghost ship in the mist.

On its front grille, someone had hung a wreath.

Most of Kulwicki's crew had come to the track. They didn't know where else to go or what else to do.

Instead of putting the team's transporter into position in the No. 1 parking spot in the tightly bunched garage in Bristol's infield, NASCAR officials had driver Peter Jellen park on the track until they figured out what to do. The poor weather would prevent cars from practicing, at least for a while, buying some time for people to think.

Roberts was allowed to use an office outside of the track to deal with the flood of calls coming in. He never saw the transporter on the track or what happened later in the morning, when crewmen gathered along pit wall and stood, heads bowed, as it took a ceremonial lap.

By early afternoon, the decision had been made for Kulwicki's team to return to Charlotte. With the light rain and even a few snowflakes still falling, Jellen fired up the truck once again and drove around to the gate in Turn 3 that provides access to the Bristol infield. Jellen turned up the steep banking of the track and pulled through the gate.

About a half-hour later, the weather broke. The rain and snow stopped. The fog lifted and the clouds partly gave way to some sunshine.

Before long, the track was dry and the cars went out to practice and prepare for qualifying. All of them, that is, except for the No. 7 Ford.

Gerald Kulwicki had tried to steer his son away from racing from the start.

"He was all that I had left," he said.

Now, Alan was gone, too, and had left no will and testament. As his son's next of kin, everything Alan had owned was now in Gerald's hands. Gerald had already talked to Hawk at the shop in Charlotte and agreed to appoint Felix Sabates as the interim administrator of Alan Kulwicki Racing.

Sabates and Alan Kulwicki had been friends for a long time, drawn together because the story of Sabates' life was possibly even more incredible than the race car driver from Wisconsin's.

Sabates was born in Cuba but fled Fidel Castro's regime. His rejection of Communism was total—there are very few more fervent capitalists than Sabates.

For a time, his family stayed up nights doing piecework—sewing collars onto shirts to put food on the table. Sabates eventually got a job selling cars in Charlotte, but he had entrepreneurial dreams of his own and the salesmanship to make them come true.

Over time, Sabates' hard work began to pay off. He managed to get in on the ground floor as a distributor for Pong, the rudimentary two-paddles-and-a-blip video tennis game. He later cashed in big with the Teddy Ruxpin line of stuffed bears. Sabates had gone, literally, from rags to riches in a classic version of the American dream.

That background gave Sabates a natural affinity for Kulwicki. Sabates himself had started a team in 1989, hiring Kyle Petty as his driver. The team had won four races by the end of the 1992 season and, at the start of 1993, Sabates had started a second team with Kenny Wallace, Rusty's brother, behind the wheel.

"Alan was my friend," Sabates said.

During the day on Friday, fans drove by the team's shop just behind Charlotte Motor Speedway. Some left flowers on the sign out front. One fan posted a poem on the front door. Several thousand fans were attending an auto fair at the track itself. Souvenir vendors were doing brisk business selling Kulwicki merchandise—much of it at prices that had been dramatically increased that morning.

In Bristol, the improving weather allowed qualifying for the Food City 500 to finally commence. Rusty Wallace won the pole.

Dale Jarrett, who was among those who had eventually made his way to the airport late Thursday night to await word about the crash victims, called Kulwicki his "hero" and said, "I don't want to be here this weekend. It's going to be hard to concentrate on driving a race car. I wish NASCAR would call it off and come back next weekend, but I know they can't do that."

There were special ceremonies honoring Kulwicki before the Busch Grand National race on Saturday, a race in which Michael Waltrip got a victory and then a "yes" to his marriage proposal in victory lane, and again before the Winston Cup race on Sunday. Wallace won the Cup race and remembered his friend and rival from ASA with his own version of Kulwicki's "Polish victory lap."

There was a lot of talk about Kulwicki that weekend, of course, with people telling stories of how determined the driver had been to learn all he could from everybody in the garage and how he could, at the same time, be stubborn about holding to his own ideas.

"He was the type of guy who always came over and asked you a question about something, and then would disagree with you," Wallace said. "He would go back and do it his way."

Kulwicki also liked to pick Larry McReynolds' brain.

"I enjoyed talking to him, even though he got on my nerves sometimes," McReynolds said.

"He'd ask what kind of tires we were going to qualify on. I would say scuffs." Scuffs is a term used to describe tires that have been put on a car for just a couple of laps, enough to slightly rough up the slick surface of a brand new one.

"Alan would say, 'One-lap scuffs or half-lap scuffs?'" McReynolds said. "'Hard-lap or easy-lap scuffs?' There was no end to his questions."

McReynolds recalled one day at North Wilkesboro after qualifying when he and Kulwicki went up into the lounge of Kulwicki's transporter to talk about setups.

"I looked at my watch and realized it was 6 o'clock," McReynolds said. "Everybody was gone and the garage was locked. A guy who looked after the place was out there and let us out. We'd been up in there two hours or more."

McReynolds still has a photograph of himself, leaning up against a post at North Wilkesboro and listening to Kulwicki.

"There's no question he was interrogating me about something," McReynolds said.

There are two Sundays in each racing season that NASCAR always leaves open—Easter and Mother's Day. In 1993, Easter fell on April 11, the Sunday after the tragic weekend in Bristol, making it easier for the racing community to participate in the services planned for Kulwicki the following week.

Friends would be received at the funeral home in Greenfield, Wis., on Tuesday night, with a funeral mass scheduled for Wednesday at St. Matthias Church. Another memorial service was scheduled for Thursday at St. Thomas Aquinas Church in Charlotte, where Kulwicki had prayed on the morning of what would be his final day.

Estes drove home the day after the Bristol race, then to Charlotte the next morning. Sabates supplied a plane to fly some of the drivers and crew members from the Charlotte area to Wisconsin for the visitation at the funeral home and the service the next day.

When the group arrived in Wisconsin, Ford officials had lined up vans to provide transportation. Somebody threw Estes a key and asked him to drive one of the vans.

After standing in long lines to pay their respects, part of the Charlotte group planned to return home late Tuesday night. Davey Allison had his own plane at the airport, too, and hitched a ride in the van Estes was driving. On the way, stories were told about Kulwicki primping before doing interviews following a pole-winning qualifying session and about other things people had seen him do or heard him say.

Allison hadn't said much on the trip, but when the van got to the airport, he said words that Estes will always remember.

"You know, a lot of people have made me wonder why I didn't win that championship last year," Allison said. "It's real clear to me right now why I didn't."

Nearly 1,200 people came to St. Matthias Church on Wednesday for Kulwicki's funeral. Father Dale Grubba, pastor for a parish in Princeton, Wis., and a racing enthusiast who had known Kulwicki for many years, led the hour-long mass.

Father Grubba spoke of Kulwicki's determination, work ethic and perseverance.

"The hero is the person who can take all of those ingredients and put them together and be a success," Grubba said. "Alan was that hero."

Grubba told a story about a Kulwicki prank with H. A. "Humpy" Wheeler, the president of Charlotte Motor Speedway, as the victim. Kulwicki had locked Wheeler onto a balcony outside Wheeler's office at the Charlotte track, forcing Wheeler to shinny two stories down a drainpipe to get back indoors.

"Nobody was a better role model than Alan," Wheeler said. "But it was never public. It was behind the scenes. Whenever I needed somebody for a speaking engagement, Alan never turned me down. He had integrity and credibility—even though he could be cantankerous."

Roberts, Lawson and Andrews were among the pallbearers. As they came into the church, they noticed large video screens set up on either side of the altar.

During the service, the "My Way" video Ken Martin had made for the awards banquet just four months earlier began to play.

Roberts didn't even bother to try to hold back his tears.

"I was sitting between Paul and Cal and we held hands and cried like babies," Roberts said. "I think that in a way that was therapy for us, a way of release. We were able to grieve and in some respects I think that was where the reality set in and the shock wore off."

The piece was played again the following morning at the memorial service in Charlotte. The crowd had quickly filled the 400 or so available seats at St. Thomas Aquinas and nearly that many more spilled out onto the lawn, where speakers had been set up so the overflow crowd could hear the service.

Kulwicki had been buried following the service in Wisconsin. In Charlotte, the driver's orange and white driver's helmet and his fireproof gloves sat on the table beneath the altar, flanked by flowers and photographs from Kulwicki's career.

Later that day, back at the team's shop, Gerald Kulwicki said he couldn't believe how many people had come to the service. "It's just hard to believe there are so many people who loved him so much," he said.

Kulwicki's status as the champion of America's most popular motorsports series made him the natural focus of the aftermath of the tragic crash. But there were three other funerals, too. The deaths of Dan Duncan, Charles Campbell and Mark Brooks left their friends and families feeling a profound sense of loss, too.

Consider Bob Brooks. The Hooters CEO lost his son, his 26-year-old protégé, on the plane. He also lost two trusted employees and friends from his company and shared that grief with Duncan's and Campbell's families.

And he lost a race car driver who had become a good friend.

"I feel like I knew Alan better than his family knew him," Brooks said. "We'd have lunch and talk for hours on end about his lives and loves. One of the last girls he was dating, I told her one day, 'You hang on to Alan, he's about to light.'"

Brooks thought about the time that he had finally told Kulwicki that the driver had cost himself $25,000 without knowing it.

"When Mark Stahl didn't make the race in Atlanta that time, I had a guy at the race track sort of keeping me up on what was going on," Brooks recalled. "He called me and said we hadn't made the race, but that he thought he would go over and talk to this Alan Kulwicki guy who had won the pole but didn't have a sponsor. He asked me how much he could offer him to put us on his car, and I told him we could go up to $50,000.

"The guy went and talked to Alan and asked Alan how much he'd do it for. Alan thought about it a minute and said he'd do it for $25,000. The next year, Alan and I were talking and I told him that story and that he'd cost himself $25,000. Alan said, 'Damn.'"

Brooks also thought about the time during the championship season when some members of the team complained about how tight Kulwicki was with a dollar.

"He put out a coffee can there at the shop and wanted the guys to pitch in money to buy the coffee," Brooks said. "Some of them were getting upset at him for things like that. I told them, 'Fellows, you're in a war if you're going to try to win the championship and I would rather go to war with the toughest general I could find. That's what you've got. I think I would suck it up and go.'"

Brooks remembered how bad things had looked after the fall race at Dover in 1992, when Kulwicki seemed hopelessly behind and out of the chase for the championship.

He thought about how many things had to fall into place to set up the drama that played out in the final race of the season. Had any one of those things not happened, there would have been no championship.

Over the next few months, as the investigation continued into the crash of the plane his company owned, Brooks also began thinking about how the same thing could be said for the tragic accident, too.

In May, the National Transportation Safety Board would say that the plane's engines were not working at the time the plane crashed, that the propellers were positioned as though Campbell had been trying to feather them to minimize drag.

It would take almost a year for the NTSB to issue a final report, which concluded that ice had been sucked into the engines during the plane's descent, causing the engines to fail, and that Campbell had failed to turn on the deicing system to guard against such an occurrence. Campbell's family would vigorously protest any implication that the former commercial airline pilot with nearly 30 years of experience was in any way responsible for what happened.

What, Brooks thought, if there had been no need for people from his sales department to go to New York and take the jet, leaving the twin turboprop Merlin for the flight to Tennessee? What if Kulwicki had signed 50 more autographs that night, or 50 fewer? Would that have been enough to prevent the Hooters plane from nearing the Tri-Cities Airport at the same time Earnhardt's plane did? If the Hooters plane had been given clearance to land first, would there have been time for the ice to form in the first place?

"A million things had to happen the right way for us to win that championship in 1992," Brooks said. "But a million things had to happen the wrong way for that accident to happen, too."

Ships That Don't Come In

With the sport still reeling from the loss of its reigning champion, the 1993 Winston Cup season resumed the week after Easter at North Wilkesboro, with Rusty Wallace scoring a second straight victory.

Wallace then made it an April short-track sweep, extending his winning streak to three the following Sunday at Martinsville.

Davey Allison, who'd won the season's first short-track race at Richmond, also ran well in April. He finished fifth at Bristol, fourth at North Wilkesboro and second at Martinsville, seemingly giving him momentum going into the first race in May, the Winston 500 at his home track in Talladega.

Bill Elliott's team, on the other hand, slogged through April still mired in a season-long funk. Elliott wrecked and finished 30th at Bristol, then after running 10th at North Wilkesboro he was 27th at Martinsville.

Eight races into the season, Elliott hadn't finished better than ninth and hadn't qualified better than 15th since the second race at Rockingham. The slump turned up the pressures that had been pulling at the team since the slide at the end of 1992 that cost Elliott the championship.

Following his heart surgery, Junior Johnson was back on the job as team owner for the Bristol race. He'd actually made it back at Darlington a week earlier, but by Bristol he once again was taking an active role in his teams' preparations. He also spent time denying garage-area scuttlebutt that he was thinking of selling his race teams.

"I've been down," Johnson said, "but we're not out."

The relationship between Johnson and Budweiser, Elliott's sponsor, began to deteriorate after some company officials suggested that Johnson try to rehire crew chief Tim Brewer, who was now working for Bill Davis' team. Johnson flatly refused, and things got worse from there. Before long, Elliott was being told privately that if he wanted to go back to Dawsonville and revive his family-owned team, Budweiser might be inclined to go along.

Elliott finished just 22nd at Talladega, where Ernie Irvan won, and was 17th the following week on the road course at Sears Point, where Geoffrey Bodine won.

Allison was seventh at Talladega and 15th at Sears Point. He had won The Winston at Charlotte in each of the previous two seasons, but ran only ninth in 1993 and followed that up with a disappointing 30th the following week in the Coca-Cola 600.

Elliott was also a non-factor in The Winston, but did get his best finish of the year so far in the 600, a sixth, despite starting 30th. Dale Earnhardt won both The Winston and the 600 and followed those up with another victory the following weekend at Dover.

During the two weekends at Charlotte, Tom Roberts and Brian VanDercook crossed paths in a parking lot as they were unloading the trunks of their cars.

VanDercook, Allison's PR man, had offered Roberts whatever help he could during the tragic weekend at Bristol after Kulwicki's crash, but they hadn't talked much since.

"He started telling me what it had been like and what he had been through," VanDercook said. "We talked about 45 minutes. He needed to talk and I wanted to hear it. I remember walking away saying to myself, 'I hope I never have to go through that.'"

Allison finished third at Dover and then sixth on a bizarre day at Pocono, where race leader and eventual winner Kyle Petty was stunned to see an inebriated fan run out onto the track during the race just past the halfway point. The fan was not injured, but he was arrested.

Despite the fact that Allison had won only once so far, he was still second in the points, 225 points behind Earnhardt, after Pocono. That all changed the next weekend at Michigan, however. Allison wrecked just 27 laps into the race that Ricky Rudd won. Allison finished 35th and dropped to sixth in the standings. Earnhardt then put him deeper into a hole by winning the July 3 race at Daytona, which marked the midway point of the 30-race schedule.

Allison, like his father, was an aviation enthusiast. He'd had his pilot's license since 1987 and the previous summer he'd also earned a license to fly helicopters. Davey was, in fact, in the process of buying his first helicopter, a Hughes 369-C, and was already training to fly it.

In between the races at Michigan and Daytona, Allison flew his plane to Indianapolis for the announcement that NASCAR would, indeed, begin holding an annual Winston Cup race at Indianapolis Motor Speedway, starting in 1994. On the flight to Indianapolis, Allison had to take evasive action to avoid a mid-air collision with another plane that had come, he said, from out of nowhere.

The second half of the 1993 season began with a new stop on the Winston Cup circuit at New Hampshire International Speedway in Loudon, N.H., just north of that state's capital city of Concord, giving NASCAR a presence in New England and its lucrative media markets.

Larry McReynolds and Allison elected to take the same car they had used for the victory at Richmond and qualified seventh with it.

After the drivers were introduced to the crowd in the prerace ceremonies, they took rides in pairs around the track in the beds of pickup trucks to wave to the crowd. Allison shared a truck bed with Irvan, one of the drivers with whom Allison had been involved in the wreck at Michigan.

Although McReynolds didn't know it at the time, a photograph he would get of that pickup truck ride would soon take on special significance.

"We had got down in a hole again, but it looked like we were starting to dig back out after Loudon," McReynolds said. "We led the race all day long, and it was best on long green-flag runs. We knew if we could get a long green run at the end, we could win."

But with about 30 laps to go, the wheel-bearing cover came off of Michael Waltrip's car and began bouncing around on the backstretch.

About the time NASCAR put out the yellow flag, another car hit it and knocked it off the racing surface.

"It was too late," McReynolds said. "We had to come in under yellow to get tires like everybody else did, but I knew right then we were dead in the water because it took about 20 laps for our car to get going. Rusty [Wallace] and Mark [Martin] ended up beating us and we finished third."

Still, the good run had buoyed the team. Allison's chief pilot, Sam Manze, had flown Davey and Bobby up from their Alabama home to Charlotte to pick up team members for the trip to New Hampshire. After the race Eli Gold, a radio announcer who also lived in Alabama, caught a ride home with Manze, the Allisons and the team.

The mood on the plane on the night of July 11, 1993, was decidedly upbeat.

Allison's car had been good enough to win at Loudon. He was fifth in the points race but the team still felt it had every chance to get things going for a run at that year's title.

Usually, Davey sat up front in the cockpit with Manze, but on this flight he decided to sit with the team and let his father ride in the cockpit. The plane landed in Charlotte, dropped off the passengers there, and continued back to Alabama.

The next day, Allison and long-time Alabama short-track star Red Farmer took Allison's new helicopter, which he had picked up and flown a few times, to Birmingham to eat lunch.

At about 2:30 in Birmingham, in the Central Time Zone, Allison and Farmer decided to fly about 50 miles east to Talladega Superspeedway where David Bonnett, Neil's son, was testing a Busch Grand National car. The trip would take about a half-hour.

At about 4 p.m. in Charlotte, in the Eastern Time Zone, McReynolds and crew member Raymond Fox were at the Robert Yates Racing shop working on the final setup for the car that had been picked for Allison to race that weekend at Pocono.

VanDercook had gathered equipment to go visit his son at Boy Scout camp, planning to spend at least part of the week there before going to Pocono. He was driving south on Interstate 85.

Allison and Farmer reached the Talladega track, which at 2.66 miles is the largest oval in NASCAR and has a vast infield. Allison piloted the helicopter toward a 108-foot wide parking lot near the garage area, a paved lot surrounded by a 12-foot high chain link fence with electrical lines not far away.

He brought the helicopter to within just a few feet of the asphalt.

Farmer was sitting in the passenger seat to Allison's right. Suddenly, the world turned upside down.

"I could see the ground, then I could see the sun," Farmer would say later.

The helicopter had suddenly shot upward off the ground and began spinning wildly. It clipped the fence, tearing off the tail section, then crashed onto its right side.

Farmer, anticipating the impact, instinctively braced himself for the blow. Allison, frantically trying to gain control of his machine, had no time to brace.

The engine was still running when the helicopter came to rest on Farmer's side. Farmer unhooked his belts, pushed broken glass from the windshield and began to climb out. Neil Bonnett had raced over and arrived in time to help pull Farmer free.

Allison, unconscious, was still strapped into his seat. Someone managed to kill the engines and the track's nurse climbed inside the cockpit to work on him.

Back in Charlotte, McReynolds heard Robert Yates being paged to the telephone. NASCAR president Bill France Jr. was calling. A few minutes later, Yates walked back into the shop looking pale. McReynolds knew instantly something was terribly wrong.

"I just got a call from Bill France and he wanted to know if I was on top of Davey's situation," Yates said.

Yates hadn't understood the question at first, thinking that perhaps Allison had said something controversial the team owner hadn't yet heard about and France wanted know what Yates was going to do about it. France told Yates that his driver had crashed his helicopter on a parking lot in the infield at Talladega and appeared to be badly injured.

VanDercook's car phone rang. It was Libby Gant, the race team's secretary.

"Brian," Gant said, "I think you need to come over here."

Wayne Estes had flown home to Georgia on a Monday commercial flight from New Hampshire. As he pulled into the garage at his house his wife, Rita, came down the stairs.

"Davey's been in a helicopter crash," she said.

"How bad is it?" Estes asked.

Rita didn't know, but it was bad.

Allison had a broken pelvis and a lung injury, but a head injury was the gravest concern. Farmer had a broken collarbone, a broken nose and a broken rib and was transported to Carraway Methodist Medical Center in Birmingham by helicopter, arriving about five minutes before a separate helicopter carrying Allison.

Friends, including Bonnett, quickly joined Allison's parents and his wife, Liz, at the hospital and began praying for a miracle.

Yates, McReynolds, VanDercook and other members of the team quickly arranged to fly in from Charlotte on a plane supplied by Felix Sabates.

"We landed and somebody who was there to pick us up told us Davey was dead," VanDercook said. That was not true. Allison was still alive, but his doctors were offering little encouragement. They had performed 45 minutes of surgery to relieve pressure from the severe bruise to his brain, but Davey's condition was still extremely grave.

McReynolds got to the hospital and someone asked if he wanted to go see his driver. McReynolds said no. He'd already been in to see Farmer, who was in critical but stable condition and was conscious. Farmer had told McReynolds what had happened.

"As much as I wanted to go back there and see him and squeeze his hand and tell him that I loved him, I guess I wanted to remember him like he was on that airplane coming home from Loudon, positive and upbeat," McReynolds said.

Allison was on the fifth floor in a neurological intensive-care unit. The hospital lobby was overrun with family and friends and media there to stand vigil, hoping there would be word that somehow Davey was going to make it.

Liz and Judy Allison stayed upstairs for hours, hoping their presence might in some way help keep a husband and a son hanging on. Around midnight, one fluttering eyelid gave them a moment of hope.

But there would be no miracle.

At 7 a.m. local time on Tuesday, Dr. Evan Zieger pronounced David Carl Allison dead of massive head injuries. He was 32 years old.

"Brandon, our son, Davey and Liz were his godparents," said McReynolds, who had lost more than a superstar driver. "We had Robby [Allison's son] and Brandon baptized together at the

Speedway Club at Charlotte Motor Speedway. Davey and Liz would stay at our house when we raced at Charlotte. In 1991, when Linda was in the hospital having Brandon, Liz came to the house and helped watched our daughter."

Allison's death was announced to the media at 7:30. Red Farmer was watching the television in his room when he heard the news.

Kulwicki's death just two and a half months earlier had shaken racing badly. Allison's death rocked it to the very core.

The sport had come to respect Kulwicki for all that he had achieved and for the way he had achieved it. But Davey Allison had grown up in the garage area. He was more than just an outstanding driver just beginning to display the full measure of his talents. He was a part of racing, a member of its most star-crossed family.

Now, just 11 months after his brother, Clifford, had been killed at Michigan, Davey was gone, too.

The racing community's reaction was overwhelming.

Fans flocked to the Yates team's shop in Charlotte, leaving flowers, cards, photos, poems and every other imaginable kind of memorial to Allison, whose final statistics would show 19 Winston Cup victories.

People drove from all over the eastern United States to the shop or to Hueytown, Ala., Davey's hometown. Radio stations in Birmingham and Charlotte and other cities where NASCAR was followed closely asked listeners to turn on their headlights to remember Allison, and thousands did.

Yates and McReynolds flew home on Wednesday and met with the rest of the team, putting off for the time a decision about when the No. 28 car would race again.

They returned to Alabama on a special flight provided by USAir, the airline with a hub at Charlotte's airport, so the team and others in the racing community could attend the funeral. The flight crew volunteered for the trip designated Flight 28 in honor of Allison's car number.

For those who couldn't make the trip, a memorial service was scheduled for 12:15 p.m. on Thursday at St. Thomas Aquinas, the same church where Kulwicki's Charlotte memorial had been held.

Cars parked up to two miles away from St. Aloysius Church in Bessemer, Ala., for the wake on Wednesday evening. A shuttle service was set up between the nearby Bessemer Civic Center and that parking lot also was full.

Junior Johnson was there. So were Mario Andretti and Bill Elliott and Jeff Gordon and Bobby and Terry Labonte and dozens of other drivers, officials and others from the world of motorsports.

The church's 600 seats were filled for the Thursday morning funeral, with hundreds more listening through speakers on the lawn outside.

Father Louis Giardino called Davey Allison the "luckiest fellow who ever walked" because he had family, friends and the career he had always wanted, and said the tragedy of Allison's death should not overshadow the glory of his life.

McReynolds spoke, too, repeating the phrase Allison often repeated and that McReynolds still keeps taped to his desk: "There's nothing that can come along that God and I can't handle together."

Along the three-mile ride from the church to Highland Memorial Gardens, fans had parked their cars and trucks and turned on their headlights in tribute. They stood and watched solemnly as the procession rolled by. Some had signs, others put their hands or caps over their hearts.

There were hundreds of floral arrangements at the gravesite. A Hueytown florist had been forced to stop taking orders on Wednesday because so many had come in.

Country music artist Joe Diffie, who had been among those performing at the going-away party for Richard Petty at the Georgia Dome the previous November, came to the graveside to sing one of his songs that Allison really liked, a song called "Ships That Don't Come In"

Allison was buried in the shade of an oak tree, less than 200 yards from where Clifford had been buried in 1992. Like Clifford, Davey was buried wearing his driver's uniform.

"Let me tell you the real irony of life," Bobby Allison said many years later. "Davey worked, worked, worked all of his life, from the time he was a little bitty guy. He was so focused on what he wanted to do and what he wanted for a career and worked and worked and worked.

"Clifford played, played, played. You could not get him to be serious. He was a good young boy and was talented at mechanical things, good at sports and swimming and all that kind of stuff. But he would not devote himself to anything.

"Clifford played, played, played and got killed working.

"Davey worked, worked, worked and got killed playing.

"That's the irony of my life."

189

The Road Goes On

The circumstances surrounding their deaths will forever link Alan Kulwicki and Davey Allison in the minds of race fans.

With the following season barely halfway completed, two of the three men who had raced so closely for the 1992 championship had been killed in separate aviation accidents. Two of the sport's most interesting stories were gone, too—Kulwicki, the against-all-odds champion and Allison, the budding superstar and torchbearer for a family dynasty.

Allison left behind a wife and two children along with parents who lost two sons within a year. Kulwicki also left a father who'd had to bury two sons.

Kulwicki and Allison also left behind Winston Cup teams that before their tears dried were expressing their determination to keep racing.

Even without the man who at times had kept the team going by the sheer force of his own will, Alan Kulwicki Racing decided to compete at North Wilkesboro on April 18, the next race after Bristol on the 1993 schedule.

Gerald Kulwicki was technically now the team owner, but Felix Sabates had been brought in to negotiate the sale of the team. Cal Lawson and Don Hawk tried to keep the business running while Paul Andrews worked on getting his crew through the shock of losing its leader.

On April 12, however, Bob Brooks announced that Hooters would not continue its sponsorship. Brooks said he disagreed with the decision to continue racing with a temporary driver while the team searched for a new owner.

"The relationship between Hooters and Alan Kulwicki was unique," Brooks said in a statement about his decision to pull out. "I started with Alan on a handshake basis, and we developed a special bond. It is unrealistic to think that such a relationship could be formed with a new owner and driver in so short of a time. While we understand the desire of Kulwicki Racing to continue to run races to preserve the value of the team as they search for a new owner, we do not feel that Hooters should be a part of this effort."

Sabates said there was another reason, saying Brooks had tried to get the team to put Loy Allen Jr., a driver Hooters was sponsoring in the Automobile Racing Club of America series, in the No. 7 Winston Cup car.

The team had other plans. Earlier that year, Kulwicki had said he liked the way that Jimmy Hensley, the rookie of the year the previous season, took care of his cars.

Hensley was without a ride after his 1992 car owner, Cale Yarborough, replaced him with Derrike Cope. Cope brought a sponsor, which Yarborough needed, leaving Hensley out of work. Kulwicki had even said that if he got sick or injured and couldn't race, he would try to get Hensley to take over for him.

That was all the endorsement the team needed.

Sabates also thought Hensley was the best driver available. As for Loy Allen Jr., all Sabates had to say was, "Loy who?"

On the same day that Hooters pulled its sponsorship, Hensley tested the No. 7 Ford at Talladega. He agreed to drive at North Wilkesboro, Martinsville and Talladega, the next three races, but Andrews said it would suit him fine for Hensley to remain in the car for the rest of the year.

That would depend on what happened with the sale that Sabates was negotiating. Sabates said he had 19 offers for the team, 11 of which he considered "serious."

On qualifying Friday at North Wilkesboro, Hensley was the story of the day.

He told reporters he had no idea that Kulwicki had noticed his ability,

191

saying he'd never really talked to the driver because Kulwicki always looked so busy in the garage.

Sabates and Hawk had worked out a deal with Bojangles', a Southeastern chain of fried chicken restaurants, to replace some of the sponsorship money lost by the Hooters defection. The car that Hensley qualified 13th fastest at North Wilkesboro carried the logos of a pair of charities.

Hensley's performance over that three-race span indicates just how strong the team really was. Hensley had been a rookie one year earlier and didn't have a ride when he stepped into Kulwicki's shoes. The crew was learning how to work with a stranger with the memory of the man they had gone to war with still fresh in their minds. Yet Hensley finished 12th at North Wilkesboro, qualified seventh and finished 13th at Martinsville and finished ninth at Talladega despite starting 29th.

As the team's sale was being discussed, Lawson felt the weight of the world on his shoulders. People asked him how he could have allowed Kulwicki not to have a will or life insurance, as though Lawson could have talked Kulwicki into either had it not been Kulwicki's idea in the first place.

All of Kulwicki's assets were frozen for 60 days after his death. While Lawson knew Gerald Kulwicki would reimburse him when the accounts were unfrozen, until then the money for the day-to-day bills was coming out of Lawson's pocket.

"Some of the people on the team came to me complaining about their per diem," Lawson remembers. "Other teams were paying their road guys $25 a day for food and Alan was still paying $20. I was keeping things just the way Alan had done them and they started talking about how things should be different. And it was all coming out of old Cal's wallet."

Brett Bodine, Ricky Rudd and Ken Schrader expressed interest in buying the team, as did Washington Redskins quarterback Mark Rypien, a longtime friend of driver Chad Little. By late April, however, two offers had come to the top of the list.

On April 24, professional golfer Payne Stewart visited the shop, spending several hours looking at the facility and equipment.

The irony of Stewart's interest would not be fully apparent until October 1999, when Stewart died when a private jet he was flying in lost oxygen in the cabin and eventually crashed after flying on autopilot for several hours. At the time of Stewart's death he, just as Kulwicki had been, was the reigning national champion of his sport, having won the U.S. Open Golf Championship earlier that year in Pinehurst, N.C.

Stewart, however, did not buy Kulwicki's team. After Talladega, NASCAR took Mother's Day off on May 9. Hensley had little road-racing experience, so the team had arranged to have road-racing specialist Tommy Kendall drive the No. 7 the following weekend at Sears Point in California. By the day of that race, Kulwicki's team members knew that Geoffrey Bodine would be the new owner.

Bodine and Sabates finalized a deal and announced it May 11 at a news conference at the team's shop. Bodine and his wife, Kathy, would purchase the team. The transaction would officially take effect at the end of the 1993 season, allowing Bodine to fulfill his contract with Bud Moore and allowing the No. 7 team to maintain its place on the NASCAR contingency programs that Kulwicki's success in 1992 had earned.

Bodine celebrated that weekend by winning at Sears Point in Moore's No. 15 Ford.

Two months later, Robert Yates Racing faced the same difficult decisions. While ownership was not an issue in that case, Yates' team now had a gaping hole in its center, too, as Allison had left difficult shoes for any driver to fill.

When USAir Flight 28 returned to Charlotte after Allison's funeral on July 15, the team members went to Yates' house, the way any family would go to a relative's home following a funeral.

They'd already decided not to race at Pocono that Sunday, a decision McReynolds knew would have angered Allison. But it would be hard enough to go back to the track the following week—when the race would be held at Talladega, the track that had helped define Allison's career and the place where his helicopter had crashed.

Robby Gordon, no relation to Jeff Gordon but a brash young driver with a background in road- and open-wheel racing, stepped in for team's first race back.

"That was probably a pretty good choice," McReynolds said. "It needed to be somebody who wouldn't feel the pressure of driving the 28 car at Davey's home track, right in his backyard. Robby didn't because he wasn't Winston Cup-oriented. He knew the elements but he didn't feel the pressure."

Lake Speed followed Gordon, and while McReynolds was pleased with the job Speed did he, along with everyone else, knew that Speed wasn't the long-term solution for the No. 28 Fords.

Yates was already talking to the driver he wanted to hire—Ernie Irvan, the same driver whose spin in front of Allison at Atlanta had wrecked the team's car and its 1992 championship hopes.

Irvan, however, was signed to drive the No. 4 Chevrolets for Morgan/McClure Racing through 1994, and car owner Larry McClure was not happy his driver wanted to walk away. Irvan, 34, had won seven races in the No. 4 car, including the 1991 Daytona 500, and McClure knew losing a driver at midseason would be a huge setback for his team.

McClure also knew, however, that a team with a driver who doesn't want to be there isn't likely to perform well. He began negotiating a release for Irvan, but made it clear to the driver and anybody else involved that he wasn't going to lose his driver for nothing.

McClure and Irvan spent parts of August not speaking to each other, but lawyers broke the impasse and negotiated a contract buyout reported at $500,000.

On Sept. 2 in Darlington, Irvan confirmed that he would drive the No. 28 Ford in that weekend's Southern 500. Jeff Purvis, who had been driving in the ARCA series, would take Irvan's place at Morgan/McClure.

With Speed now out of the Yates-owned cars, Ford engineered a switch that allowed Bodine to leave Moore's Fords early and to drive the No. 7 Thunderbird in the season's final seven races, beginning at Dover on Sept. 19. Speed would move into Moore's cars in preparation to run there full-time in 1994.

As the '93 season continued, there were some poignant moments.

At Pocono on the Sunday after Allison's death, Kyle Petty and Rusty Wallace had both stashed flags bearing Allison's No. 28 into their cars. After Earnhardt edged Wallace for the victory, Wallace joined Earnhardt on the victory lap holding the Allison flag out his window in tribute. Petty gave his flag, a larger one than Wallace had, to Earnhardt's crew. Earnhardt stopped at the start-finish line, took the flag, paused while his crew knelt to pray, and then carried the larger flag around once more, this time running in the reverse direction in tribute to Kulwicki.

On Aug. 1 at Michigan Speedway, Terry Labonte filled in for Allison in the final event of the 1993 International Race of Champions series, which Allison had led after three races. Labonte finished sixth in the final leg, earning enough points to allow Allison to edge Al Unser Jr. for the IROC title. The $175,000 first prize that was donated to a trust fund for Allison's daughter, Krista, and son, Robby.

Earnhardt finished fifth in the race and fifth in the series as a substitute for Kulwicki to earn $50,000, which was donated to three of Kulwicki's favorite charities.

After Irvan and Bodine moved to their respective new rides in September, they earned the front-row starting spots at Martinsville on the final weekend of that month—Irvan on the pole in the No. 28 with Bodine alongside in the No. 7.

On the Wednesday after Allison's death, Brian VanDercook had walked out of a team meeting at the shop in Charlotte to say that whenever the team returned to action, it would have in mind the goal that Allison had set for them. "Win the pole, lead the most laps and win the race, every week," VanDercook said.

At Martinsville on Sept. 26, Irvan did just that.

"I can still see the picture in my mind," McReynolds said. "The 28 coming down pit road with the window net down and Ernie waving his hand. It was like there was nobody else there, just that car coming down pit road. And Bobby Allison walked out there to give Ernie the 'thumbs up.'

"It was hot that day, it must have been 100 degrees." Irvan was among several drivers who struggled to finish the 500-lap race in the heat. "I remember Ernie undoing that uniform and tying it around his waist. His T-shirt said, 'In memory of Davey Allison.' I knew we had the right guy."

The No. 7 Ford that Bodine drove in that race was the same No. 8 chassis that Kulwicki drove in the 1992 Hooters 500. Bodine wrecked it, damaging the car badly enough that the team decided to retire it from competition.

Later that year the chassis was purchased from the team by a couple from Florida, who spent years lovingly restoring the "Underbird," to the condition in which it had raced in that 1992 season finale. With the help of team members, they got the original engine block, cylinder heads and other equipment from that race. The car still had the glove box inside the driver's door, and when the seat was being patched they found a St. Christopher medal that Kulwicki carried in his cars as a good luck charm in the seat's frame. They left it there.

Irvan won again two weeks later at Charlotte, giving Irvan the only two victories in the season's final 16 races not scored by the three drivers who would wind up atop the seasons points standings.

Earnhardt's win in July at Pocono and the following week at Talladega gave him six for the season. Despite consecutive wins by Martin at Watkins Glen, Michigan, Bristol and Darlington, Earnhardt went into the final eight races with a 304-point lead on Wallace and a 307-point edge on Wallace.

Wallace would make it interesting, winning five of those final eight races. Martin won again, too, at Phoenix, but Earnhardt's consistency kept him in command. He led by 126 points going into Atlanta, needing only to finish 34th or better to win the title.

Wallace won that race, but Earnhardt finished 10th and won his sixth championship by 80 points over Wallace, with Martin third, Dale Jarrett fourth and Petty fifth. Irvan, whose driver points total included his races in both the No. 4 and the No. 28 cars, was sixth.

At the end of the season's final day, Earnhardt and Wallace once again rode around the track in a clockwise direction, with Earnhardt holding a flag carrying Kulwicki's No. 7 and Wallace flying Allison's No. 28.

Elliott was eighth in the final standings, but for the first time since 1982 he did not win a race. He came close at Richmond, finishing three car-lengths behind Wallace, and closed with a late surge—third at Rockingham, fifth at Phoenix after winning his second pole of the year and fourth in defense of his 1992 Hooters 500 victory at Atlanta.

Tragedy rocked the sport again in February of 1994. Neil Bonnett, who had raced twice the previous year in a comeback attempt many of his friends tried desperately to talk him out of, died in a crash during a Daytona 500 practice session.

Larry McClure's new driver, Sterling Marlin, won the '94 Daytona 500. Irvan picked up where he'd left off late in 1993, taking the No. 28 Ford to victory lane at Richmond, Atlanta and Sears Point. He was in the thick of the championship race when, at Michigan in August, he crashed almost head-on into the wall at more than 180 mph.

The team must have felt like it was reliving a horrible nightmare when doctors gave Irvan, who'd suffered a serious head injury, only a

10 percent chance to survive his injuries. Irvan beat those odds, however, and although he wouldn't race again until late the following season, he survived.

Elliott and Johnson stayed together for 1994 with Budweiser remaining as sponsor. Jimmy Spencer replaced Hut Stricklin in the McDonald's car and won at Daytona and at Talladega in July. But Spencer also failed to finish 11 times and came in 29th in points.

Elliott finally broke his victory drought on Labor Day weekend with a win in the Southern 500 at Darlington, giving him his 40th career victory. But he finished 10th in points, two spots worse than in 1993, as Earnhardt won yet another title to tie Richard Petty's career record of seven.

The back-to-back titles for Earnhardt, repeating his double from 1990 and 1991, provide only a façade of constancy for the sport during 1993 and 1994, however. The reality is that the sport's pace of change was increasing as rapidly as its popularity, and that the remarkable race that concluded the 1992 season was truly a crossroads in the history of stock-car racing.

On some levels, that point is obvious. The fact that Richard Petty's final race as a driver came on the same day Jeff Gordon made his Winston Cup debut is a remarkable coincidence.

During the broadcast of the Hooters 500, ESPN's Bob Jenkins had drawn a parallel using Gordon to illustrate just how long Petty had been part of the sport. Petty's final start was No. 1,185 of his career. At a rate of 29 or 30 races per season, Jenkins said, Gordon would make his 1,185th career start at the age of 61.

Gordon finished second twice on his way to the 1993 rookie of the year award and won his first pole at Charlotte in October. The next year, he got his first Winston Cup victory in the Coca-Cola 600. He also won the inaugural Brickyard 400 at Indianapolis and the next year won the championship.

He won the points title again in 1997 and won the Winston Million, too, joining Elliott as the only drivers to ever win that bonus. The next year, he won a third championship and 13 races, tying Petty's modern-era record for wins in a season.

Gordon's team began a major transition in September of 1999 when Ray Evernham, his crew chief and the man given credit as the architect of the No. 24 team's dynasty at Hendrick Motorsports, left to lead

Dodge's return to Winston Cup racing after an absence of nearly two decades.

Robbie Loomis, who had been Petty's crew chief in 1992, left Petty Enterprises and took over as Gordon's crew chief to start the 2000 season. Gordon won three times that year but finished ninth in the points race, his lowest finish since his rookie season. In 2001, however, Gordon and Loomis returned their team to the top of the sport, winning six races and adding a fourth championship to Gordon's résumé. Only Petty and Earnhardt, with seven each, have more.

Gordon came into the 2002 season with 58 victories in 293 career starts. He won a record $10,879,757 in 2001 to move into first ahead of Earnhardt on the career money list with $45,748,580—an average payday of $156,138 per race. By comparison, Petty ended his career with earnings of $7,755,409—an average of $6,544 a start.

Would Gordon have won all of those races if Allison and Kulwicki had still been alive, or did their demise open a door of opportunity through which Gordon and his team stepped? For the next decade, fans also couldn't help but wonder how fierce a Gordon-Allison rivalry might have become.

As improbable as Kulwicki's championship was in 1992, from the moment that season was over it was every bit as unlikely that such an underdog operation ever could win the title again. The financial deck was already stacked against Kulwicki's team and the gulf between the haves and have-nots widened rapidly as the decade wore on.

Would Kulwicki have clung tenaciously to his desire to do things his way? The difficulties of the driver-owner role would eventually wear down Darrell Waltrip, Elliott, Ricky Rudd, Bodine and others. Could Kulwicki have endured those challenges, or would he have seen the landscape changing and found a way to meld his philosophy into one of the sport's well-funded multicar operations?

Elliott spent six years as a driver-owner and finished as high as second in only one race. He finally won for the first time since the 1994 Southern 500 at Homestead-Miami Speedway in November of 2001, driving a Dodge owned by Ray Evernham.

The 1992 season also marked the effective end of Junior Johnson's racing dynasty.

After the dismal season in 1993, Johnson's cars won three races in 1994—including the Elliott victory at Darlington. But his sponsorship contracts with Budweiser and McDonald's ran out after that year. Budweiser left outright and McDonald's offered Johnson only an incentive-laden package with payments contingent on the team's performance in 1995. Johnson wanted no part of a deal like that, and McDonald's went with Elliott, who became a driver/owner for 1995.

Johnson sold what was left of the McDonald's-backed team to Bob Brooks, the Hooters restaurants CEO, and got Lowe's, a chain of home improvement stores based near his home in Wilkes County, N.C., to sponsor Brett Bodine for 1995. Midway through the season, Bodine asked Johnson if he would sell him the team. Johnson said yes and walked away from the sport. He says he doesn't miss it nearly as much as most people figure he would.

After Irvan's crash at Michigan in August of 1994, Kenny Wallace finished the season in the No. 28 car. Dale Jarrett, who'd won only once in the Joe Gibbs-owned car since the '93 Daytona 500, jumped to Yates' team for 1995. That opened the seat in the No. 18 Gibbs car for Bobby Labonte, who wasn't unhappy driving for Bill Davis but was looking for security since Davis' sponsor—Maxwell House—was leaving after '94.

If Allison had still been in the No. 28 car, Irvan would not have been in it that August day at Michigan in 1994. Had Irvan not been hurt, where might Dale Jarrett be today? Or Bobby Labonte?

Jarrett finally brought Robert Yates Racing the championship that team missed out on in 1992, holding off Labonte to win the 1999 title. Labonte came back to win the 2000 title in a season in which his Joe Gibbs racing teammate, Tony Stewart, led the circuit with six victories. Ironically, the first Winston Cup race that Stewart saw in person was the 1992 Hooters 500 at Atlanta Motor Speedway, back when Stewart was a 21-year-old sprint-car racer from Indiana. He stood near Richard Petty's team on pit road that afternoon.

How different would NASCAR's top series have been at the end of the 20th century had Kulwicki and Allison not died so tragically?

As different, perhaps, as the sport would have been without the equally tragic deaths in 1964 of Joe Weatherly and Glenn "Fireball" Roberts. Or as different as the future might have been had Adam Petty, Richard's grandson and Kyle's son, and Kenny Irwin, who also had a turn as driver of the No. 28 Ford, not been killed in crashes at New Hampshire two months apart in 2000.

No one knows those answers, of course.

If any lesson is to be learned from the events of the 1992 season and the months that followed the climactic race at Atlanta, perhaps it is that life is not lived in a straight line. It comes, instead, in a series of circles that change constantly as they ripple across the circles made by the lives of those around us.

Earnhardt's death in a crash on the final lap of the Daytona 500 on Feb. 18, 2001, will ripple through the sport in years to come. That tragedy left fans looking for some of the same kinds of answers they searched for when Kulwicki and Allison were taken. A decade has passed since the 1992 Hooters 500 and the full impact of the events set in motion that day are just now coming into clear focus. It may take even longer to develop a full appreciation for the impact of Earnhardt's death.

But as much as racing changed between its earliest days and the end of the 1992 season, and as much as it has changed from then until now, one basic premise remains.

Running a race is all about going as hard as you can from start to finish and doing what you can to be the best along the way. While the starting line and the finish line are ultimately the same place, the honor and the glory comes in going the distance and giving it all you have.

So, too, is living a life.

Notes and Acknowledgments

Many people who were there for the 1992 Hooters 500 are still involved in racing and have vivid memories of the events chronicled in this book. I owe a great debt to all of those who took time to share some of their memories. I was not covering NASCAR in 1992 and didn't have the chance to know Alan Kulwicki or Davey Allison. After hearing what these people have said about those two fallen heroes, I wish I had.

- Larry McReynolds stayed at Robert Yates Racing as crew chief on the No. 28 car until 1996, going back to victory lane with Ernie Irvan twice that season after Irvan's return from his injuries in the crash at Michigan. McReynolds went to Richard Childress Racing in 1997 and, the following year, was crew chief when Dale Earnhardt finally got the Daytona 500 victory that had eluded him for so long. McReynolds switched to Mike Skinner's team later that year, then left the pit box at the end of the 2000 season to begin a career as a television analyst with Fox Sports.

- Irvan stayed with the Yates team through 1997, then retired during the 1999 season after being injured again in another crash at Michigan the previous year.

- Richard Petty and Kyle Petty continue to guide Petty Enterprises, with Kyle driving one of the team's three Dodges.

- Bill Davis owns a two-car Dodge operation.

- Cal Lawson is team manager in the NASCAR Craftsman Truck series.

- Paul Andrews is crew chief for one of three Winston Cup teams owned by Dale Earnhardt Inc.

- Ty Norris is director of motorsports for Dale Earnhardt Inc.

- Wayne Estes is director of communications at Bristol Motor Speedway.

- Brian VanDercook and Chip Williams have their own public relations companies and both are still active in NASCAR.

- Richard Sowers is the author of two books about NASCAR and a third about horse racing.

- Michael Kranefuss sold his interest in his Winston Cup team in 2000, but is still involved with the sport through his son's developing career.

- Len Thacher provides a valuable media service by preparing a weekly statistical update book distributed at each race.

- Bob Brooks is still chief executive officer for Hooters and sponsors a stock-car racing series, the USAR Hooters ProCup. The circuit's final race of the season is named in Alan Kulwicki's memory.

- Benny Parsons is a NASCAR analyst for NBC and Turner Sports telecasts. He, Ned Jarrett and Bob Jenkins were enthusiastic when told about this project and graciously offered their recollections.

- Jenny Nickell and Ken Martin are still with Lingner Productions in Indianapolis. They spent an entire afternoon explaining their role in the broadcasts of the Hooters 500 and the 1992 banquet in New York, and set me up to review a videotape of the banquet broadcast.

The information in the book is based on interviews with dozens of people who attended the 1992 Hooters 500 or who were involved in or connected to the subsequent events.

Accounts of these events written by the staffs of *The Charlotte Observer, The Atlanta Journal-Constitution, The Birmingham News, The Knoxville Sentinel,* and *The Bristol Herald-Courier* and from wire service reports and other publications were also used in researching this book. I would especially like to thank the staffs of NASCAR Winston Cup Scene and National Speed Sport News for allowing me access to their archives.

The majority of the quotations are based on the recollections of those interviewed, while others come from notes compiled by manufacturers' representatives and the staff of the Atlanta track, from broadcast coverage of these events and from the publications mentioned above. Whenever two recollections of the same story or quotation were markedly different, and these differences could not be reconciled, those accounts were either not used or both versions were included.

This book began as an idea for a story in *The Charlotte Observer* published on the weekend of the season-ending race at Atlanta Motor

Speedway in November of 1999. After just a couple of days of working on that story, it was immediately apparent there was more to it than could be included in a newspaper feature.

It never would have become a book, however, without the interest shown by Lonnie Herman of Albion Press, and by the editor he assigned to this project, Pete Williams. Pete's guidance through the early stages of organizing the information was invaluable, as were his suggestions about the direction and structure of the work.

This book also never could have happened without the support and help I received from my editors and colleagues at *The Charlotte Observer,* a newspaper that takes its coverage of stock-car racing seriously. Mike Persinger, my supervising editor at *The Observer,* and Jim Utter, who shares racing coverage duties with me for the newspaper and its companion Internet site, www.thatsracin.com, were especially supportive and encouraging during this project.

Mike Tate, a friend and a true NASCAR fan from my hometown of Gastonia, N.C., had held on to his videotape of the broadcast of the 1992 Hooters 500 and provided me with a copy. That tape is now well worn. Mike also was a sounding board as I progressed through the book, as were dozens of others among my family, friends and colleagues, who listened patiently to my endless chatter about the book for the year it took to write it.

I am also indebted to Monte Dutton, the outstanding racing writer for the newspaper in my hometown. Monte helped me through some of the early intricacies of turning an idea into a book, and he did it with skill and his usual good humor.

Jim Hunter, the president of Darlington Raceway and one of the most colorful and interesting men in the sport, came to my rescue at a particularly critical point in the writing process. Hunter allowed me to use his beach house to get away from the telephone and fax machine during a rare open weekend in the Winston Cup schedule in October 2000, allowing me to complete a large portion of this project.

Finally, and most importantly, I must thank my wife and the love of my life, Karen, for her patience and support during the time it took to write this book. A moral of the story told here is that the time we have in this world is precious and that we have no business squandering it. Karen understood how important it was for me to tell this story, even if it meant sacrificing some of the time we have together. There's no way I can ever repay that gift or find sufficient words to tell her how much her love and support mean to me every day of my life.

David Poole
December 2001

Appendices

The 1992 Season Events Summary

A summary of the 28 Winston Cup events leading up to the 1992 Hooters 500 at Atlanta Motor Speedway:

Daytona 500

Davey Allison avoids a crash just ahead of him on Lap 92 and goes on to lead the final 98 green-flag laps to open the season with a victory in the Winston Cup circuit's biggest race.

Bill Elliott and Richard Petty, in the first start of his final season as a driver, are among those whose cars are damaged in the big wreck, which Allison avoids with a turn to the outside.

Also knocked out or damaged in the wreck are Dale Jarrett, Chad Little, Ken Schrader, Sterling Marlin—who started from the pole—Dale Earnhardt, Mark Martin, Darrell Waltrip, Elliott, Hut Stricklin and Richard Petty.

Allison, who leads 127 laps in all, becomes just the second second-generation driver to win the Daytona 500. His father, Bobby, won it three times, including in 1988 when Davey finished second. Lee and Richard Petty were the first father-son combination to win the race.

Allison's victory comes in a backup Ford after he wrecked his primary car in practice on Wednesday. He earns $244,040 for his 14th career win.

Goodwrench 500

At Rockingham, N.C., Bill Elliott leads the final 213 laps in a dominating victory, going to victory lane in just his second start in the Junior Johnson-owned Ford. Elliott had started second alongside Kyle Petty, whose usual strength at North Carolina Motor Speedway did not materialize this time around.

Allison and Harry Gant finish behind Elliott and are the only other cars on the lead lap at the checkered flag. Allison's finish leaves him 56 points ahead of Morgan Shepherd for the early-season points lead. Elliott is seventh in points, 88 points back. Alan Kulwicki finishes 31st.

Pontiac 400

At Richmond, Bill Elliott edges Alan Kulwicki by 18 inches to earn the second-largest winner's purse in Winston Cup history: a $272,000 payday swelled by a $190,760 bonus for winning from the pole.

Elliott and Kulwicki touch at least twice over the final 10 laps as they race for the victory. Harry Gant is third with Davey Allison fourth, allowing Allison to take a 63-point lead over Gant. Elliott moves up to third, 68 back.

Kulwicki finishes second for the ninth time in his career.

Motorcraft 500

At Atlanta, Bill Elliott gets a little bit of luck to help him make it three straight wins. He stays out longer than the leaders and gets a huge break when Mike Wallace spins to bring out a yellow flag on Lap 284. Because Davey Allison, Harry Gant, Alan Kulwicki and Dick Trickle had already made green-flag stops, Elliott winds up leading them by almost a full lap.

He wins by 22.6 seconds over Gant, with Dale Earnhardt third and Allison fourth.

Transouth 500

At Darlington, S.C., Elliott ties Harry Gant, Dale Earnhardt, Darrell Waltrip and Cale Yarborough for the modern-era record with his fourth straight victory.

A conservative approach proves pivotal for Elliott, who takes the lead when Gant has to make an extra pit stop for fresh tires late in the race. Elliott takes the lead at that point and holds on, with Gant finishing second for the second straight race.

Mark Martin gets third and is the only other car on the lead lap.

Allison leads 160 laps but winds up fourth when his Ford tightens up when clouds cover the sun and cool the track. Kulwicki is running second with nine laps to go but blows an engine.

Elliott pulls into second in the points, 48 behind Allison.

Food City 500

Alan Kulwicki ends Bill Elliott's winning streak but extends Ford's string of victories to 10 straight races with the win at Bristol, Tenn.

The victory, the fourth of Kulwicki's career, is his second straight at Bristol and puts him in NASCAR's Winner's Circle plan, making him eligible for money for appearing in the season's final 23 races.

Kulwicki passes Dale Jarrett on Lap 474 of 500 to take the lead after twice deciding to stay out on used tires to gain track position while others came in for new tires.

Jarrett and Ken Schrader are the only other cars on the lead lap behind the winner.

Davey Allison, racing four days after the death of his grandfather, is penalized a lap for pitting outside his stall on Lap 270, and then 12 laps later crashes and suffers an injury to his ribs. Sterling Marlin finishes in the No. 28 car and winds up 28th.

Elliott spins on Lap 31 and wrecks on Lap 251, limping home to a 20th-place finish in his damaged Ford.

Allison's lead over Elliott shrinks to 29 points. Kulwicki moves to fifth, 99 back.

First Union 400

With Jimmy Hensley standing by for relief driving duty, Davey Allison withstands the pain from his sore ribs and lower back to score a two car-length victory over Rusty Wallace at North Wilkesboro, N.C. Allison takes the lead on Lap 313, beating the other top challengers off pit road during a yellow flag.

Alan Kulwicki leads 182 of the first 187 laps but finishes seventh. Bill Elliott finishes two laps down in 20th and falls to third in points, 106 behind Allison.

Hanes 500

On a day at Martinsville, Va., when broken axles plague many would-be contenders, Mark Martin takes a 1.13-second victory over Sterling Marlin.

Alan Kulwicki leads more than 200 laps early in the race, building a lead of up to seven seconds, but breaks an axle and finishes 16th. Axle failure also wrecks the hopes of Dale Earnhardt and Ernie Irvan.

Davey Allison crashes on Lap 386 and finishes 26th, but holds the point lead by 16 over Harry Gant, who finishes fifth.

Winston 500

At Talladega, Ala., Davey Allison gets two-thirds of the way to winning the Winston Million bonus by edging Bill Elliott by two car-lengths.

Allison, who extends his points lead to 67 over Elliott, makes it nine straight wins for Ford in 1992 and 13 straight overall. It is Allison's seventh top-five finish in nine races. Dale Earnhardt finishes a fast-closing third. Alan Kulwicki finishes sixth.

Coca-Cola 600

Dale Earnhardt breaks Ford's winning streak with a victory in Charlotte, N.C. Earnhardt holds off fellow Chevrolet driver Ernie Irvan by about three car lengths. Kyle Petty is third in a Pontiac that led 141 laps.

Davey Allison, bruised up from a crash as he took the checkered flag to win The Winston all-star race a week earlier, finishes fourth and builds his points lead to 111 over Bill Elliott, who finishe 14th. Alan Kulwicki finishes seventh and stands fourth in the points, 132 behind the leader.

Budweiser 500

Harry Gant wins at Dover, Del., by making it 98 laps on his final tank of fuel. Gant's Oldsmobile runs out of gas as he rolls down the backstretch on the final lap, and he cuts off the ignition and coasts home. He still wins by nearly a lap—Dale Earnhardt passes Gant just before the finish line to get back on the lead lap.

Davey Allison finishes 11th after being penalized for exceeding the pit road speed limit on his final green-flag stop. Gant moves past Elliott into second in points. Alan Kulwicki wrecks two cars in practice, then wrecks a third during the race.

Save Mart 300

Ernie Irvan becomes the seventh different winner of the season, overcoming a first-lap penalty for jumping the start and passing Terry Labonte in the later stages to win his second straight road-course event in the race at Sears Point, Calif.

Davey Allison, who had won the race a year earlier, spins into a tire barrier on Lap 10 and damages his Ford. He finishes 28th and sees his points lead shrink to 28 over defending champion Dale Earnhardt.

Champion 500

The three drivers who would wind up battling for the championship on the season's last day move into those positions in the standings for the first time all season in a race at Pocono, Pa., that Kulwicki wins.

Kulwicki rallies past Bill Elliott and Mark Martin in the final laps to pick up the victory and moves into third in the standings, 58 behind Allison. Elliott finishes third in the race and is second in points, 21 behind Allison, who is fifth in the race.

Miller 400

Davey Allison dominates at Brooklyn, Mich., coasting to victory by more than 3 seconds in a race that wasn't even that close. Allison tops the $1 million mark in earnings faster than anybody else in the sport's history.

Allison's fourth win of the season ties him with Bill Elliott for the most on the circuit. Kulwicki is third in the race and Elliott is 10th, leaving Allison with a 67-point lead.

Pepsi 400

Richard Petty qualifies second and leads the first five laps, but there's no miracle for The King as he races for the last time at Daytona Beach, Fla. On a day when temperatures reach 95 degrees, Petty is forced to get out of his car early and winds up finishing 36th.

Ernie Irvan, meanwhile, leads 118 of 160 laps to get the victory.

Bill Elliott is fifth and moves to within 46 points of Davey Allison, who is 10th in the race. Alan Kulwicki finishes 30th but remains third in the points race.

Miller 500

The season takes a dramatic turn at Pocono, Pa., in a race won by Darrell Waltrip.

Davey Allison had led 115 laps and appears to have a dominant car, but after a restart on Lap 150 of the 200-lap race he gets tapped from behind by Waltrip's car as they exit the treacherous Tunnel Turn at Pocono.

Allison's Ford slides into the grass, flips backward and begins a barrel roll. After 11 rolls, with parts spewing off the car, the Ford bounces off a guardrail and slams down on its top.

Allison suffers a broken right collarbone, forearm and wrist and, for the first time all season, loses the lead in the points race. Elliott moves nine points ahead with a 13th-place finish while Kulwicki's third-place finish leaves him third in the standings but just 47 points out of the lead.

Diehard 500

Ernie Irvan wins for the third time in six races, but it is once again Allison's team that steals the headlines.

Allison, battered but unbowed after his horrifying crash at Pocono, comes to Talladega, Ala., and starts the race in his No. 28 Ford with Bobby Hillin standing by to relieve him in the car.

Just five laps into the race, a caution allows the team to make the driver switch without losing a lap. Hillin then drives the car to a third-place finish, joining Irvan and runner-up Sterling Marlin as the only cars to complete all 500 miles.

Bill Elliott finishes fifth and falls one point behind Allison in the points race. Allison is credited with the points from the third-place finish because he started the race in the car.

Budweiser at the Glen

Kyle Petty gets the victory at Watkins Glen, N.Y., in a race delayed by rain for more than three hours at the start and then shortened to 51 laps by more rain. Petty becomes the ninth different winner of the season.

Dorsey Schroeder is the relief driver for Davey Allison this weekend and finishes 20th. Elliott finishes 14th, to take a 17-point lead. Kulwicki is seventh.

Champion 400

Harry Gant takes the victory at Michigan Speedway by making a gas gamble pay off big. Gant stops to top off his fuel tank on Lap 98 of the 200-lap race and goes the rest of the way with just one more pit stop as the race stays green. Everyone else stops twice after Lap 98 and Gant steals the victory.

Darrell Waltrip edges Bill Elliott for second, but Elliott still picks up ground on Davey Allison, who finishes fifth despite his injured arm and despite the fact that his brother, Clifford, was killed in a crash during practice on Thursday afternoon. One day after the race, Davey attends his brother's funeral.

Budweiser 500

Just days after the birth of his daughter Sarah, Darrell Waltrip goes to victory lane once again at Bristol, giving him 12 career victories at the track but his first win there since 1989.

This race is the first one run on the new concrete surface at Bristol. The track removed its asphalt surface and replaced it with concrete after the race there earlier int the season.

Bill Elliott finishes sixth and Davey Allison, who is caught up in one of the accidents on the new surface, finishes 30th. That moves Elliott's points lead from 37 to 109 over Allison. Alan Kulwicki finishes fifth in the race and is third in points, 133 behind the leader.

Southern 500

Davey Allison comes to Darlington with another chance to win The Winston Million bonus, but Darrell Waltrip and Mother Nature deny him the $1 million prize.

Allison had led 63 laps in his bid to add the Southern 500 to the Daytona 500 and Winston 500 victories from earlier in the year. But just before the 400-mile mark he had to come to pit road for a green-flag stop for fuel.

The rest of the leaders had pitted, too, but Waltrip decides to stay out, hoping his fuel will last until rain that has been threatening all day arrives.

That's exactly what happens, and Waltrip is leading when the race is red-flagged after 405 miles. The race is not restarted and Waltrip, in his 19th try, finally gets his first Southern 500 victory.

Allison finishes fifth and, in addition to not winning the big bonus, loses 10 points to Bill Elliott's third-place finish. Elliott's lead is now 119. Alan Kulwicki is eighth and drops another 28 points behind.

Miller 400

Rusty Wallace, who has had only two top fives in the season's first 21 races, finally gets a victory to become the season's 10th different winner. Wallace leads the final 139 laps for his third career victory at Richmond and his 31st career win overall.

Darrell Waltrip, coming in off two straight wins, finishes third behind Wallace and Mark Martin.

Bill Elliott finishes 14th, one lap down to the winner, but still picks up ground in the points race. Alan Kulwicki is 15th and Davey Allison is 19th after spinning out twice. That leaves Elliott with a 124-point lead over Allison and a 164-point edge on Kulwicki.

Peak 500

Ricky Rudd wins at Dover to conclude a weekend that seemingly knocks Alan Kulwicki out of the championship chase.

Rudd comes in on Lap 481 for his final pit stop and takes fuel only. Bill Elliott, who had stopped for tires and fuel about 15 laps earlier, eats into Rudd's lead of nearly six seconds over the final laps, but falls about 50 feet short of catching him at the checkered flag.

Elliott's second-place finish is enough to put him 154 points ahead of Davey Allison, who finishes fourth.

Kulwicki, meanwhile, drops behind Harry Gant into fourth in points, 278 behind the leader. Kulwicki wrecks in practice but win the pole in his backup car, then is involved in a wreck with Chad Little during the race and finishes 34th, saying afterward that result probably ends his chances of being the champion.

Goody's 500

Geoffrey Bodine has to wait an extra day because of rain, but on a Monday at Martinsville, Va., he adds his name to the roster of winners for the 1992 season.

Bodine, driving for legendary car owner Bud Moore, gets his 12th career Winston Cup win and his fourth at Martinsville by leading the final 43 laps and holding off Rusty Wallace and Brett Bodine, Geoffrey's brother.

The season's larger picture begins to get interesting as Bill Elliott suffers a blown engine just 158 laps into the 500-lap race. Elliott finishes

30th in a 31-car field and sees his points lead shrink to 112 over Davey Allison, who finishes 16th.

Alan Kulwicki makes up ground with a fifth-place finish and is now 191 back.

Tyson 400

For the second straight weekend, Sunday is a washout because of rain and the race is run on Monday. And for the second straight weekend, Geoffrey Bodine goes to victory lane at North Wilkesboro, N.C. Remarkably, this time he does it in a 400-lap race that was run without a single caution flag. Bodine leads 312 of the 400 laps and passes Bill Elliott eight times under green.

Elliott never gets his car adjusted right and finishes 26th as the points races tightens once more. Davey Alison finishes 11th and Alan Kulwicki is 12th, leaving Elliott just 67 points ahead of Allison and 144 ahead of Kulwicki.

Mello Yello 500

The season's final race at Charlotte Motor Speedway helps to create the greatest late-season points race scramble in Winston Cup history.

Mark Martin gets his second victory of the season, with Alan Kulwicki finishing second and Kyle Petty third.

Elliott, meanwhile, can't shake his string of bad luck. On Lap 295 —just 39 laps from the finish—he is running sixth when he hits the Turn 4 wall and breaks a sway bar. He spends 18 laps on pit road having his Ford repaired, then returns to run 16 more laps before parking with four laps to go. He finishes 30th for the second time in three races.

Davey Allison finishes 19th but still makes up ground. At the end of the day, there are six drivers in the race for the championship with three races to go. Elliott still leads, but by just 39 points over Allison. Kulwicki is 47 behind. Martin is fourth and just 91 points behind Elliott. Harry Gant is now 94 back. Petty, who has made up 274 points on Elliott in three races, is 106 out of the lead.

AC-Delco 500

Kyle Petty dominates at Rockingham—leading 484 of the 492 laps —to continue his late season run at the title. His victory is his fifth straight top-five finish and his 11th top-10 finish in 12 races since the midway point of the season.

Bill Elliott rights his ship with a fourth-place finish, however, so none of the other title contenders can make up ground on the leader. Elliott now leads Davey Allison by 70 points, Kulwicki by 85, Petty by 94 and Gant by 113. Mark Martin finishes 30th to drop back out of the thick of the race.

All Elliott needs to do is finish sixth or better in the final two races to win the championship.

Pyroil 500

The stage for the final drama is set in the season's penultimate race at Phoenix, as Davey Allison takes the race victory and regains the points lead after Bill Elliott has yet another problem.

Elliott's Ford cracks a cylinder head and begins to overheat. He finishes 31st and drops from first in the points, where he has been since Watkins Glen, to third.

Allison wins at Phoenix for the second straight year, with Mark Martin second and Alan Kulwicki fourth. When the points are all added up, the teams head for Atlanta with Allison 30 points ahead of Kulwicki and 40 ahead of Elliott. Harry Gant is 97 back, one ahead of Kyle Petty, while Martin is 113 out of the lead.

APPENDIX 2

Career Records

Richard Petty

Year	Races	Wins	Poles	Top 5	Top 10	Earnings
1958	9	0	0	0	1	760
1959	21	0	0	6	9	8,111
1960	40	8	2	21	35	41,873
1961	42	3	2	19	24	25,239
1962	52	2	4	26	33	60,764
1963	54	14	8	30	39	55,964
1964	61	9	9	37	43	114,772
1965	15	4	7	10	10	16,450
1966	39	8	16	20	22	94,666
1967	48	27	19	38	40	150,197
1968	49	16	12	31	35	99,535
1969	50	10	6	31	38	129,906
1970	40	18	9	27	31	151,124
1971	46	21	9	38	41	351,071
1972	31	8	3	25	28	339,405
1973	28	6	3	15	17	234,389
1974	30	10	7	22	23	432,020
1975	30	13	3	21	24	481,751
1976	30	3	1	19	22	374,806
1977	30	5	5	20	23	406,608
1978	30	0	0	11	17	242,273
1979	31	5	1	23	27	561,934
1980	31	2	0	15	19	397,318
1981	31	3	0	12	16	396,072
1982	30	0	0	9	16	465,793
1983	30	3	0	9	21	508,884
1984	30	2	0	5	13	257,932
1985	28	0	0	1	13	306,142
1986	29	0	0	4	11	280,657
1987	29	0	0	9	14	445,227

1988	29	0	0	1	5	190,155
1989	25	0	0	0	0	133,050
1990	29	0	0	0	1	169,465
1991	29	0	0	0	1	268,035
1992	29	0	0	0	0	348,870
	1185	200	157	555	712	$8,541,218

Bill Elliott

Year	Races	Wins	Poles	Top 5	Top 10	Earnings
1976	8	0	0	0	0	11,635
1977	10	0	0	0	2	20,575
1978	10	0	0	0	5	42,065
1979	13	0	0	1	5	57,450
1980	11	0	0	0	4	42,545
1981	13	0	1	1	7	70,320
1982	21	0	1	8	9	226,780
1983	30	1	0	12	22	479,965
1984	30	3	4	13	24	660,226
1985	28	11	11	16	18	2,433,187
1986	29	2	4	8	16	1,069,142
1987	29	6	8	16	20	1,619,210
1988	29	6	6	15	22	1,574,639
1989	29	3	2	8	14	854,570
1990	29	1	2	12	16	1,090,730
1991	29	1	2	6	12	705,605
1992	29	5	2	14	17	1,692,381
1993	30	0	2	6	15	955,859
1994	31	1	1	6	12	936,779
1995	31	0	2	4	10	996,816
1996	24	0	0	0	6	716,506
1997	32	0	1	5	14	1,607,827
1998	32	0	0	0	5	1,618,421
1999	34	0	0	1	2	1,624,101
2000	32	0	0	3	7	2,580,823
2001	36	1	2	5	0	3,618,017
	659	41	51	160	293	$27,306,174

Alan Kulwicki

Year	Races	Wins	Poles	Top 5	Top 10	Earnings
1985	5	0	0	0	0	10,290
1986	23	0	0	1	4	94,450
1987	29	0	3	3	9	369,889
1988	29	1	4	6	8	448,547
1989	29	0	6	6	10	501,295
1990	29	1	1	5	13	550,936
1991	29	1	4	4	11	595,614
1992	29	2	6	11	17	2,322,561
1993	5	0	0	2	3	165,470
	207	**5**	**24**	**38**	**75**	**$5,059,052**

Davey Allison

Year	Races	Wins	Poles	Top 5	Top 10	Earnings
1985	3	0	0	0	1	11,715
1986	5	0	0	0	1	8,070
1987	22	2	5	9	10	361,060
1988	29	2	3	12	16	844,532
1989	29	2	1	7	13	640,956
1990	29	2	0	5	10	640,684
1991	29	5	3	12	16	1,712,924
1992	29	5	2	15	17	1,955,628
1993	16	1	0	6	8	513,585
	191	**19**	**14**	**66**	**92**	**$6,689,154**

Jeff Gordon

Year	Races	Wins	Poles	Top 5	Top 10	Earnings
1992	1	0	0	0	0	6,285
1993	30	0	1	7	11	765,168
1994	31	2	1	7	14	1,779,523
1995	31	7	8	17	23	4,347,343
1996	31	10	5	21	24	3,428,485
1997	32	10	1	22	23	6,375,658
1998	33	13	7	26	28	9,306,584
1999	34	7	7	18	21	5,858,633
2000	34	3	3	11	22	3,001,144
2001	36	6	6	18	24	10,879,757
	293	**58**	**39**	**147**	**190**	**$45,748,580**